There's No José Here

There's No José Here

Following the Hidden Lives of Mexican Immigrants

GABRIEL THOMPSON

Nation Books
New York

THERE'S NO JOSÉ HERE
Following the Hidden Lives of Mexican Immigrants

Published by
Nation Books
An imprint of Avalon Publishing Group, Inc.
245 West 17th Street, 11th Floor
New York, NY 10011

AVALON
publishing group incorporated

Nation Books is a copublishing venture of the Nation Institute
and Avalon Publishing Group, Incorporated.

Library of Congress Cataloging-in-Publication Data is available.

Cloth edition
ISBN-10: 1-56025-978-7
ISBN-13: 978-1-56025-978-7

Trade paperback edition
ISBN-10: 1-56025-990-6
ISBN-13: 978-1-56025-990-9

9 8 7 6 5 4 3 2 1

Book design by Maria E. Torres.

Printed in the United States of America
Distributed by Publishers Group West

For my parents,
Jim Thompson and Sandra Hietala,
who have supported my various wanderings without
ever asking that dream-killer of questions:
and just how do you plan on making money doing that?

Contents

Introduction

IT HAPPENED OVER and over again:

"Hi, is José there?"

"Uh, there's no José here."

"Yes there is. Can you please ask someone if he's there now?"

"Let me see . . . ummm . . . I'm pretty sure we don't have a José."

"Do me a favor, just ask."

"Fine." Getting agitated now. "Hold on a second." Several minutes pass.

"Hello?"

"Hola, José, soy yo, Gabriel."

"Hola, Gabriel. ¿Qué onda?"

My friend José, from the southern Mexico state of Puebla, has worked for eight years at a Manhattan company that produces low-end jewelry. Still, whenever I called him at work, I was told he wasn't there. I'd have to insist that whoever answered the phone inquire into the existence of a José in their shop. Eventually, they would discover that—lo and behold—a José did indeed work at their company, and had in fact put in more than twenty-four thousand irretrievable hours of his life laboring for their benefit. The first few times this occurred I made a note of it. After half a dozen identical interactions, I stopped keeping track.

• • •

There is another José story, a story that was told to my father by one
of his friends. A man who ran a construction company would refer to
all of the Mexican workers—or, to be more precise, all those who
appeared Mexican—as José. As in: "I've got to get myself a couple of
Josés for this job if we're going to have that roof patched up by Saturday." In his mind it was nothing but a convenient, logical short-
hand. Thus, my friend José supposedly doesn't exist at a shop where he
has worked for nearly a decade, but at a worksite somewhere in California right now a bunch of Josés exist, even when they actually don't.

In April of 2005 a group calling itself the Minutemen made international news when they gathered approximately 150 people on the
U.S.-Mexico border and sat on lawn chairs looking through binoc-
ulars into the empty desert.[*] I spent a week living with them on the
campus of a bible college, which the Minutemen quickly attempted
to turn into a military compound. By the second day they had
rechristened the church cafeteria as the "mess hall," and the grounds
were transformed into the "perimeter." The volunteers were white,
mostly men but also a good number of woman (who nonetheless
insisted on being called Minutemen), and all of them were angry.

My main desire, reporting on their activities at the time for an
online news magazine, was to discover what it was that they were so
angry about. They were small in number, for sure, but one couldn't
dismiss their dedication. All had decided to take time out from their
normal lives to trek to Arizona. Some came from as far away as New
York, as I did—paying their own way to live in primitive conditions
and face sunburns and scorpions. Why?

* Though news reports usually echoed the Minutemen's claim that "thousands" of volunteers
had shown up, by my own estimation—and according to the only newspaper that actually
bothered to count—roughly 150 participants came, and this number was cut in half several
days into the project.

They were mostly angry about abstractions and generalizations: Mexicans refused to learn English. They were lazy and came to the United States to get on welfare. Or else they came to the States to steal jobs from U.S. citizens. They were drug dealers. Violent. Disease spreaders. Child molesters. Immoral.

I wasn't interested in battling abstraction against abstraction. Instead, I asked the same question over and over again: "Do you actually know any Mexican immigrants?" Although one wouldn't expect any of the Minutemen to have attempted to make serious relational inroads in the Mexican community, most were from the immigrant-heavy state of California. Surely a few of them had some sort of contact with Mexicans, or so I figured. Yet each volunteer I spoke with drew a blank; none knew any Mexican immigrants personally. There was a battle raging over Mexican immigrants, but the Mexican immigrants themselves were somehow ignored, like my friend José at the jewelry factory. At the same time, they were regularly referred to, but as an abstraction, like the many "Josés" at the construction company.

The problem is, politically charged abstractions don't necessarily tell us anything useful. Though I don't personally know any Mexican immigrants who are drug dealers or child molesters, they undoubtedly exist. The same can be said about born-again Christians, police officers, Boy Scout leaders, surgeons, lifelong Chevy drivers, and residents of Arkansas.

Abstractions are ultimately dehumanizing, and in the U.S. debate over how to handle the "problem" of Mexican immigrants, the competing narratives crashing up against one another remain at arm's length from the immigrants themselves. Americans are so busy catapulting statistics at one another, fighting tooth and nail over the "goodness" or "badness" of Mexican immigrants (and, for that matter, nonwhite immigrants in general) that immigrants get buried under the deluge, their voices suffocated beneath a mountain of footnotes and policy papers.

There are two general perspectives of immigrants. The first view, shared by mostly conservative whites, and perhaps best exemplified by the Minutemen participants, is of immigrants as lawbreakers, as moral degenerates who present a clear and ever-growing threat to what is referred to as our "way of life," in itself another abstract notion that is rarely actually explained. People within this camp usually have a glorified notion of a pristine past, where things were somehow better (in practical terms, sometimes all this means is that one didn't have to overhear conversations in Spanish while purchasing groceries). Throw in the so-called War on Terror, and such people suddenly have another reason to fear, and loathe, immigrants. In our country, there is a long tradition of nativism, and that tradition persists today.

The second, more sympathetic view is of immigrants as innocent and exploited victims, as a nameless mass of misery. According to this caricature, immigrants are honorable, hardworking people who come to the United States in order to better their lives but are taken advantage of because of an unjust social order. They are humble, thankful, grateful. Simple folk. Again, though more sympathetic than the conservative caricature, this view simplifies the immigrant reality and is ultimately condescending. Throughout the history of the United States, immigrants have suffered special exploitation, of course, but they have also been among our most dedicated fighters for social justice. They are not passive and they are not resigned—at least no more than any of us. To treat them as a perfect people is ridiculous. To pretend that things simply happen to them, that they naturally assume the mantle of victimhood, is as inaccurate as to pretend that they are more prone to lawbreaking than U.S. citizens.

Call my friend Enrique a victim, and he will laugh in your face; call him an asshole, and he'll nod and say, "You're right, but so are you." Mexican immigrants fall somewhere between angels and assholes—again, as we all do.

My own journey into the world of Mexican immigrants came about as most life-altering developments do: by pure chance. After graduating from college in California I moved to Brooklyn to work as a community organizer. The primary focus was tackling the problems of low-income tenants living in poor housing or facing eviction. It quickly became obvious that the people living in the worst housing conditions, and who felt least comfortable taking action, were the Mexican immigrants.

My closest Mexican friend soon became a man named Enrique. This book is largely his story. As his adventures in Brooklyn progressed, I got to know his wife, his children, his parents, his friends, his uncles, his cousins, his nieces, and his nephews. I should state here that this book has been made possible only through the openness and patience of Enrique, who was forced to suffer through thousands of my questions—often inane, as he liked to correctly complain—and who welcomed me with open arms into his life. With him I attended court dates, funerals, weddings, and births. I traveled with him by car from Brooklyn to his hometown in southern Mexico, and to Fort Bragg military base to say good-bye to his best friend, who was being deployed to Iraq. At times Enrique and I drove each other a bit crazy—long, sleepless road trips will do that—but still, whatever he was going through, he wouldn't fail to call, and his message was always the same: "*Güero,*" he would begin—white boy, my unofficial nickname. "You've got to come along with me if you really want to be able to understand what it's like to be an immigrant." And we would be off—sometimes to housing court, sometimes to a celebration of some sort, sometimes just to eat a large meal of beans, rice, and tortillas while bullshitting for an hour or two. This book, then, is not an authoritative study on Mexican immigrants; this is not a book that says *Here is what Mexicans are like.* My goal is more modest, more focused. I am telling the story of several friendships, several hardships, several interesting lives.

To err on the side of caution, most of the immigrants in this book are identified by their first names only. I don't know if the Department of Homeland Security would attempt to track down the people within these pages who are living in the country illegally. Probably not; I would hope the department has better things to do. Either way, I don't care to find out. In addition, for privacy reasons several characters are given pseudonyms, and when this occurs I make a note of it.

Finally, a note on terminology: Labels can be politically explosive, as one quickly learns when writing about Mexican immigrants who are in the United States illegally. On one side are the people—overwhelmingly Anglo—who prefer to call such people "illegal aliens" or even "invaders." These labels, often purposefully, conjure up images of exotic outsiders who are subversive and have criminal tendencies. A more succinct variation of the term "illegal immigrants" is simply "illegals." This, too, is dehumanizing, boiling down an existence to one of illegitimacy. Someone who drives without a license is breaking the law, but we don't call that person an "illegal" driver, and we would never think of shortening this label to an "illegal." In my book, the same should go for immigrant status.

One evening while watching the news I saw a white man shouting, "Go home, illegals!" at a group of immigrants who were demonstrating for their right to have driver's licenses. As the camera panned the crowd of protesters I could see many broad Indian faces, faces that are indigenous to the continent we all share. The irony was lost on the red-faced Anglo, whose ancestors grew up thousands of miles away.

Partly in sympathy with my Mexican friends, partly in wishing to disassociate myself from the red-faced Anglo, I choose not to use the term "illegal" in this book, except when quoting others. The truth is that the vast majority of the immigrants I know in New York City, including Enrique, are descendents of the Mixtec, one of the major pre-Columbian civilizations in the Americas. Their indigenous blood runs deep.

I once saw an old Latino man wearing a T-shirt that read "Who's the Illegal, Pilgrim?" The man has a point, and in this book I refer to the Mexican immigrants who are here without the blessing of the United States government as *undocumented*. Hopefully, this book will play a modest role in their documentation.

PART I:
USA

CHAPTER 1

Loud

I FIRST MET Enrique while eating lunch at a Mexican restaurant in Brooklyn called Flaco's. *Flaco,* which means "skinny" in Spanish, may accurately describe the owner, but it is a misleading title for a restaurant that serves up hearty meals of beans and meat laden with lard. Tall, with close-cropped hair and a constant smile, Flaco is usually the only person in the place without a sizable paunch. His restaurant is one of those hole-in-the-wall eateries that are spread out across New York City, achieving the impossible: in a space the size of a studio apartment, he serves up complete meals to dozens, sometimes hundreds, of people each day. From dawn till dusk, a diverse group of customers move in and out, some sitting down to eat, but most picking up food and wandering off to their destinations.

I noticed Enrique because he was, in a word, loud. He threw the door open with a grin, announced his presence with a rowdy but friendly greeting directed at Flaco, and plopped down on the stool next to mine. Seated, his forehead came up only to my chest, but his wide shoulders, meaty forearms, and large face gave the impression of a compressed giant. We began talking—actually, he began talking, in a mixture of Spanish and English—and I quickly learned he was having problems with his landlord. At the time, in the summer of 2002, I was working with tenants for a local nonprofit organization, so I invited him into our office the following week, where he could meet with a legal services attorney.

Enrique grew up in the *campo,* or country, in a village called Cuicatlán. Cuicatlán is near the town of Chinantla, where his mother lives. He has dark skin because he is indigenous, an Indian. He used to be skinny and strong, but now he is fat because all he does is eat and drive a cab around the city. Got to New York City in 1986, when he was sixteen. Crossed in Tijuana without getting caught. He didn't speak English, didn't know anything about the United States. But that didn't stop him. Fucking *mojados* have to be smart. Mojados, you know, wetbacks. Lived with his sister in the Brooklyn neighborhood of Borough Park. Washed dishes. Worked all the time, seven days a week. The restaurants only paid a few dollars an hour. Fucking thieves. After a few years, he moved into a building on Broadway Avenue in Williamsburg, still in Brooklyn. Started driving a car instead of washing dishes. Made a bit more money, but still not much. Gas prices were out of control. And the Broadway building was horrible, with rats and cockroaches. His daughter got lead poisoning in that building. Now she is failing classes at school and receiving disability checks every month. Next he moved into a building in Bedford-Stuyvesant, but now the landlord hasn't paid the bills and there's no fucking hot water. *Pinches* landlords. And the city doesn't give a shit, because they don't care about Mexicans. Or blacks. They only care about the rich, people who have money. Like you, maybe. No, probably not. *No hay ricos aquí en Flaco's.* Rich people make the rules, poor people . . . *hijo de su pinche madre,* poor people are the ones who suffer. Only way we're gonna get anything done is if we come together. But *los pinches mexicanos* never work together. Jews, now there is a group that knows how to get things done. Are you Jewish? They take care of each other, Jews. Not Mexicans. That's why we're always having problems, always working for nothing, living in the worst housing. Everyone talks about going back to Mexico, but they stay. Year after year after year. Never think to get together and fight. *Estúpidos* keep saying, *Just a little more money, then I'm going home.* Look at me, been here twenty years, don't have shit to show for it. I'll come to your office. See what happens.

He tells me all this on that day at Flaco's, while gobbling up a huge meal. In less than ten minutes. From that day forward, we are friends.

On my first trip to Enrique's apartment I am floored by the smell and step back from the entryway of the three-unit building for a moment to regroup. Enrique laughs. "A-ha, now you see what I'm talking about. That's from the water down in the basement. It's been like that for weeks." It's not just water—the unmistakable odor of liberated sewage is overwhelming. We enter again and walk quickly up creaky stairs to his second-floor apartment. As he fiddles with the lock he says to make sure to close the door behind me as soon as we get in, so that the smell stays out. I am eager to oblige.

Juana, his *esposa* (though not officially, I learn, since they haven't been married), is a short and sturdy woman with a gentle, smooth face and long black hair. She is from Mexico, too, but her facial features appear Native American. I mention this, and Enrique reminds me that she *is* Native American: Mexico is part of the North American continent. "You didn't know that? We're all *americanos* here, güero, except for you. Juana and I *somos americanos indigenas.* Where are you from?"

"You mean like my family? They're from Norway and Finland, mostly."

"*Noruega y Finlandia,*" Enrique comments, nodding to Juana. "Well, güero, welcome to our country. We welcome immigrants here, and we're going to do our best to help you." He lets out a quick burst of laughter and then, pleased with his geography lesson, motions for me to sit down at a small kitchen table. As I take a seat, a child starts crying from another room. Juana leaves for a moment and returns with a young boy in her arms, who wiggles free from her grip and runs over to Enrique, plopping down on his lap. He looks at me with curiosity.

"*Hola*, Junior," Enrique whispers. "Say hello to our new friend." The child takes another quick glance at me and then turns away and buries his sleepy face in his father's chest. Enrique runs his chubby fingers through Junior's hair. "He's tired now, but it won't last. Give him a few minutes and he'll be running circles around the house. Just like his dad, he can run and run without getting tired. When we take him out to the park he runs around for hours, and he's not even two years old yet. He's going to be a *fútbol* star someday. Isn't that right, Junior?" Junior keeps his face buried and doesn't answer.

While Juana prepares a pot of coffee, Enrique recounts the major developments of the previous year. When they moved in six months ago, in December 2001, they were satisfied with the small but clean apartment. Located on a desolate stretch of Dekalb Avenue in the neighborhood of Bedford-Stuyvesant, it was true that they were surrounded by boarded-up homes and drug dealers, but a grocery store was nearby, and living on the second floor meant the noise of the street usually didn't reach them, except for the occasional gunfire. With a rent of one thousand dollars a month, it wasn't exactly cheap, but it could have been worse, especially considering how quickly the rents seemed to be going up everywhere. Plus, Enrique explains, previously the family had been renting a single room in a nearby apartment, which housed the three of them as well as Abram, Juana's thirteen-year-old son from a previous relationship. They needed a place of their own.

Juana interrupts his narrative with cups of coffee. Enrique puts Junior down and takes a big sip. "You work with tenants?" he asks.

"Yes."

"Poor people, right? Who have problems with landlords?"

"Yes."

"Then how come I've never seen you around? This whole neighborhood is full of tenants getting fucked. Where have you been?"

My face turns slightly red. "Uh, well, I just started. And it's a big area we're working in. There are only a few people in the office."

"Anyway, never mind. No one can do anything all by themselves. But you got to get more fucking active if you want to keep your job. They keep kicking all us poor people out, you won't be needed anymore. You think the white families that pay two thousand dollars rent are going to need your help? They get rid of the poor people, you've got to find new work. *Simple y sencillo.*" Plain and simple.

"I agree. So what do you think—

"Forget it for now, we're working together. That's good. We'll figure something out later. But I still haven't told you everything about our case."

Through that first winter, heat and hot water were plentiful; sometimes the apartment got so hot that Enrique and his family would have to open the windows to keep from sweating. Before they moved in, the landlord had completed cosmetic repairs and given the apartment a fresh coat of paint, which gave the appearance of quality construction. Though ideally the two-bedroom railroad apartment would have been a bit larger, it at least made for a cozy home, a home where one could raise a family, all things considered. Enrique knew many others who were living in far worse conditions—he had lived in far worse conditions himself—so he had no right to be unhappy.

It wasn't until the springtime that things began to fall apart. The landlord, who had promised quick repairs when the lease was signed, now failed to return phone calls about a bathroom leak or broken lock on the entrance door. Strangers started hanging out in the first-floor apartment, which had previously been sealed and vacant. Soon the unit was full of squatters, and on weekends the steady traffic of unknown people suggested that a good-sized drug-dealing operation was going on beneath their feet.

"If it was just Juana and myself, we could handle it," Enrique says of the problems. "But now that we have Junior, things are different. It is not safe to raise a child here. The assholes downstairs are always fighting, and each time Juana walks in with Junior something bad could happen. Those people don't even know what they're doing when they're fucked up. One day last week when I got home from work, two guys were barbecuing in the hallway. Barbecuing indoors! Fucking *pendejos*. The smoke was everywhere. It was a miracle they didn't burn the place down."

Since the barbecuing incident, new problems have emerged. A heavy rain flooded the basement, causing the stench. Soon after, a number of leaks began to form throughout the apartment. Each phone call to the landlord went unanswered, so Enrique began to lodge complaints with the city. The city was slightly more responsive, eventually sending out inspectors to write up violations. They also were attempting to contact the landlord, but still no progress was being made. Anyone could cite violations—what mattered was to fix them.

"Hold on a second," he tells me, and disappears down the hallway, returning with a thick packet of papers. "Each one of these is a violation for the building. I call the city, they send inspectors, and all they do is write up more violations. And I'm the one who is showing them where the violations are in the first place. It's just a fucking game they're playing with me. The landlord plays his game, and the city plays their game."

"Look behind you,." he says. I turn around in my chair and for the first time notice dozens of papers tacked to the wall. "Those are the newest violations. I've got so many, I don't know what to do with them anymore." He chuckles, but not happily. Where other households might hang paintings or family photographs, he has constructed an exhibit commemorating the city's bureaucratic ineptitude.

"Tell him about the rat yesterday." Throughout our conversation Juana has remained quiet, tending to Junior as he buzzes around the apartment; as advertised, he is a bundle of raw energy. She motions toward the bathroom and repeats her request. "Tell him about the rat in the bathroom."

Enrique hops up from the table and signals for me to follow him into the tiny bathroom. Small pieces of plaster are scattered about the floor, and a gaping hole in the ceiling reveals several large and rotting planks crisscrossing above. "Yesterday morning this whole thing fell, and Juana heard it and looked in. Fucking rat this big just sitting on the toilet, staring at her." He holds his hands two feet apart, emphasizing the length of the creature with a low whistle. "I got one of my boots and went in after the bitch."

"You weren't afraid of the rat?" I ask.

"Of a rat? Of course not." He looks at me quizzically, as if this is the craziest question he's ever been asked. "All I had to do was hit it over the head with my boot. What's a rat going to do about that?" He picks up one of his boots that is on the floor by the front door and demonstrates his downward striking technique. "Actually, I had to hit it a few times to kill it. The asshole was huge." He smiles, recounting the humorous—to him—episode. "The damn thing even clogged the toilet when I tried to flush it down."

"You should have heard the rat crying," Juana adds, looking more horrified than amused. "Crying and crying, until it was dead. I didn't know rats could make that much noise."

Before driving me home, Enrique gives me a tour of the apartment, pointing out the many leaks and rat droppings, and smacking several cockroaches that are scurrying about with the back of his right hand. We end up in the kitchen, where we began, looking out the window into the backyard. The ground is covered in trash, in places several feet thick. One could jump safely from the fire escape if need be, cushioned by the refuse—though there was the risk of being pricked by one of the hypodermic needles that glisten below. Enrique opens the window, and the smell of sewage retreats from our nostrils, overtaken by the fumes of rotting trash from outside. The rats holed up along this stretch of Dekalb Avenue must think they've died and gone to rat heaven.

"Welcome to our beautiful home," Enrique says, moving his right hand with a flourish in front of the view. "But it won't stay like this forever. When we have a chance we're going to clean up this mess in the yard. You ever been to Mexico?"

"No, not really. Only Tijuana."

"Well, next year we'll have corn growing back there, and you can enjoy a real Mexican meal. We're going to clear out all this shit and plant rows of corn. Tortillas, tamales, everything. Juana can cook anything, learned from her mom. We'll feed you so much corn, you'll get a nice belly like me."

Enrique had very little use for the tenant attorney when he met with her a few days later in our office. She told him what he already knew: to seek repairs one needed to lodge complaints with the city (he had), make sure to be home when the inspectors knocked (he was), and keep all of the paperwork well organized (at this point he raised his folder of violations in his defense). He knew what he was supposed to do, he had done it, and nothing had happened. Before leaving the office, though, Enrique made sure the trip hadn't been entirely pointless. He noticed a box of tacks on my desk and asked if he could have a few. "Some more violations arrived today, and I've run out of things to post them up with." Much more of this, and the supplier of wallpaper for his entire apartment would be the New York City Department of Housing Preservation and Development (HPD).

During the following weeks I ran into Enrique at Flaco's nearly every day. Mostly he discussed the current crisis in his apartment. The electricity went out, then the boiler stopped working, then another rat was bludgeoned to death and—remembering the backed-up toilet—its corpse flung out the window by the tail. Enrique was also engaging in an arms race of sorts with the first-floor junkies. Each time they broke a lock and entered the unit, he would buy a larger one and lock it back up. He almost seemed to relish the challenge, though beneath the joking manner he adopted to chronicle his adventures for his audience at Flaco's—he was a natural storyteller and often attracted a lunchtime crowd—lay a simmering frustration.

During these conversations Enrique spoke often of his journey to the United States, and my allotted hour-long break was often stretched as I listened to his tales. The youngest of eight children, he was born and raised in Cuicatlán, a rural village of a few hundred people in the state of Puebla, located southeast of Mexico City. When he was sixteen, his brothers Juan and Angel, already in New York, agreed to pay eight hundred dollars to a well-known *coyote*, or human smuggler, who went by the name of Antonia. None of the clients ever saw Antonia; her operation was large and anonymous, with many workers on the ground in Mexico and New York, according to Enrique. Indeed, four years earlier, in 1982, Juana had also entered illegally with the help of the Antonia network.

There were five people from Cuicatlán in Enrique's group, including his older sister Sabina and her husband, who had already spent a number of years living in New York City and had returned for a short visit. From Cuicatlán the group took a bus to Mexico City, and then to Tijuana. Once in Tijuana they were joined with another group of twenty hopeful migrants and waited several days in a cheap motel.

They crossed the border one evening on foot, following two coyotes to a small safe house somewhere outside the U.S. border city of San Ysidro. From the safe house, the group was loaded into two separate pickup trucks, hidden under partitions in the back. Enrique was stuffed into one pickup, his sister and her husband in another. Enrique's truck passed through the immigration checkpoint without notice, and an hour later they were safely unloaded in a San Diego house. They waited for an hour, but the second truck didn't arrive. Eventually they were told the other truck had been apprehended and its migrants deported. Enrique wasn't concerned about Sabina's long-term fate—he knew they would simply be dropped off in Tijuana and would attempt to cross again (which they did, arriving in New York a week later). But Sabina's husband was holding Enrique's food money for the next several days.

"I told the coyote that my money was with the other truck, but he just laughed. He said it wasn't his problem, that he didn't care if I didn't eat for a week. Coyotes are ignorant brutes, that's what I learned. But there was another man from my hometown who was in my truck. He gave me money so I could buy food when we got to Los Angeles."

Two days later Enrique's group took a plane from Los Angeles to Las Vegas, and then on to Newark International Airport. At Newark he was greeted by his older brothers Angel and Juan, and moved into a small apartment in the Borough Park section of Brooklyn, which he shared with Angel and, a week later, with Sabina and her husband. Within several weeks he was working as a dishwasher at a nearby restaurant, earning what seemed to be a healthy sum but was actually a few dollars less than the minimum wage. He would spend three years living with Sabina and Angel, and would eventually pay off the eight-hundred-dollar debt for his safe passage north. And the process of crossing illegally and evading *la migra* was an event that he would regularly cite as a rite of passage, as evidence that he—and every other undocumented immigrant in the United States—wasn't afraid of making sacrifices to progress in life. Even after he became a legal resident, and then a U.S. citizen, he still considered himself a *mojado*, an immigrant who was up against various U.S. authorities. To this day, someone who reaches the message on his cell phone will hear the following greeting in Spanish: "Hello, my name is Enrique. I'm sorry that I can't come to the phone right now, but I am being chased by la migra. Please leave me a message, and I'll get back to you in the event that la migra doesn't catch me." Friends thought it was funny; acquaintances didn't know what to make of it. It was trademark Enrique, finding humor in a topic he took seriously. An immigrant was someone who was always being chased in one way or another, whose duty it was to outsmart the authorities.

Through sheer chance, Enrique arrived in the United States in 1986, the same year that Congress passed and President Reagan signed the Immigration Reform and Control Act, a provision of which allowed undocumented immigrants to become permanent residents if they had arrived in the United States before January 1, 1982. Ultimately, of the 1.7 million applicants who legalized their status under this provision (1.2 million also applied under a specific provision set aside for farmworkers), 70 percent were of Mexican origin, with the next largest groups coming from the war-torn countries of El Salvador and Guatemala. Of course, Enrique didn't technically qualify for permanent legal status, having arrived four years too late. Nonetheless, he was the first of his siblings to become a permanent legal resident, and then a citizen, through the legislation.

When asked about this feat, he throws the question back at me, disappointed by my denseness. "How did I do it? What do you think? I lied, pendejo." He had spent so many hours instructing me on the immigrant reality, and still I couldn't figure out the simplest of solutions. Soon after arriving in the United States, Enrique was washing dishes at a Brooklyn restaurant named Tiffany's when he overheard other Mexicans speaking about the amnesty program. He explained the situation to the Greek owner—one of the few bosses Enrique describes as a "nice, nice man"—who wrote a letter of rec-ommendation for him, stating that he had been working at the restaurant for an inflated number of years. Other workers at the restaurant also wrote him letters of support. Armed with these papers, he made his way to a church in the Brooklyn neighborhood of Sunset Park, where church volunteers assisted people in filling out applications. It was that easy.

Enrique was similarly underwhelmed by the citizenship process that followed. "The immigration officials asked me some stupid questions, like who George Washington was. I told them everything they wanted to hear, and I passed." For Enrique, the event lacked the glamour and stirrings of patriotic pride that it is meant to invoke. "On the evening that I passed I didn't feel any different than before. It's just a piece of paper. I was always an American—I don't need some stamp from immigration telling me that. Mexico is a part of America, and I'm an Indian, so why should I feel special because some white guy tells me I'm legal? Citizenship doesn't mean anything to me, except that I can visit my mother without having to run from la migra every time I come back."

If Enrique's refusal to cede a single moral inch to immigration laws was notable when compared to other "legal" Mexican Americans who criticized those who crossed without papers, his steadfast class-consciousness was even more unique—at least when compared with many other Mexican immigrants who lived in his neighborhood. In Bedford-Stuyvesant, Hasidic Jews who had been crowded out of the adjacent neighborhood of Williamsburg were purchasing many homes and evicting tenants, the majority of whom were Mexicans. The trend was predictable and logical: Hasidim needed to be within walking distance of their synagogues in Williamsburg, since they didn't drive on the Sabbath, and with so many smaller buildings in Bedford-Stuyvesant—where tenants could more easily be evicted because the rent laws didn't protect them—it was a natural neighborhood to move into.

The result was also predictable: many Mexicans began to view "*los judíos*"—the Jews—as the cause of all their problems. From the president on down, the U.S. power structure has always been Christian, and the political muscle of the far-right evangelicals has been rising dramatically, but Mexicans living in Bedford-Stuyvesant tended to see all strings being pulled by Jews—an idea that all too many neighborhood preachers were happy to confirm. It wasn't a sophisticated criticism, but it proved convincing for many who had spent their entire lives in the United States living within a small radius of blocks in Brooklyn. They saw Hasidic Jews cruising by in vans, dressed in strange outfits and looking for new properties to buy, while they themselves received eviction notices and went to court with only a vague idea of what their rights were; judges in court always sided with the landlords, with the Jews: the Jews controlled everything.

It was less a systematic racist ideology than an outgrowth of the insular nature of Brooklyn neighborhoods, and of two groups—Mexicans and Hasidic Jews—that had little common ground upon which to develop understanding and very many opportunities for mutual distrust. Without a shared language, even honest communication was difficult. It didn't help, either, that the only consistent interaction that Mexicans had with Hasidim was through the tenant-landlord relationship, an overflowing fount of animosity in New York City for decades.

But where others saw conspiracy, Enrique saw cooperation. "We complain, but it is our own fault. When we come here, we don't get together as Mexicans and save our money. We don't buy our own homes. We don't take care of each other. That is what the Jews do. They say, 'Look, we don't have that much by ourselves, but if we work together we can accomplish something.' That's what they do. Simple y sencillo."

At the same time, the problem wasn't fundamentally one of race—though Enrique always reminded me that immigrants were exploited more ruthlessly than others. Race wasn't unimportant, but the real barometer was class. "High-class people" was Enrique's catchall phrase for the wealthy elite, who were the real controllers of the country (and who were, both in Mexico and the United States, usually light-skinned). "It's no different in Mexico. You have a small group with lots of money, they control the politicians. Then you have everyone else, who have almost nothing. In Mexico, you know, we have the Indians, the indigenous, who are the poorest. Here, I guess you have the blacks and the immigrants. But it's no different."

Enrique was poor, indigenous, and an immigrant, but this was less an excuse to assume the mantle of victim than a challenge to rise to the fight for the side that was actually *honorable*. And this idea, that there was an ongoing battle being waged between "high-class people" and everyone else, was at the core of his self-identification. He told me that this perspective had come naturally to him, was instilled while growing up as an Indian in poverty, having to grow food to survive and eventually migrate north out of necessity. Seeing fair-skinned Mexicans flaunting their wealth on television, watching darker-skinned politicians buy his mother's vote with a few pesos and never returning or fulfilling any of their campaign promises: these experiences were transformative. Skin color was worth noting, but not nearly as important as whether a person was "high class"— corrupt, distant from the people, arrogant, or *una persona del pueblo*—someone of the people, modest, hardworking, principled, a populist. At one point, when asked about his political perspective, Enrique answered that he was a Democrat. He thought for another moment. "Well, here I vote for the Democrats. But I'm really probably a Zapatista."

CHAPTER 2

Day in Court

THE CAR IN front of us is slowing down, which is the sensible thing to do, as the stoplight at the corner is yellow. Enrique, trailing the vehicle by a good twenty feet, stomps down on the accelerator. The light turns red. Inches before we slam into the car's rear bumper he swerves to the left, now in the wrong lane entirely, and darts through the intersection. Cars on our left and right slam on their brakes, but we emerge unharmed, like a movie action hero slipping through sliding prison doors at the last moment.

"That was fun," Enrique suggests. "What did they say the number was?"

"Four-oh-seven Washington Avenue."

"No problem. Hey, what's wrong with you?" I try to relax my facial muscles, unclench my jaw.

"With me, nothing. Except that I'm in the car with a madman." Huge laughs from Enrique; he's in a very good mood for some reason.

Good mood or not, he shouldn't have taken the call. When it came in over the two-way radio, he was on the other side of Brooklyn. There aren't many rules at Speedy Car Service,* where Enrique has worked as a livery cab driver for a decade. The most

* Not the real name of the company.

important rule is simple: if a driver takes a call, he or she must arrive at the location within five minutes. If the customer has to wait more than five minutes and phones the base to complain, the driver is suspended for three hours, during which time he cannot take calls. Have it happen twice in one week, and you're suspended an entire day. If that doesn't do the trick, you'll eventually be told to find employment elsewhere. Time isn't simply money for livery cab drivers—once they take a call, their very job is on the line.

The passenger, a white woman looking to be in her late forties, is outside when we arrive, dressed in a beige business suit. Seven minutes have passed since Enrique took the call, but the woman doesn't appear agitated. "Where are you heading to, ma'am?" he asks. He loves switching from crass to sophisticated, takes pride in his ability to adapt.

"Union Square," she answers quickly, pulling out her cell phone.

"No problem." He smiles broadly. "And how is your day going?"

"Fine, thanks." She's already on her cell phone, but Enrique doesn't notice.

"That's a nice building you live in. Is the rent expensive?"

She shushes Enrique and begins to talk into her phone. Enrique turns to me and complains in Spanish. "You white people are all the same, too busy to talk. Get a Latino or black and they'll be friendly. But not the high-class people. Think they're too important to talk to a *taxista.*"

A few hours with Enrique in the car, and one can't miss noticing that he enjoys his job. Had he the opportunity to attend high school and college, with his native intelligence he could have probably been a first-class lawyer or engaging teacher. Instead, he completed the schooling available to him in Cuicatlán, graduating into the fields after sixth grade to plant crops and tend to the family's goats. The nearest town, Chinantla, did have a secondary school, but the trip was forty-five minutes one way on foot, and almost no families in Cuicatlán could afford the school uniforms and textbooks. Plus, there was always the need for another body to work the land.

Still, it's hard to feel sorry for him. He's a people person who enjoys speeding around, and in this life, at this moment, driving a cab is what he was born to do. Even when in a dark mood, he never fails to do his best to strike up a conversation with his customers, and his queries are far from the artificial interest of a Wal-Mart greeter. He genuinely wants to talk. Sometimes he'll even listen.

As a livery cab driver, the financial rewards for his labor are meager.[*] To observe the amount of money that passes through his hands each day might lead one to conclude that the taxi business is decent, perhaps even modestly lucrative. Yet about half of every fare dollar gets sucked up in gasoline, insurance, car payments, car repairs, and the weekly deductions from the base that all drivers must endure. All told, each year Enrique earns approximately twenty-three thousand dollars—which lands him well below the poverty line. And for good measure, it's one of the most dangerous occupations around.

Immigrants like Enrique dominate the New York City cab scene. According to a 2004 study, nine out of ten drivers are foreign born. In one year the typical driver lodges sixty-five thousand miles behind the wheel, which means the cars must be replaced frequently. But Enrique isn't the typical driver. Each year, along with his city driving, he makes numerous trips to states like South Carolina and Virginia, escorting Mexicans who are moving away and

---

* Livery cabs, sometimes called "car services," are neighborhood-based fleets, usually outside of Manhattan, where a passenger must call the base ahead of time to be picked up. Yellow medallion cabs, on the other hand, are flagged down on the street. Livery cab drivers like Enrique are forbidden from picking up random passengers that flag them down. Enrique picks such people up during nearly every shift.

would rather stuff their belongings into a car than take the bus. He also makes one trip a year to Mexico, sometimes two. There have been years when Enrique has driven more than one hundred thousand miles, the equivalent of roughly thirty cross-country trips.

The woman doesn't stop chatting on her cell phone during the entire ride to Union Square, but when she pays she leaves a decent tip of five dollars. Enrique thanks her, she nods and hustles off to her destination, and we head back to Brooklyn. "That's a hundred and fifty for the day," he says, adding the money to a thick wad held together with a rubber band. "Not bad, not bad at all. I'm hungry. Let's go to Flaco's."

By summer's end the situation in Enrique's apartment was causing him to grow increasingly bitter, and our time at Flaco's was usually spent discussing possible solutions to his housing predicament. An inventory of the building's three-month accumulation of violations reflected a living hell, though sifting through city papers isn't the best way to grasp such a reality. The language of the building inspector is spare and disinterested; one imagines they could describe genocide and make it seem like a low-key, unremarkable affair. Yet the sheer number and repetition of violations made for an impressive tally, only to be topped by the coming winter's crises.

The first official violations in Enrique's apartment were recorded on May 22, 2002. An inspector that day found exposed electric wires in the kitchen, emerging from a crumbling wall. The window in the bedroom was broken. The smoke detector was also defective. Less than a week later an inspector returned and added to the list a lack of hot water throughout the unit and an unlawful gate in the kitchen window, making it impossible to get to the fire escape. And even if a person *could* get to the fire escape, he or she would have found a chain and padlock around its ladder, at least ten feet aboveground. Most of these citations were written up as class-C violations, the most severe category, which pose "an immediately hazardous condition" to the tenant—and which according to New York City's housing code must be repaired within twenty-four hours. While inspecting the fire escape, the inspector also noted that the backyard had accumulated "refuse and/or rubbish."

An inspector returned to the building the following week, several days after my initial visit to Enrique's apartment. None of the violations had been fixed, and this time the inspector found the courage to follow his nose into the basement. Upon what was most assuredly a hurried affair, he glanced around long enough to scribble up an order that the landlord "cleanse and disinfect to the satisfaction of the department after removing the accumulation of raw sewage." In less sanitized parlance, to clean the shit up. After three sizzling June days, an inspector returned to the basement. The only change was the composition of the feces; a citation was written to remove what were now collections of "dry" sewage.

A blitz of violations followed. During the rest of June and July city inspectors returned to Enrique's apartment to find repeated instances of no hot water; a collapsing and rotting floor in the kitchen; repeated infestations of mice, rats, and cockroaches; an exposed electric socket in the bathroom; and a collapsing ceiling in the bathroom. They also cited the landlord twice more for new accumulations of raw sewage and water in the basement, which sat below exposed electric wiring. It would be difficult to conjure up a more "immediately hazardous" situation.

Despite the widespread violations—immediately hazardous and otherwise—almost nothing was actually done. Occasionally someone would show up at the building and claim to have been sent by the landlord to take care of a specific issue. But such visits were infrequent, and the solutions, though at times creative, were far from permanent. After a particularly nauseous and sweltering week, an employee of the landlord carted two large barrels full of dried garlic into the basement. For several days the sewage smell was eliminated, covered up by the strong stench of garlic. After that came a weeklong period where the two odors battled fiercely for supremacy; some days the smell was of garlic with a whiff of sewage—on others the stench of shit with a hint of the pungent herb. But a week later, with the sewage faction receiving significant reinforcements from a recent rainfall, the garlic had surrendered. Sewage reigned supreme. The smell seeped into walls, ceilings, floors; clothing, sheets, blankets, even shoes. Hair, though, was by far the worst.

And while the sewage was an unpleasant violation to live with, the most dangerous issue was the threat of fire, especially with the strung-out junkies barbecuing on the first floor. During the next several months, the city inspectors wrote up six unique violations in Enrique's apartment for the "obstructing bars or unlawful gates from window to fire escape" that the landlord had installed, which didn't allow the family to exit. The bars in the kitchen were never removed. They found eleven instances of exposed electric wires, located both in Enrique's apartment and in the basement. Eleven separate violations were sent to the landlord; the landlord didn't respond. Even the simplest of solutions, needing only a quick snip of the bolt cutter, seemed out of reach. On May 22 the inspector found the ladder for the fire escape padlocked. A letter was sent. The follow-up inspection, on May 28, found the same condition. Another letter was sent. The padlock remained.

"Family" is the answer most people give when asked to identify what matters more than anything else to them. Enrique was no different; his family was a source of both priceless support and endless frustration. And if one had to choose a specific event that defined

Enrique, that was never forgotten, it was when his father abandoned his mother.

At Flaco's, when we weren't talking about his housing situation, we were talking about family. Enrique was very curious about my parents. "What did they think when you moved all the way to New York?" he asked, when he learned that I had grown up in San Jose, California.

"It's pretty normal," I said. "Kids leave their parents all the time. Look at you. You left your mom back in Mexico. That's a lot farther away."

"I did *not* leave my mother," he said. His voice had dropped a level; it was the first time I had heard him truly angry, and I flinched. "I *had* to go. There wasn't anything to eat. There was no work. I went because I had to take care of my mother, and I couldn't take care of her in Mexico, because I couldn't earn money. I came here out of *necesidad,* not for a vacation or *aventura.*"

"Okay, sorry, I didn't mean anything. I was just saying that lots of people my age live far away from their parents. I still go home to see them."

When Enrique was seven months old, his father, Angel, left Cuicatlán and traveled to Tijuana, where he crossed legally with a visa. It was 1971.

Angel followed the same path as the other men from Cuicatlán, making his way to Brooklyn, where he found work at a plastics manufacturer while living on Myrtle Avenue, only several blocks away from Enrique's current apartment. Not long after, Enrique's sister Sabina crossed the border illegally and joined Angel, finding employment at the same factory. After several months, Sabina injured her hand at work and was forced to take a week off to recuperate. The accident was fortunate. Immigration agents raided the factory during her absence, and Angel, who had overstayed his visa, was deported.

When Angel returned to Cuicatlán for what would turn out to be a two-year stay, Enrique was a small, precocious four-year-old. His memories of that period are less than happy. "Angel would beat on everyone," he explained.

"Why?"

"How the fuck should I know? I was just a kid. He didn't need any reason. He just thought that everything had to go his way." Enrique went on to tell me that Angel beat his wife, Angela, in front of the kids, but he didn't elaborate, and I didn't pry. By this point he had put down his fork and was sitting tensely on a stool at Flaco's, clenching and unclenching his right fist unconsciously. We moved on.

Midway into his second year back in Mexico, Angel was again talking about leaving for Brooklyn. Angela was against the idea. She had married him, so he should stay with his family, be a responsible father and husband. But the decision was never really Angela's to make. Angel was a Mexican man, and he made his own rules. He crossed again in Tijuana, this time with the help of a coyote. As Mexicans say, Angel *fue de mojado*—went as a wetback, illegally.

He didn't return to Angela again until after the 1986 amnesty, though they did speak nearly every month on the phone. The amnesty legalized not only Angel's and Enrique's status, but also the status of Enrique's five other siblings who were in the United States at the time: Juan, Sabina, Maria, Sergio, and Angel, Jr. After several months of living with Angela, Angel told her he had to return to the United States one final time to fill out his retirement papers with the janitor's union, which he had been a member of during the decade that he cleaned floors at the Port Authority transportation hub in Manhattan. The plan was for him to return and retire with Angela. On the morning that he left, he promised that he would be back soon, and that with his retirement checks they would both be set for life. That was the last time she had heard from him.

Enrique had never forgiven Angel for abandoning Angela, or for initially leaving her alone when he was just a newborn. The anger was fresh, and even during periods when he and Angel were on good terms, interactions between the two were always delicate, as if they both knew that the current truce would most likely be short-lived. Yet Angel's abandonment of Angela was also something they never spoke about directly, as if making mention of what had happened was too painful to bear, and might even lead to a fight.

During our discussions at Flaco's Enrique frequently spoke of his trips to Mexico to visit his mother; he made the drive south at least once a year and sent money home regularly. Eventually he had learned to tolerate Angel's new girlfriend, Leticia, who later became his father's second wife. But it had been a long and often difficult process for Enrique, and he still placed his ultimate loyalties firmly with his mother. Though he was living thousands of miles away from her, he still saw his role as being her absolute protector. "Fuck Angel," he would say whenever he and his father were arguing. "I don't need him for anything. I've got Angela." During these episodes he could go months, sometimes years, without speaking with his father. But every Sunday, Enrique and Angela spoke for hours on the telephone, without exception.

By October, conditions in Enrique's apartment were reaching a breaking point. The electricity went out for a week, and when a city inspector came on Halloween he found the entire building dark, with tenants and squatters using candles and flashlights to get around. Rats and cockroaches scurried about, using the refuse still piled up in the backyard as a headquarters. There was no hot water. It was beginning to get cold.

By now inspectors were coming to the building every week, thanks in part to a lawsuit filed by Enrique. When Junior had become sick after a string of cold September days without hot water, Enrique grew frustrated enough to travel to Brooklyn's housing court, located downtown on Livingston Street, and initiated a "Housing Part Action" for lack of repairs—the last resort for tenants seeking redress. After Enrique spent the day filling out paperwork and listing the violations, he sent a summons to the landlord and was given a return date to see a judge.

On the date of his case Enrique arrived early. This was his chance to finally say what he wanted to say, and his papers were meticulously organized—with violations listed in chronological order, the most serious hazards first. He wasn't going to be one of those tenants who arrive unprepared, with only their own words to back them up. No, when Enrique walked into court, he was walking in armed with *evidence*. He might not have gone to law school, but he knew everything there was to know about housing code violations, and he wasn't about to let a smooth-talking slumlord get off the hook. "In Mexico corruption is everywhere," he told me a few days before the court date. "Here, you have to follow the rule of law. And I know what the law says." He was optimistic.

But instead of confronting his landlord face-to-face, he spoke briefly in the hallway outside of the courtroom with an attorney for the owner, who acted surprised to learn about the conditions. When they were called in front of the judge, the attorney launched into a defense of his client, stating that no one had been aware of the conditions that existed. Enrique then began to chronicle his experiences in the building, but the judge hushed him and simply asked for a report of the code violations in the building. While the judge looked over the paperwork, Enrique tried again to explain the living conditions; pieces of paper couldn't fully capture what his family had endured during the past six months. Again the judge told him to be quiet. After reviewing the violation printout, the judge ordered the landlord to complete the needed repairs. The landlord's attorney promised that the work would be done, repeating his belief that his client hadn't been aware of the problems before today. Enrique thanked the judge and left, upset that he never had the chance to talk. "The judge never told the lawyer to be quiet," Enrique recounted. "And I knew from the moment he opened his mouth that the lawyer was full of shit."

The judge's deadline passed. Enrique waited on the dates that the attorney had promised a worker would come by, which caused him to miss hours he could have been working. No one came to fix the violations.

Enrique returned to court. The same attorney was there again and promised that it wouldn't happen again. It did. Enrique returned a third time. This time the attorney arrived late and asked for a postponement, which was granted. On the fourth date the attorney never arrived. Now the judge was finally beginning to share some of Enrique's anger and found the landlord in contempt, fining him twenty-five thousand dollars in civil penalties.

Still, this was of limited solace to Enrique—his apartment was falling apart. Waving his violation papers in front of the judge's face, he demanded action and then listened in frustration to the judge's advice. "He told me, 'Look, why don't you just move? Why are you still living there?' I don't need him to tell me where I should live—that's not his job. His job is to make sure they fix my apartment, to *enforzar la ley.*" Enrique had recently read about the "warranty of habitability," a city code that said all tenants had the right to safe housing. Yet here he was, being told by the judge that it didn't apply in his case.

Instead, the judge told Enrique that if he wanted he could attempt to collect the fine by starting a case in civil court. Not yet completely disillusioned with the city's court system, Enrique did as he was told. But no one could locate the landlord, and the case went nowhere. "It was pointless," Enrique said, reflecting on his experiences. "You go to court and miss a day of work, sit around all day waiting to talk to the judge. The landlord just has to send his attorney, who sits there with a fucking smile on his face. The judge tells you to come back another day, give them more time. Then the same thing happens. It's just a game to them. The landlord plays, the judge plays, and then they say, 'Oh, we didn't know,' or, 'Oh, just come back to court again.' Fucking stupid. Real fucking stupid."

According to the City-Wide Task Force on Housing court (referred here as "City-Wide"), a nonprofit organization that monitors the court, Enrique's case was far from unique. Housing Court in New York City was established primarily to protect tenants by codifying their legal rights and forcing landlords to take certain steps in order to proceed with an eviction. Before the court was established, a tenant's primary resource when living in substandard housing had been to simply withhold the rent, and landlords frequently evicted tenants by employing "hired muscle" to physically remove a person's belongings—with or without cause. With the establishment of a housing court, however, tenants could sue their landlords for lack of services and were granted a legal process (and therefore, at the very least, time) if the landlord was attempting to evict them.

Yet over the years, the court system evolved into an institution that did little to enforce the city's housing code; it became instead a debt-collection agency for landlords. The institution designed originally to level the playing field remained highly slanted toward landlords, who were almost always represented by counsel. Tenants, on the other hand, almost always proceeded alone, arriving in court with limited knowledge of their rights. Tenants who spoke little English were even less prepared to navigate the system, and were routinely intimidated into signing their rights away by overbearing landlord attorneys outside the courtroom, what the late *Village Voice* journalist J. A. Lobbia referred to as "hallway justice." And even for those who were confident and informed enough to proceed with legal action, the system regularly failed.

An investigation by City-Wide into HP Actions (lawsuits for repairs) filed during 1999 found that three years later nearly half of the units still had the original violations—and 22 percent still had *some* of the original violations. What is more, the financial penalties for such inaction on the landlord's part were practically nonexistent. Of the 672 tenant-initiated HP Actions analyzed during 1999, City-Wide found that only 16, or 2 percent, resulted in landlords actually having to pay a fine—and that many times these fines were sharply reduced from their original amounts.

Timeliness was also a crucial component, as many of the violations were "extremely hazardous" and therefore demanded quick attention. When landlords like Enrique's asked for more time, or disputed the tenant's claims that repairs hadn't been completed, the average wait from the first court date to second inspection was forty-four days—a lifetime when one is forced to endure a New York City winter without heat or hot water. City-Wide's conclusion was overwhelmingly discouraging. "Overall, we found that it took tenants a significant number of days to get a court-ordered inspection and court date," they wrote, "and over 55 days to have the court order fines when repairs were not done and almost no financial penalties to the landlord for not making court-ordered repairs in a timely fashion."

They continued: "Unfortunately, the people who are best situated to stem the tide of housing deterioration are the ones worst treated by our enforcement system. Far from being the linchpin of our code enforcement effort, tenant plaintiffs at Housing Court are treated as if they are somehow to blame, paying court costs, enduring delays and postponements, and often pursuing cases to little avail."

By the winter of 2002, one year before the report was published, Enrique could have already told them that.

CHAPTER 3

A Corn Stalk
Grows in Brooklyn

SUPERAR. IN SPANISH the word can have several related meanings: to excel, to overcome, to surpass, to transcend. To speak of immigrating to the United States from Mexico is to speak of the hope of *superando,* of breaking new ground, building a better life for oneself and one's children.

The stories of immigrating, of superando, may include adventure, risk, adrenaline, sacrifice, and even loneliness or boredom. For Enrique's own notions of superando the checklist was by most standards modest. He wanted to work and save money and send some back to his mother. He wanted to find a wife and have a family, raise children who were every bit as smart as the richest, whitest Americans, and who didn't have to do manual labor. "Spend all day in an office, on a computer" is how he envisioned their soft-hands, sweat-free existence. And he wanted to one day have a nice place to live, a home he could be proud to show off to visiting relatives. "I don't need to be rich," he said. "But I want to live comfortably." Though he didn't use the phrase, Enrique wanted to become a member of the middle class: to shrug off the world of food stamps and Medicaid, collapsing ceilings and cockroach infestations.

To break out of his current poverty, he always seemed to have a scheme or two kicking around in his head. One was to purchase a

second car and incorporate his own taxi business, which he could
eventually expand. Enrique's employer, a man named Candelario,*
was from a Mexican town only ten miles from Cuicatlán, and his car
service business had been good to him. He now had a fleet of eighty
cars and had purchased a house in the Bay Ridge section of
Brooklyn. Enrique liked the idea of owning his own business, and
though he had filed papers to form the company—which he called
"Enrique's Limousine Corporation, Inc."—he hadn't gotten
together the money for another car.

Another idea had been to purchase Flaco's restaurant. Enrique
knew how the restaurant business worked and prided himself in
his cooking abilities. "I've done it all: I've washed dishes, I've
waited tables, and I've cooked," he said. "I can make omelets,
chicken, tortillas, pasta, anything you want." The long hours of a
restaurateur didn't worry him; he'd always worked long hours. At
one point, when business seemed to be floundering, Flaco had
contemplated selling his equipment to Enrique. But business had
picked up as the neighborhood continued to gentrify, and Flaco
had lost interest in selling.

Enrique was talking about these plans less now. Instead, he was
beginning to see his housing court experiences as a metaphor for his
time spent in the United States: despite his determination, life
seemed to be repeating itself without any discernible improvement.
"Let me tell you, this life is not easy," he said to me one afternoon
after spending the morning in court. He appeared to be in a reflec-
tive mood—an uncommon experience for someone who was always
on the go. "Mexicans here have it very hard." He looked at me, his
face a mixture of anger and apathy. I fully expected him to continue.
Instead, he let his comment drift off unattended. It was as if he didn't
have faith that he could make his words really reflect how he was

* Not his real name.

feeling. Or maybe he had said everything that he felt needed to be said: Mexicans here have it very hard.

Part of the reason for Enrique's depression was that he thought he had turned the corner on his housing problems, left them back on Broadway Avenue. In 1987, after a fire, Enrique's father was forced out of his apartment in the Broadway Avenue building. Without a home, the city relocated Angel to an apartment building in Williamsburg. Enrique, still living in the crowded apartment in Borough Park with Sabina and Angel, Jr., saw the fire as an opportunity to get his own place. He spoke with the property manager of the low-income co-op, who was a friend of Angel's and also from Mexico, who agreed to give him a lease. Though the building was in a permanent state of disrepair, the rent was an affordable two hundred dollars a month. Only two years after crossing the border, Enrique had his own apartment. His superando seemed to be on pace.

In the building lived a woman named Paula, from the medium-sized city of Izúcar de Matamoros, located in western Puebla not far from the border of Morelos. Though she was fourteen years older than Enrique—thirty-two to his eighteen—they had immediately hit it off, and Paula moved into apartment number six, joining Enrique. Two years later, in 1990, Paula gave birth to Cristina, the first of three daughters they would have together.

In his own estimation, Enrique was not entirely ready to be a father. Twenty years old, he was drinking too much and spending time with a group of other young Mexican men who more often than not found themselves getting into fights come Saturday night. The son of the building manager, a young man about the same age as Enrique, was named Manuel,* and the two quickly became best friends, drinking and fighting together.

In 1993 Christina came down with a fever and cough. Enrique and Paula took the two-year-old to Woodhull Hospital, but the doctors incorrectly diagnosed her condition as pneumonia. When the antibiotic medication failed to work, the parents, who were already skeptical about the quality of care at the large facility, brought her to a private physician. A doctor ordered a series of tests, one of which showed that their daughter was suffering from severe lead poisoning. Her blood lead level was 48 micrograms per deciliter, nearly five times the threshold of 10 that the Centers for Disease Control defines as lead poisoned. Representatives from the health and housing departments came out to the building and discovered numerous lead paint hazards, especially in one of the bedroom closets.

According to Enrique, the representatives were of no further assistance. "They didn't do anything for me," he recalls. The super of the building, a man named Gilberto, was the father-in-law of Enrique's brother Sergio, who now lives in Alaska. "HPD came out and found lots of lead, but me and Gilberto were the ones who took out the closet that had lead paint and put up the Sheetrock." Cristina was given various medicines until her blood lead level dropped, but the doctors warned Enrique and Paula that their daughter had probably suffered permanent brain damage and would likely exhibit behavioral and learning problems in the future.

Later that year Enrique and Paula were married in downtown Manhattan on a hot August day. In 1994 their second daughter, Dalía, was born. In 1997 Paula gave birth to another girl, Lourdes. It was a bad time to bring a new child into the family: Enrique and Paula were constantly fighting over "just about everything," according to Enrique. By 1998, with their relationship growing increasingly strained, Enrique decided to move out, joining his father in his Williamsburg apartment. Though I've asked many times about the details of their breakup and about the issues they fought over, Enrique remained vague, preferring not to re-create the experience (Paula declined to speak to me). "I moved out, that was all there was to it," he said. He was glad to be able to crash temporarily at his father's apartment, but he knew that eventually the two would begin to fight again, so he kept his ears open about cheap rooms for rent in the neighborhood.

Juana had even worse luck than Enrique when it came to relationships. In 1982 her first daughter, Anayeli, was born in Juana's hometown of Santa Ana Coatepec, a village several hours north of Cuicatlán. The father left Juana soon after Anayeli's birth, and without the means to support herself Juana crossed the border two years later, leaving her daughter with her grandparents. In 1989 Anayeli would join Juana in Brooklyn and eventually become a legal resident after marrying a U.S. citizen and moving to New Jersey.

Not long after arriving in Brooklyn, Juana met a man named Apolonio, and in 1985 she gave birth to her second daughter, Sandra. Apolonio was a heavy drinker who was also prone to violence. He beat Juana regularly. After Sandra's birth Apolonio traveled to Mexico and came back with another woman, whom he had wed in the interim. Juana was glad to have gotten rid of Apolonio, though he would sometimes stop by the apartment she shared with her older sister in Coney Island to check in on Sandra. "I told him that I wished he would stop coming around," Juana said, "but he told me that nothing would stop him from seeing his daughter." Eventually, however, something would stop him. In 1994, after being severely beaten in a fight, Apolonio went into a coma, and when he recovered he had suffered significant brain damage and was unable to walk. His brothers, afraid the gang that had administered the beating might return, took him back to Puebla, and Juana hasn't heard from him since.

Juana's problems continued, however. She met a man named Guadalupe who lived in her Coney Island building, and soon they were a couple. In 1988 Juana gave birth to Abram. Guadalupe shared two key characteristics with Apolonio: he was an alcoholic, and he was violent. Family life was chaotic. Guadalupe was drunk most nights, and though Juana was successful in keeping him away from Sandra, she herself was beaten numerous times. One night Juana found the courage to call the police during one of Guadalupe's violent episodes, but when they came Juana was too afraid to file a report. Guadalupe grew angrier.

Understated by nature, Juana rarely uses language that evokes much emotion, but the following years—between 1990 and 1996—she describes as "*absolutamente horrible.*" Only a near disaster released Juana from the grips of her second abusive relationship. In 1996 she received a call from a social worker at Sandra's school. Sandra had told the worker that Guadalupe had recently attempted to sexually assault her while Juana was working at the garment factory. Both Abram and Sandra were placed in the custody of the state for two weeks, and Guadalupe disappeared. "He probably went to Mexico," Juana said. "But I'm not really sure, 'cause I never heard anything from him again." After a series of interviews, Juana's children were placed back in her custody, and she moved into an apartment on Central Avenue in Bushwick.

It was while living on Central Avenue that Juana first met Enrique. By 1998, with her hours at the garment factory cut (it would go out of business within the year), Juana began working afternoons at the house of a friend, who had three sewing machines in her living room and did piecework for local department stores. This friend was from Chinantla and frequently hired Enrique to drop off her bundles of clothing at the department stores. One day Juana was asked to go along in the car as well, in order to help unload a large delivery.

"I remember him talking that first day about his hometown," Juana said. "He kept saying he was from Cuicatlán and Chinantla, and how his mother still lived there. I just stayed quiet and listened to him. You know, he doesn't need anyone else; he can just keep on talking and talking. I remember thinking it was strange that he was talking so much about Mexico, since he's here living in Brooklyn."

Eager to move out of Angel's apartment, while transporting clothing to the store one day Enrique asked Juana if she had any housing leads. For whatever reason, Juana was finding that she liked Enrique, and she was also having a hard time coming up with the money for the room that she rented. Enrique agreed to help with the rent and joined Juana, Sandra, and Abram in an apartment they shared with several other Mexicans on Willoughby Avenue. Six months later they moved into another small room on nearby Kent Avenue. At some point during that year the two roommates became a couple. On January 3, 2001, Enrique and Juana celebrated the birth of their first child together, Junior. It was a joyful experience, but it added to their real estate problem. Now squeezed into a single room were Junior, Abram, Sandra, Enrique, and Juana. So not long after Junior was brought home from the hospital they moved again, this time into Leticia's apartment in the Tompkins housing projects, where Angel was now living.

Enrique knew the living situation with Angel wouldn't last; extended contact with his father always resulted eventually in yelling matches and promises never to speak again. So while driving his cab around town he kept his eyes open for available apartments, and one fall day he saw a rental sign in front of a decent-looking building on Dekalb Avenue. On December 5, 2001, the family moved into the building. "Finally I thought that everything was going to be good, nice," Enrique said. "After we moved in, the divorce papers went through between Paula and me, so I didn't have to worry about her so much anymore. And then, just when we're getting settled, all this shit starts happening again in the building.

I'm not just going to let Junior get poisoned like Cristina. I'm not just going to keep suffering like I did before."

After the winter of complaining to the city without results, Enrique's strategy began to shift. He stopped calling the city. He stopped leaving messages with the landlord. The paint was peeling in the bedrooms, and the floors were rotting throughout the apartment—and he had numerous pages of violations and his own common sense to confirm that these were serious breaches of New York City's housing code. But if the city wouldn't do anything, at least he didn't have to pay rent, which got him thinking about creating his own solution. He wasn't going to suffer through another freezing winter. If the definition of insanity is doing the same thing over and over again and expecting different results, Enrique had tired of playing the part of the lunatic.

Boiling water in teakettle increments to bathe Junior was a long, tedious affair: the first thing they needed was a dependable stream of hot water. Enrique saw a special for hot water heaters at Home Depot, and one spring morning he drove over to Queens to pick one out. He settled on a forty-five-gallon model, more than large enough for the family, and shelled out $250.00.

The previous week Enrique had made a final complaint to the city, but this time he didn't assume anything would actually be fixed. He was doing research, gathering intelligence. When the inspector came, Enrique was more interested in peppering him with questions than adding to the long list of standing violations. If one were to install a hot water heater, what types of regulations would a person need to follow? What does the New York City housing code say about the type of foundation needed to support such a contraption? Can it be placed in the kitchen, for example? How about right here, next to the sink? Anything wrong with that?

The next week, after trudging the hot water heater up the shaky flight of stairs, Enrique began to work. He poured a cement slab of three square feet next to the sink, making sure it was the required five inches thick. After it dried he went out and purchased pipes from a hardware store and began to tear down sections of the Sheetrock. Then he purchased welding equipment. With the kitchen looking like a construction zone, Juana was beginning to wonder just exactly what Enrique had in mind, but she kept her concerns to herself.

As a teenager, Enrique had worked in construction off and on for several years, and though he hadn't done any welding himself, he had watched others do the work and was a quick study. For three days he welded the new pipes from his hot water heater to the building's water supply. The fumes from the welding caused him some dizziness, but if he kept all of the windows open and a fan going he was able to work in thirty-minute increments. As he labored, Juana kept Junior away from the area, occasionally running requested materials to her sweating, light-headed husband.

Above Enrique lived his friend Refugio, who also drove a cab for Speedy Car Service. Enrique had told Refugio about his plan and decided to install piping from his water heater along the kitchen wall and up through the floor of Refugio's apartment so that his friend could also have hot water. "That way the hot water would run along our wall and on his kitchen floor, so it would also help heat the apartments," Enrique explained later. "And it actually worked—both of our kitchens stayed warm."

Encouraged by the successful installation of the hot water heater, with the assistance of Juana and Abram, Enrique spent the next three months continuing to rebuild the apartment. The floor of the bedroom was covered with stained brown carpet, and the kitchen with peeling plastic tiles. It was also uneven, dipping in certain areas and with plenty of baseball-sized bumps scattered throughout. Enrique tore out the carpet and the cheap tiles and made another trip to the hardware store, buying three-quarter-inch plywood and a level. Over the course of several weeks he pulled up the rotted wood floor and nailed down fresh lumber to the joists, making sure to remove all of the bumps. The entire family made a trip to Home Depot, and they selected shiny tiles of blue and white for the bedrooms and black and white for the kitchen.

A week later, when I visit, the tiles have been glued down, and the effect is extraordinary: with a new and flush floor, the apartment is beginning to actually look inviting, even pristine. Enrique walks me through the rooms, smiling at his handiwork and explaining the various steps of the project.

"But this is only a beginning," he says, a wide grin on his face, running his right hand along the cracks in the bedroom walls. "There's still a lot to be done. The walls, the bathroom, the backyard . . ." He is not complaining—he is excited, almost giddy. "I told you we would fix this place up, didn't I? I told you, we're fucking mojados, but we aren't as stupid as we look! Didn't I tell you? Fucking mojados are the smartest pendejos in the world!"

Hearing his father yelling, Junior runs into the room. Enrique scoops him up. "Isn't that right, Junior?" Junior smiles at his nodding father. "That's right, mojados like your *papá y mamá, la gente más inteligente en nueva york.*" And he laughs loudly at his inadvertent rhyme, looking happier than I have seen him in months.

During the next several weeks I see Enrique infrequently. Work, partly because of the seemingly endless number of Mexicans that Enrique had referred to my organization, keeps me busy. I had given him a bunch of my business cards to hand out to his passengers. "Every Mexican has a problem with their landlord," he had told me—and he didn't seem to be exaggerating. Enrique is likewise occupied, pounding nails and painting walls.

The few times I do run into Enrique, his mood continues to be ebullient. He has successfully turned the tables on his housing predicament, turning a threat (landlord abandonment) into an opportunity (with no rent to pay, he can do the work himself). Other tenants might have been indignant, upset about having to do so much work that was technically the landlord's responsibility. But Enrique was a man who liked to get his hands dirty, who relished physical and intellectual challenges. He had a task to do—something that proved he was self-reliant, something that was for the benefit of his family. Enrique craved tangible results, and after nearly two decades in the United States he was finally seeing them.

It wasn't just the housing improvements: in other ways Enrique's life was as stable as it had ever been. He had a new son, a woman he loved, and a quiet home life (notwithstanding the construction ruckus of his own making). Most important, he had the opportunity to put his previous problems behind him and start over; he had a new family. Recently, after prodding by Juana, Enrique had even given up drinking. He had a collection of self-help tapes in Spanish that he would listen to while driving his cab, as well as several books with titles like *Power Without Limits* and *Secrets for Success and Happiness*. He swore by these books and often tried to get me to read them. Not only did they help him stop drinking, he insisted, but his temper was also kept in check through the breathing exercises they suggested.

Since I had met Enrique I had never actually seen him drunk, but I had seen him angry, and it was a frightening experience; I could only imagine how much more so it would be when alcohol was added to the equation. Most striking was how quickly his temper could overtake him: we would be driving along, laughing about one thing or another, and a person would cut him off—sending him into a rage that I did my best to dissipate, often without success. Though he was carefree about many things and often laughed about his misfortunes, whenever he felt that someone was doing him wrong he could quickly shift gears and become a different person entirely. He had been in more fights than he could remember, and when calm he spoke about his temper in a detached manner, as if he were describing something that existed independent of himself, over which he had little control. "He got his temper from his father," Enrique's sister Sabina once told me when the topic of anger management came up. "All of the men in the family are the same, they all are hot-blooded."

His anger could also be provoked when people within his circle of friends and family were slighted. One day Abram had left his bicycle outside for a moment and ran into the apartment to grab something. When he returned he found that his bike had disappeared. Naturally nonconfrontational, Abram wanted to just forget about the incident, but once Enrique learned what had happened he went downstairs and walked around the neighborhood, searching for the bike. Eventually he saw a stocky man resting atop its seat in front of a liquor store.

Without a moment's hesitation, Enrique confronted the man, demanding to know where he had gotten the bike. The man made the mistake of growling something along the lines of "What the fuck do you care?" That was all Enrique needed to hear. He picked up the bike, with the man still attached, and gave it a violent shake, tossing him onto the ground. Suddenly the tough guy wasn't feeling so tough, and he walked away without a word. Abram got his bike back.

In fact, Enrique could go to battle even for people he hardly knew. Once, when he was driving an acquaintance in his cab they passed a group of people beating up a young man. "Oh shit," the passenger said to Enrique. "That's my friend they're fucking with."

Enrique stopped the car and without asking a question jumped out and ran toward the group, swinging wildly. Although he was outnumbered, after landing several hard punches to the faces of the attackers, they turned running and Enrique helped the bruised man to his feet. It was only then that he realized his passenger was still back in the car. "Can you believe that?" Enrique asked, reflecting on the cowardice. "What kind of 'friend' just sits there and doesn't do anything?" At the time, I had shared Enrique's indignation, though the truth was that I had never had my worthiness as a friend tested in a fight and wasn't all too certain I'd have gotten out of the car, either. And Enrique barely knew his passenger.

Though I worried that Enrique's temper could eventually come back to harm him, I was also glad to have him as a friend. There was no doubt in my mind that if I found myself threatened, Enrique would do everything in his power to protect me. Without trying, he was fearless; an instinctive warrior. He had some sort of code that separated his world distinctly into good and evil, and he was unquestioningly loyal to those he saw as good—even when at times there didn't seem to be any rational reason for his beliefs. One of his passengers had a friend who was being beaten up: the passenger was *his,* so he sprung into action to defend the friend. *His* stepson's bike had been stolen, an insult that demanded he stalk the neighborhood for the thief. In both of these situations Enrique's actions might have gotten him seriously injured, even killed. "What if one of the guys on the street had had a gun?" I asked. "What if the man on the bike was a member of a gang?" Enrique shrugged the questions off. He hadn't had time to worry about those possibilities back then, and he sure as hell wasn't worried about them now.

"I've been shot before, you know."

I didn't know. "What?"

"Yeah, it was back when I was living with Paula on Broadway. I think in 1990, the same year Cristina was born. I was coming home from work at Tiffany's and a black guy tried to rob me with a gun. He said, 'Give me your money.' I told him no. But his gun wouldn't work, it was jammed. So I took out my steak knife that I had in my jacket from work and started running after him."

"You ran after a guy with a gun?"

"Yeah, fuck it, I was young and stupid. So I chased him away and then went back to the building, but I didn't have my keys. I was hitting the buzzer, and the guy came back with one of his friends, who had another gun. He was maybe ten feet away and shot me once, and then they took off running."

Enrique rolled up his right sleeve and showed me his thick forearm. Halfway up his elbow was a white dime-sized scar from the bullet's entrance, and on the backside of his arm was another circle from the exit. After being shot he went inside, grabbed a handful of napkins to hold over the wound, and walked to the hospital several blocks away.

"You chased a guy with a gun?" I was having a hard time with the facts he was laying out.

"Fuck it, like I said. Why should he have my money? Fucking pendejo thought he could just do whatever he wanted to a stupid *mexicano*. But he learned: not *this* mexicano. Back then the Puerto Ricans and the blacks always thought they could rob any Mexicans they wanted. They thought we wouldn't fight. Fuck that."

Confronted with the same situation today, I got the feeling that Enrique would choose the same questionable tactic, to run after an armed man with a steak knife. But though he didn't seem able to change this tendency—this inclination to defend his honor—he insisted he was doing his best to turn over a new leaf and not resort to violence as his first solution to problems. "When I was younger

I could have gotten into a lot more trouble," he admitted. "I was lucky that things turned out as good as they did. Now I think I am smarter, especially since I'm not drinking. I have to do a better job of staying in control. I have Junior and Juana to look after. But I'm not going to let some asshole just rob me."

Summer is about to begin when Enrique calls me to say that the work in the apartment has been completed. A year has passed since my first visit, and when I arrive and begin to walk up the steps I can still smell something rotten in the basement, but the odor isn't nearly as strong. Inside the apartment the gray and grimy walls are now a gentle baby blue. "When I knocked them down there were many holes, which is where the rats would come through," Enrique tells me while he and Juana give me a tour. "Since I put them up we haven't seen even one rat. And I fixed the bathroom ceiling, where that one rat fell. Remember that *pendeja?*" I nod. "Remember, Juana, *esa pendeja rata?*" Juana nods; I think it would be safe to say that Juana will go to her grave with that memory intact.

"Anyway, no more rats, simple y sencillo. We covered up the holes and we cleaned up the backyard—that's all you've got to do. Come look." I follow Enrique and Juana across the glistening kitchen floor, which Juana has just mopped. "You remember how much *basura* there was in the backyard before? Well, look at it now."

The apartment itself has been radically redone, but by far the most dramatic change is in the backyard. I whistle and then follow Enrique through the kitchen window and onto the fire escape. (He'd finally removed the illegal gate himself.)

"You see, I said we'd fix this up," Enrique says, admiring the fruits of their labor. To our left and right are trash-strewn backyards, but ten feet below us is a healthy garden of waist-high cornstalks. "You should have been here to see all the bags of garbage we collected," he says. "I think we threw out something like fifteen bags—me, Juana, Abram." The scene has a surreal quality to it; in the gritty streets of Brooklyn, a plot of cultivated land is emerging amid urban decay, like a stubborn weed poking through solid concrete on a basketball court. There is much talk of immigrants coming to the United States and bringing their customs. Here, it seems, Enrique and Juana have actually unpacked a small section of Mexico, dirt and all.

Making Them Hurt

WHEN ONE IS forced to deal with problems alone they can seem insurmountable. A key principle of organizing, then, is to connect discouraged people who are suffering from the same issues so they can learn that they are not alone and that perhaps it's time to actually do something about the issue, together.

Linking people together is especially important when one is working within communities that have special reasons to fear retaliation for their activities. Undocumented Mexican immigrants, for example. Often landlords would brazenly threaten to "call immigration and have them deported" if their immigrant tenants complained about their housing conditions. In four years I never saw any evidence that this had ever occurred, but it was nonetheless an effective technique of intimidation.

"Too many Mexicans don't stand up for themselves," Enrique would often complain. "They think that just because they're mojados they have to suffer abuse. But if we've got enough of us together, who's going to do anything to us? But *la clave*"—the key—"is that we've got to organize, to fight *juntos, unidos.*" Though he was sometimes frustrated with what he saw as the Mexican community's reluctance to assert their rights, he never truly gave up on the chance for them to come together. For one thing, he almost

never missed a single event held by the Pratt Area Community
Council (PACC), the nonprofit organization that I worked for.
Each month we would facilitate meetings, which Enrique chaired
several times, where we discussed ongoing organizing campaigns,
learned about recent problems that people were experiencing, and
began to get to know one another. Since they had joined PACC,
Enrique and Juana made a point of coming to the meetings and
usually purchased soda for the group. On cold nights Enrique often
drove our older members, mostly African American women, to the
church where the meetings were held.

My organizing strategy, having known Enrique for a year, had
evolved to this: meet hesitant Mexican immigrants who are intimidated by their landlords, invite them to our monthly community
meeting, and have them speak with Enrique. It was simple, but it
worked. One family was afraid to call in a complaint to the city
about the leaks and rats in their apartment. "The landlord said that
if we did, he would call la migra," the husband said to the group in
a hushed tone during one of our winter meetings, while snow piled
up outside. "I want my son and wife to live in a good home, but I
don't want us to get kicked out of the country."

"Your landlord is a liar," Enrique responded. "He's just afraid that
he'll be forced to actually do what the law says he has to do." And
Enrique explained how housing inspectors would come and simply
cite violations, how they never asked any questions about the
tenant's immigration status. How if all the Mexicans stopped being
so afraid, they would finally find themselves making progress, living
in good conditions. How this man should not only call the city but
also join our organization and fight for new laws, better enforcement, equal rights.

The family called me the next day; they had contacted the city.
It was one thing for a white man like me to say that the housing

inspectors wouldn't question them about their immigration status. It was another thing entirely to see an immigrant like themselves tell them that they had the right—indeed, that they were obligated for the good of *la raza*—to stand up and fight back.

By the spring and summer of 2003 a battle was brewing in New York City over an issue with which Enrique was intimately familiar: childhood lead poisoning. Councilman Bill Perkins, from Harlem, had introduced a piece of legislation that would significantly strengthen the regulations that protected children from lead poisoning. According to the health department's own statistics, 94 percent of lead-poisoned children in New York City were children of color, which meant it was not only a health issue, but an environmental justice cause as well. And the highest incidents of lead poisoning occurred in Central Brooklyn, where Enrique had lived for nearly two decades.

It was no mystery how children became lead poisoned. Poorly maintained apartments, built around the turn of the century before lead paint was outlawed, were the culprits. Leaks, collapsing ceilings, peeling paint—all increased the chances that a young child would ingest dangerous amounts of deteriorated paint during the normally healthy hand-to-mouth developmental stage. Once poisoned, the effects were irreversible, leading to consequences like a reduction in IQ, problems in comprehension and concentration, and even juvenile delinquency, according to medical experts.

As a housing advocacy organization located in the middle of the so-called lead belt of Brooklyn, in the spring of 2003 we implemented a participatory research project. One dozen high school students were trained to collect samples in homes for lead dust, and we knocked on enough doors to test sixty units. Our results confirmed a crisis: one out of every three homes tested was discovered to have lead levels in excess of the federal safety guidelines. The vast majority of the dangerous homes had young children growing up within them. This was not just a housing problem—this was a public health nightmare. One of the only good pieces of news was that Enrique's renovation and cleanup work had been a success. There was no lead found in his apartment.

We called a meeting of all of the parents, which Enrique attended, and decided to hold a press conference where we would release a report outlining our findings and demanding action, including the passage of the new lead bill introduced by Perkins. Although Enrique's home hadn't been found to be dangerous, he agreed to be one of the speakers, as a parent whose child had been poisoned. "It's been so long since Cristina was poisoned," he told the group. "This could all have been prevented, but they still haven't fixed the problem."

By mid-morning on the date of our press conference, Enrique is in his taxi, making a second trip to Brooklyn's Borough Hall, where we will be releasing the report. He dropped off Juana and two other Mexican parents twenty minutes ago, and now his car is filled with another Mexican family—whose parents are undocumented—who have two children recently diagnosed with lead poisoning. Their apartment was found by the students to contain lead levels more than one hundred times the safety threshold. Enrique had volunteered to bring the family directly to the event, because he wanted to make sure parents whose children were poisoned would be well repre-sented, and he was afraid the family might back out if they were not personally chauffeured. "We need them to testify," he said to me sev-eral days earlier. "I can speak, but Cristina was poisoned a long time ago. We need new families. We need to show them that children are still being poisoned, so they can't just say we're making it up." Today he was going to make sure the Mexicans were well represented. "This is too important," he stated. "We need to hit them hard," and he smacked his right fist into the palm of his left hand, ready for war.

Organizers have helped parents to develop testimony for today. I was in charge of working with Enrique, but he hadn't been all that interested in preparation; his preference was to just get behind a microphone and start speaking, to trust his instincts. Besides, he did have his own notes to rely on if he needed guidance, in the form of the dozens of violation printouts he liked to carry around. I wasn't worried about his testimony; my concern was whether any news organizations would actually show up to cover the event.

By the time we arrange the order of the speakers—several parents and several high school students—an unbelievable number of press representatives are lined up. The *New York Times* had run a piece on our project this morning, and it seems to have triggered interest among every major English and Spanish television network, along with a host of other newspapers.[*] It also didn't hurt that across the plaza, at Brooklyn's Supreme Court, some sort of important case is scheduled to begin, so TV crews assigned to Borough Hall are able to wander between events.

Enrique is the last parent to testify. Holding Junior in his arms and looking out at the half-dozen cameras and numerous reporters with notepads in hand, he strikes a defiant note. While the other parents have spoken about their experience as a tragedy, Enrique is accusatory.

"When blacks and Latinos get poisoned, the city sits back and says it can do nothing," he begins, his voice booming. "But they need to remember that we aren't talking about animals here, we're talking

---

[*] "One-third of Children in Part of Brooklyn Are Exposed to Lead Dangers, Study Finds," by Diane Cardwell, New York Times, June 9, 2003.

about children. They say it will cost too much to fix the problem, but how much do they want to spend on our poisoned children? Ten years ago my daughter was poisoned, and now she needs special schooling because she can't concentrate. And it was something that could have been prevented if the housing agency had done something. We've known about lead poisoning for a long time—but still nothing happens. Why?" he shouts, pausing before answering his own question. "Because the kids who are poisoned are black and Latino; because they are poor." He holds Junior a little higher, making sure the cameras get a good view. "We are here right now to say that the time has come to protect *todos los niños.*" All of the children.

As soon as the press conference concludes, English- and Spanish-language TV crews surround Enrique as he continues to blast away at politicians and housing officials, still holding Junior. After spending so many months attending his fruitless case in housing court and repairing his apartment without assistance from the city, he is relishing the attention.

The press conference spurred immediate action from the housing department, who agreed to meet with us as soon as possible. They were in crisis mode, as their press person had received numerous calls regarding our report, and the local ABC station had interviewed the department commissioner for the evening news in a special report on lead hazards in Central Brooklyn.

Organizers know that a lot of planning is needed whenever a group meets with politicians or corporate public relations representatives. In life, we are taught at an early age to respect authority—be they parents or teachers, caseworkers or supervisors. An army of upset people who are unprepared can walk into a meeting with a smooth-talking bureaucrat and leave feeling like the person is an old friend—without actually winning any concessions. Organizers stress with their members the need to focus on the demand that they are pursuing and not get distracted with irrelevant counterarguments that are designed to go nowhere. "Their job is to tell you all kinds of nice, reasonable things," I told our group during a planning meeting, "but not actually agree to give you anything."

Enrique didn't need this advice. He had an organizer's instincts and could sense patronizing attitudes before a person opened his or her mouth. But more than that, he had something that was even more invaluable: he could not be intimidated. He had traveled alone from Mexico to make a new life, survived harsh conditions and frequent violence, and it would take more than an expensive suit or accent-free English to impress him. Stated a different way, he was an instinctive democrat. He had a right to be wherever he wanted and say whatever he wanted, and so did everyone else. His was a level playing field, always.

At the meeting Enrique and several other parents spoke about how lead hazards were making it dangerous for children to live in Central Brooklyn, and we handed over the list of buildings in need of repair to the agency. The agency immediately sent out a team of inspectors, who confirmed that indeed the lead violations existed. One of the higher-ups in the housing department, a bearded man who had been in the agency for as long as anyone could remember, had repeatedly said that the main action we were asking for—a vigorous and proactive inspection program—was "impossible," which angered Enrique. The two had a few words in the meeting, and on the subway back to Brooklyn Enrique is still upset.

"If a call comes in and they need a car to pick up someone, do I say 'No, impossible?'" he asks. "It is my job to drive people around, so I have to do my job. It is their job to protect our children from lead poisoning. So they can't sit there and say, 'Impossible, impossible, impossible.' You have to find a way to make it possible. If you can't do your job, then we'll find someone who can." We would see the same administrator in numerous meeting in the coming months as the city debated new lead paint legislation (which eventually passed over the housing department's objections and Mayor Bloomberg's veto). Each time we ran into him, Enrique would refer to the man as "*Señor* Impossible."

In July a judge threw out the city's previous lead bill, which created an opening for the coalition's efforts and led to a series of negotiation meetings. Most of the meetings that summer were between politicians, agency bureaucrats from the health and housing departments, and advocates. Whenever he could, Enrique came along as well. Twice Enrique was the only parent in the room who had been directly affected, and it was interesting to see otherwise smart people completely underestimate Enrique's political analysis. At the end of every meeting we held with housing and health officials, they would make a point of approaching him directly to ask for more information about his building—as if the only reason he was pushing for a new law was to take care of his own case. In fact, he already had done so—in spite of the city's inability to help.

Traveling with his bundle of violations, Enrique soon came to expect the onslaught of eager bureaucrats, and he wouldn't mince words. "I've been to so many meetings, and still you guys haven't been able to fix anything. And I'm someone who has done everything possible, gone to court over and over again, and can't get repairs. Just think about all the other immigrants who don't have the time to do what I have done. What can you possibly do for them?" The bureaucrats would begin to mount a defense citing specific clauses in the housing code or some other technical information that Enrique wasn't familiar with, and he would dismiss them. "Exactly. You can't do anything. You think I'm here to get your help, but I'm not. I'm here to tell you that you aren't doing a good job.

I'm here to tell you that your laws and regulations don't mean anything to real families living here."

Enrique had never taken a political science class, but he had a mind for politics. He felt that fine-tuned, articulate arguments didn't change anything. He wasn't appreciative when the city's representatives listened patiently with sympathetic nods as he recounted his experiences—in his mind, the niceties that were extended toward him by people in the health and housing departments were meaningless, inconsequential. When leaving one meeting with which he was particularly unsatisfied, he laid out his philosophy in the elevator ride down from the offices of the city council. As tended to happen when he got passionate, he used his hands to illustrate his point.

"Güero, those assholes aren't listening to anything we're saying," he said angrily. "The problem is simple: we're not hurting them enough. We have to push harder." Enrique took his right palm and placed it against the side of my face. As if dreaming of mashing it against a curb, he then pushed, hard enough to force me to shuffle my feet in order to keep from falling.

"Okay, okay, I get your point."

"And then, with one group pushing on one side, when they're not looking we get another group that pushes them from the other side." With his left palm he now pushed against my left cheek. I felt like a fish; both of his hands were now pressing into my contorted face. It didn't help that a few other advocates were in the elevator, watching our interaction with curiosity.

"I get it, I get it."

"Good. I'm just saying, I think we need more protests, less meetings. These pendejos like it when we're sitting in their stupid offices, playing their games. We can't let them get too comfortable."

When the city council finally decided to hold a hearing on the proposed lead bill, it took some convincing to get Enrique to city hall to testify. He didn't see the use in speaking into a microphone in front of more politicians. But several weeks before the hearing he had enjoyed a protest held in front of a tony townhouse in Greenwich Village that was hosting a fund-raiser for Gifford Miller, the council's speaker and a then-mayoral hopeful. Miller had been dragging his feet on scheduling a hearing for the bill, and our group of advocates and parents marched in front of the building chanting, which forced the arriving attendees, dressed in suits and a few tuxedos, to navigate through our crowd.

When Gifford Miller arrived he was visibly agitated: Enrique loved the protest. "That is the kind of action we need if we're going to win this fucking fight," he said when I asked him about testifying at city hall. He had especially appreciated the Spanish chant that we used: "*Miller, racista, te tenemos en la lista!*" (Miller, you racist, we have you on our list!)

But speaking at city hall held little appeal for Enrique; he had already shared his story so many times. Still, I eventually cajoled him into coming. Instead of getting to testify, however, he and the other parents sat through hours of testimony against the bill from the commissioners of the housing and health departments and went home without being able to make any public remarks. "See, I told you," Enrique said on the ride back. "These things don't mean shit."

Later, when Miller agreed to support the bill, eventually rallying enough votes in the city council to make it law, Enrique decided his political instincts had been vindicated. "It was plain and simple. We scared Miller that day when all the high-class people were meeting to give him money in Manhattan. I could see their faces. 'Holy shit!' they were thinking when they got out of their limousines. 'What the fuck are all these blacks and Mexicans doing here?' They thought we were going to rob them!" Enrique laughed loudly at this happy memory. "That's exactly what we need to do. *Los pobres* need to forget about all the games and all the meetings. If you want to get anything done, you've got to scare people; you've got to hurt them."

CHAPTER 5

Missing School

AFTER THE LARGE amount of Spanish-language press PACC received regarding our housing work, we started fielding even more calls. Before, most of the calls would begin like this: "I was in a cab the other day, and the driver said to call you if I have problems with my landlord. We don't have heat or hot water right now. . . ." Now, people were calling because they had seen our work on the television channels of Telemundo or Univision, or read about it in *El Diario* or *Hoy*, New York City's two Spanish-language newspapers.

One morning a few months after the lead campaign, I receive a phone call from a man named José, who says he saw us on the news and is also a fishing buddy of Enrique's. José tells me that—like Enrique, Flaco, Juana, and seemingly every other Mexican I encounter—he is from the state of Puebla. I mention this observation to him.

"*Sí*, everyone from Puebla is coming here. We call it Puebla York," he says. "Or *Manhatitlán*."

In fact, two out of every three Mexicans in the New York metropolitan area originate from the Lower Mixteca region, a hot, low-lying land peopled by descendants of the pre-Columbian Mixtec. The Lower Mixteca, which includes sections of southern

Puebla, northern Oaxaca, and eastern Guerrero, is one of the poorest areas of Mexico, and its dry land is among the least arable in the country.

Rural, hot, indigenous, isolated—how did this section of southern Mexico end up with so many of its original inhabitants navigating the hustle and bustle of *la Gran Manzana*—the Big Apple? According to the foremost expert on Mexicans in New York, Professor Robert C. Smith, a Baruch College sociologist, the exodus has its origins in a chance meeting between two brothers from the town of Chinantla (where Enrique's mother, Angela, lives) and an Italian American tourist. The year was 1945, and Pedro and Fermín Simón had been attempting without success to become *braceros*, or guest farmworkers, in the United States. A friend of the Simón brothers introduced them to the Italian American tourist in Mexico City, who agreed to allow them to travel back with him to the United States. Instead of Texas, which had been their original destination of choice, they rode all the way to New York with their new friend, who not only found them work at a restaurant but also paid for their hotel stay. According to a *New York Times* interview with the late Pedro Simón in 1998, on the day that the brothers decided to remain in New York City, they emerged from the hotel feeling triumphant and then found confetti raining down on them: it was V-E Day.* Fighting in Europe had ended. The first Mexicans from Puebla, called *poblanos,* had arrived.

A trickle of neighbors followed the pioneering Simón brothers, but it wasn't until the late 1960s that a sizable number of poblanos began to venture north; Angel, Enrique's father, was one of the mostly young men who made up this group. Still, the real exodus

* "A Mexican Town That Transcends All Borders," by Deborah Sontag, *New York Times*, July 21, 1998

from Puebla—and the Mixteca area generally—didn't get under way until the late 1980s, when the region was hit hard by an economic recession. Thousands of residents streamed north, to a city where Mexicans—with their impressive work ethic and willingness to accept low wages—were rapidly becoming the workers of choice among employers. Between 1990 and 2000, according to the U.S. Census, the number of Mexicans in New York City tripled, making them the fastest-growing immigrant group. Generally thought of as a center for Puerto Ricans and Dominicans, New York City was becoming increasingly Mexicanized.

José was one of the Mexicans who had come during the surge of the 1990s. He lived with his wife, Esther, and daughter in a six-unit building several blocks from Enrique. Though he told me that his building wasn't in the best shape, when he called he was more concerned with the new landlord's recent demand.

"He asked us to list all of the members of the household and to put our social security numbers next to the names," he said over the phone. "Is that something he can ask us to do?" I told him it was not. "But he says if we don't give him the information, he will call immigration." Ridiculous, I say. Let him try. "But could you come take a look at the papers?" No problem.

The next week I take a train into midtown Manhattan to meet José at his workplace. His boss had recently increased his schedule to twelve-hour shifts while continuing his six-day workweek, so we decide to meet during his hour-long lunch break. As I emerge from Madison Square Garden, music is in the air. Crossing Broadway, I look for its source and see an old Korean man tapping melodic notes from a drum of some sort. I arrive at the address José has given, finding one of those gray Manhattan buildings a person could walk by for years and never notice. I call him on his cell phone and he comes down to greet me.

On the elevator ride up to the ninth floor, I ask José for the second time whether his boss will mind my wandering in. On the phone he had told me that all of the workers in the shop, which produced low-end pieces of jewelry, were being paid under the table— and much less than the minimum wage. This sounded like it fit the definition of a sweatshop, and I assumed management wouldn't look kindly upon an unannounced white man walking about. On the phone José hadn't seem concerned. He still isn't.

"Don't worry, don't worry," he tells me in his high-pitched voice. Over the phone I had guessed from his squeaky voice that he was a slight man; instead, though he has a gentle face, he is nearly six feet tall and weighs well over two hundred pounds.

"You're my friend, right?" José says. "So we just tell them you're my friend. No problem." When we arrive on the ninth floor, he opens a door and we enter a room full of Korean supervisors, who, despite José's assurances, all look up from whatever it is they are doing and eye me with suspicion. José, however, doesn't seem to notice and begins to introduce me around the room. Each person stands up and shakes my hand in what feels like an overly formal manner, as if I am here on official business. Toward the back of the room José brings me over to a Korean man who is just finishing up his lunch.

"Good afternoon," José says to him in heavily accented English. "I would like to introduce my friend, Gabriel." The man looks up and quickly stands and offers his hand.

"Very nice to meet you," he tells me, also with a heavy accent. "You're José's friend?"

"Yes, I have been working with him on his housing situation," I answer, not knowing what else to say. "Nice to meet you, too," I add, and José and I continue on to the next room.

"Who's that guy?" I ask. "He seemed nice enough."

"That's my boss," he answers over his shoulder, now in his native tongue. "And no, he's not nice." We pass through an empty room and into a large, windowless space. A dozen brown-skinned women, several of whom don't look like they have yet entered their teenage years, are bent over a long table. Most are stringing colorful beads onto strings that are becoming necklaces, their fingers guiding the string through the tiny holes. The task demands concentration, attested to by their squinting eyes and craning necks, and only a few look up from their work in our direction.

When we arrive in the last room we sit down at a small table. Around the table are large metal contraptions and plastic tubs full of a clear liquid that emits an odd odor. José pulls out a manila folder that, like Enrique's paperwork, is meticulously organized. "Here is what the landlord gave us," he says, handing over a nearly illegible piece of paper. "He wants names, ages, social security numbers, and birth dates for every person."

The landlord, of course, has no right to most of this information. I suggest we write a letter to him, explaining that he is attempting to collect information that is private, which José seems to think a worthy idea. I mention that perhaps we should ask the landlord for the names of all of *his* family members, along with *their* social security numbers and incomes, and José chuckles.

"Can you make a copy of the letter for my files?" he asks. "Just to make sure I have it in the apartment if the landlord comes." This emphasis on organization is a trait that José shares with many Mexican immigrants. Whether it is rent receipts, phone numbers, old leases, hospital records, or letters from the landlord, people didn't seem to throw away—or even temporarily misplace—such mountains of paperwork. There was one piece of paper, of course, most would never find in their files—one that would enable them to legally live in the United States. But it seemed that to compensate for this gap, they were determined to file everything else away for safekeeping.

Before I leave, José pulls out one last piece of paper, upon which are scrawled a series of numbers. "I've been trying to figure out how much I am getting paid," he explains. "Right now they are paying me three hundred and fifty dollars a week, which is the same thing they paid when I was working less hours." I do my best to calculate his earnings. Twelve-hour days, six-day workweeks equals seventy-two hours a week. Divided by $350, it means he's making less than five dollars an hour—and this is without factoring in the overtime he should be earning for the thirty-two hours he puts in after the standard forty.

After adding my numbers to his sheet, I tell him they've paying well below the minimum wage of $5.15 an hour. José nods. "See, that's what I thought. Way below. I'm going to ask them to give me four hundred dollars, or else I'm going to go back to my normal hours."

"Has anyone from the Department of Labor ever come up here to check in on the workers?" I ask.

He shakes his head. "No, not since I've been working here they haven't. I wish someday they would come up so that they could see what these people are paying the workers. I've worked here for a long time. I'm trained to use the equipment that paints all of the jewelry, so I get more than the others." He motions toward all the machinery around us. "But most of the women here work Saturdays, too, and they only get paid two hundred and thirty dollars. That is something the Department of Labor should know about, no?"

Several weeks later, at one of our organizing meetings, both José and Enrique are in attendance. Nearly fifty people are seated on folding chairs in the community room of St. Luke's Church, in the neighborhood of Clinton Hill. It is our largest gathering to date. Normally Enrique would be excited about such a turnout—on a chilly evening, no less—but tonight he remains quiet, seated next to Juana. While Junior joins a group of equally hyper children who race around the circle of seated adults, parents share their stories of housing troubles. At the end of the meeting Juana gathers up Junior and the family leaves, not waiting even to eat the dinner that will arrive shortly from Flaco's. I give Enrique a call the next day to check in.

As I suspected, there is a new problem, and it involves Enrique's daughter Cristina. I knew he had recently received multiple calls from the school informing him that Cristina wasn't in class, but initially he wasn't concerned, because when he checked in with Paula she had told him that their daughter had been sick. But two days ago the school called again, and when he contacted Paula she told him she had dropped Cristina off at school that morning. When he heard this he grew angry and drove over to pick up Paula en route to the school, where they were told that Cristina had been absent many more days than either of them realized.

After the meeting with the school representative, Paula told Enrique that Cristina had a boyfriend and that he would probably know the whereabouts of Cristina. Hearing this, Enrique grew angrier—he knew the young man Paula was talking about, and he was several years older than Cristina. Too old to be involved with his daughter.

Cristina's two younger sisters, Lourdes and Dalía, went to a nearby school, and it was Cristina's responsibility to pick them up and walk them home each day. Enrique and Paula went over to the school, hoping to find Cristina. When school got out, Lourdes and Dalía emerged, but no Cristina. Together they drove around the block, and it was then that Paula spotted Marcos, the boyfriend, walking along the sidewalk. Enrique hopped out of the car and confronted Marcos.

"I asked him, 'Where's Cristina?'" Enrique recounted. "He tried to play dumb, like he didn't know. When I asked him again, he told me, 'That's none of your business.' Fucking bitch, that *is* my business!" Enrique, enraged, had struck Marcos twice across the side of his face. Marcos, who Enrique guessed was around seventeen or eighteen, started crying and took off running. Enrique hopped back in the car, following Marcos even when he turned down a one-way street, into oncoming traffic. Enrique somehow avoided hitting any of the cars, and a block farther he finally saw Cristina, waiting for Marcos.

Enrique jumped out of the car and dragged the crying Cristina inside. "As soon as I started to take Cristina away, Marcos walked up, like he was going to do something. I yelled at him again and said, 'What, you want some more, you fucking bitch?' After that he left, but on the ride home Cristina was yelling and crying, saying that I didn't have any right to do what I was doing."

In his house, Enrique was old school: his children were to follow his directions, always. Nearly every time the subject turned to his kids, he would begin his sentences with the same phrase. "When you're living under my roof, you had better . . ." The problem was, Cristina was no longer living under his roof, and even though he was angry with his oldest daughter, he wasn't so blind not to realize he was only pushing his daughter further away with his violent and domineering outbursts. "If she wants to skip school and mess around with men, fine," Enrique concluded at the end of our telephone conversation. "She can get on welfare and have lots of kids if that's the kind of future she wants."

It wasn't fine, of course. But Enrique's parenting skills were limited. His father had been abusive and violent—when he was present—and Enrique had no other model to follow. The two most important parenting facts he knew were that a father was supposed to protect his kids and be around for them, not abandon them like Angel had done. But beyond that he wasn't sure how to proceed with Cristina. Enrique wanted Cristina to understand how fortunate she was to have been born in the United States, to not have to grow up in the campo and toil in the fields. But yelling at her and beating up her boyfriend wasn't helping her to see things from his perspective.

Enrique's desire for his children to finish school was only made stronger when he considered what had happened to Juana's two daughters, Sandra and Anayeli. Both had dropped out of high school and settled down with boyfriends to have children and were receiving welfare. Indeed, data from the 2000 U.S. Census on high school dropout rates finds that U.S.-born Latinos drop out in higher numbers than both whites and blacks (14 percent for U.S.-born Latinos, 11.7 percent for blacks, 8.2 percent for whites). Still, this number is much lower than the 33.7 percent of immigrant Latino youth who drop out—which is not an entirely accurate reflection on the quality of schooling, because teenagers coming to the United States are, obviously, here to work, and many never set foot inside a classroom.*

Enrique was a poor Mexican immigrant in the United States; he had been a poor Mexican in Mexico. He had always worked hard: determination alone wasn't enough to break free from poverty. Education. Schooling. Math. Computers. English. These were the keys for improvement, for achieving a level of material comfort that had always remained out of reach. He had sacrificed for himself, yes, but

---

* Based on data from a 2003 report by the Pew Hispanic Center, "Hispanic Youth Dropping Out of U.S. Schools: Measuring the Challenge," by Richard Frey.

the eventual goal was always to provide a better life for his children. Now, here he was, an immigrant with children who had every advantage in the world—free schooling, U.S. citizenship, speakers of English and Spanish—yet his oldest daughter seemed on the brink of throwing it all away.

CHAPTER 6

Dreaming of the Minimum Wage

THROUGHOUT THE LEAD paint fight, Enrique's building still didn't have a real owner. With the number of violations on the property, and the unpaid taxes for the building, the city began the legal process of seizing the building and transferring it to a new, presumably more responsible owner. As a tenant organizer with a group that also managed and owned low-income housing, I would frequently check the listings to see if anyone had tried to claim the building. Month after month it remained abandoned. I considered this a good thing, knowing that if anyone did purchase the property from the current slumlord, they would in all likelihood immediately evict the tenants, Enrique and Juana included.

During these months of waiting, Enrique and I spoke frequently about the possibility that my organization would inherit the building, which could ensure that the rents would remain affordable. The longer there was no activity, the greater the chances that the city would commence legal action and remove the building from the owner, and since it was a small building in a not-so-great area of Bedford-Stuyvesant, near other properties that the city had granted PACC, I felt optimistic about our prospects. A prospective buyer would see the damage and smell the sewage, maybe encounter a few of the strung-out squatters, and likely be dissuaded from any potential business deal.

In fact, a few people did come snooping around the property, glancing up at the building and taking photos with digital cameras. Several men even knocked on Enrique's door and claimed to be the new owner, but when Enrique demanded to see the deed, they left quickly and were not heard from again.

A more important knock on Enrique's door came in July: a new landlord had finally purchased the building, violations and all. A representative for the owner went door-to-door, informing residents that from now on he would be coming by each month to collect the rent. He was pleasantly surprised to find that amid the wreckage, apartment 2-R was in fine shape, and he agreed to grant a two-year lease to Enrique and Juana, something he refused to give to the other tenants in the building.

The catch was the rent. Enrique knew from his previous housing court experiences that living in a three-unit building meant the landlord could begin an eviction proceeding at any time, and that a lease was his only protection against quick displacement. Yet the landlord's agent demanded a monthly rent of $1,150; anything less, and Enrique would find a thirty-day notice to vacate on his door. This wasn't an empty threat. Within a week the other two tenants had been served such notices. Stability could be bought, but at the price of a yearly rent of $13,800, more than two-thirds of Enrique's annual earnings.

Though he waited two weeks to respond to the landlord's offer, there really was no decision to make. After all the labor, Enrique was not about to abandon the apartment—and where could he and his family go, anyway? To move they would have to pay a new landlord the first and last month's rent, and probably a deposit as well, and there was no guarantee that the new owner wouldn't be just as bad. Better to put in extra hours at work and stay put. Enrique managed to convince the landlord to waive one month's rent, in compensation for all the repairs he had made in the apartment, and signed the lease. He remembered a phrase from one of the motivational tapes, a phrase he had immediately agreed with: where there's a will, there's a way.

Before having Junior, Juana had worked at a garment factory on Park Avenue in Bedford-Stuyvesant, where she sewed clothing for young girls. Now that her son was two, and money was going to be tight, she decided it was time to return. She visited a nearby day-care center, but the amount they charged would completely wipe out her earnings. Next she visited the local Head Start office, but the receptionist told her that Junior wasn't yet old enough to enroll. He would have to go to work with her at the factory.

It is sunny the first day I visit Juana at work. The large factory building towers above the public housing development across the street, and its windows are tinted less by design than by sheer grime. Taped to the front gate is a piece of torn cardboard with a hand-written sign, "*Se Solicita Trabajo,*" informing Spanish speakers that work is available within. I make my way past the gate and descend the stairs into the basement, walking along a corridor until I come to a door that is propped open slightly.

Juana had told me that I wouldn't be stopped by anyone, but I still had concocted a story if the need arose: I was the speech thera-pist for Junior and needed to visit with him for several hours each day. It was true that Junior was behind in his speech development; the few words he did know came out as a mishmash of English and Spanish, and Juana was trying to have him evaluated through a neighborhood school, but had so far been unsuccessful. It was not true, of course, that I knew the first thing about speech therapy, but the cover seemed believable enough. Still, my heart was beating fast when I walked through the door and found myself in the middle of the factory floor, looking for a guard to chase me away. Thankfully, Juana was right about the security. During my numerous trips to the factory, I never ran into anyone who asked me what the hell I was doing in the building.

When I arrive, Juana is one of nine brown-skinned women stitching together pink and gray fabrics that are in the process of becoming T-shirts for young girls. The words "Dangerously Cute" are emblazoned across the chest of each item, the white letters outlined in silver glitter. Butterflies and stars swirl around the sassy slogan. Most of the twenty-five machines are dormant, forming a rectangle on the shop floor that is illuminated by flickering fluorescent lights. Over the gentle sounds of the whirring of the nine machines in use, a radio is playing a Spanish love song. And then, amid the calm, a child darts out from behind one of the spools of fabric and begins sprinting around the rectangle of silent workers.

"Junior, *¡ven acá!* yells Juana, looking up and noticing me out of the corner of her eye. She is just in time to witness Junior's next brazen move, which is to push a stack of T-shirts off a nearby table and then bounce into an empty box; his attempt to hide given away by his uncontrollable giggling. *"¡Siéntate!"* Junior pops his head up, his face now serious, sensing a punishment on the horizon. He looks at Juana and sees me standing several feet from his mother, then sprints over to us and plops down on one of the stools by Juana's machine, grinning guiltily. I grab him and sit down on the stool, putting him on my lap, but he squirms free to continue running around the makeshift track. Juana sighs with a smile and turns back to her work.

"He's a little monster," she says, more in appreciation than exasperation. "But he only gets like this when someone else is here. If it's just him, he'll go into the room over there and watch television." She points to a doorway just off the shop floor. "Did anyone say anything to you when you came in?"

"No, it was like you said, no one was around."

I volunteer to take Junior for a walk around the block. "Don't bother," Juana advises me, "he'll just tire you out"—but I decide that I owe her at least a few minutes of work without distraction. After chasing Junior twice around the block he is only more energized. Giving up, I grab him in my arms, push the front door of the factory open, and carry him down the flight of stairs. I escort Junior to the small room Juana had pointed out and settle him down on a large mattress in the middle of the floor.

The room is sparsely furnished but seems to be someone's home. A small fridge stands in the corner, a mirror hangs on the wall, and an alarm clock and television sit atop two dressers. Junior quickly becomes absorbed in a rerun of a Tom and Jerry cartoon, and I return to the shop floor and join Juana, asking her about the room.

"That is the room of the woman in charge. She lives here sometimes, or maybe all the time—I'm not sure."

"What are you sewing?"

"This stuff?" Juana shrugs and raises a T-shirt up, as if looking at it for the first time. "They're all clothes for girls. You can tell from the fabric that they're no good." She hands me the shirt. "But I guess someone is buying them, somewhere."

I ask her how much she makes an hour.

"They don't pay by the hour, but by the piece," she replies, throwing another completed shirt in her pile. "We do it by the dozen. We usually get paid a dollar-thirty or a dollar-forty for each dozen."

Juana explains that it takes an hour to an hour and a half to make a dozen shirts, and as she answers my questions about pay her voice betrays no anger; she might as well be describing last night's weather. Instead, she's telling me that she earns about one-fifth of New York's minimum wage, or one dollar an hour. After putting in two sixty-hour weeks, she recently received a cash payment of $150. For each item of clothing she completes she will make about a dime.

Like her older sister Eva, who lives in the nearby Brooklyn neighborhood of Bushwick, Juana came to the United States in search of work. Though she hardly spoke of her parents, whenever Enrique mentioned his visits to Mexico he stressed the fact that they came from a poor family. "At home I couldn't make money" was how Juana described the situation. "Men might work construction, but they don't get paid much. But here, people said there was always work that would pay well."

And for a while there was. Before meeting Enrique, Juana had worked at a unionized garment factory in Brooklyn that paid her five dollars per dozen pieces, more money than she could hope to make in Mexico. But after the terrorist attacks of September 11, 2001, the factory either closed down entirely or reconstituted itself overseas—Juana isn't sure which—and is now being converted into housing.

According to the Fiscal Policy Institute, the recession after September 11 caused the largest one-year drop in manufacturing jobs in the last twenty years: 15.7 percent. In 2002 it fell another 11.5 percent. Still, New York State's Department of Labor estimates that in 2003 there were nearly forty thousand people producing apparel in the state, and the garment industry remains the largest manufacturing sector in New York City.

It is also an important source of employment for immigrants, who across the nation constitute 75 percent of the apparel workforce. Although having much higher labor costs than countries like China or Mexico, New York City garment factories are able to persist because they contract with stores that are looking for smaller orders and quicker turnaround times. And, of course, shops like Juana's increase their competitiveness by breaking the law, paying wages that are actually below that of many factories on the Mexican border. A lack of opportunity compelled workers like Juana to migrate to the United States for higher wages; not long after, they've found that the *maquiladora* wages have followed suit.

Exploitation runs rampant in New York City's apparel industry. In his book *Slaves to Fashion,* sociologist Robert Ross estimates that in 2000 there were approximately 265,000 sweatshop workers in this country, concentrated most heavily in Los Angeles and New York City.[*] In 2003 New York State's Department of Labor conducted 1,321 investigations of apparel companies and found that 526 shops, or 40 percent, were in violation of wage laws—paying below-minimum wages or failing to pay overtime. The problem of the sweatshop, thought of as a pressing issue in developing countries like China and Indonesia, has yet to be solved here at home.

I meet Cecilia on my second visit to the factory two weeks later. A fair-skinned Costa Rican woman in her early forties ("That's more than enough information, señor," she laughs when I ask her age), she is anything but the stereotypical boss who "sweats" employees for maximum output. For one thing, she has no problem with my hanging about, even when I tell her I am writing about the sweatshop. In addition, though she is technically in charge, Cecilia does essentially the same work as everyone else and is on good terms with the other women. And when not working at a feverish pace, Cecilia would often chase after Junior—who was constantly getting into trouble—sweeping him into her arms and laughing as she brought him back to her room. She had even christened Junior with an appropriate nickname: *terremoto,* or "earthquake" in Spanish.

---

[*] Robert J. S. Ross, *Slaves to Fashion: Poverty and Abuse in the New Sweatshops* (University of Michigan Press: 2004)

Indeed, it was difficult to discern any sort of hierarchy on the shop floor: when the boss lives in a sweatshop, she's none too high on the economic totem pole.

I arrange to interview Cecilia at the factory a few days after we are introduced. It is dark outside, well past eight o'clock, but when I arrive I find her still at work, punching tags that read "Hot Shots," the brand name of the garments, onto blue and white T-shirts. During our discussion she rapidly folds and tags clothes, then moves the massive bundles of shirts from one place to another.

"I came to the U.S. seven years ago," she says, then opens her mouth to continue, but pauses. "Wait, seven years? Has it been that long?" She looks up, and for the briefest of moments her hands stop moving. "Yes, I guess it has." She nods to confirm her math. "And I've been doing this work ever since."

At her previous job Cecilia earned seven dollars per dozen pieces, nearly twice her current wage. Her work consisted primarily of pulling off labels like "Made in El Salvador" or "Made in China" and replacing them with tags that read "Made in the U.S.A." Two years into the work, however, immigration agents raided the factory and rounded up twelve workers who were in the country illegally. Eleven who had no documentation were deported. However, Cecilia, who had overstayed her tourist visa by eighteen months, was able to stay with the help of a local church that had assisted her in filing for an extension. "Without the church, I would have been kicked out," she says. "Without God, we can't do anything."

I ask Cecilia about her current working arrangement.

"Payment is made in cash, always," she tells me. "We all get paid by the dozen. I get the money from the boss and hand it out to the workers. I make more than the others, since I'm here all the time and in charge. For every dozen pieces I get four dollars. Others make even less."

"Who pays you?" I ask.

"The boss, Herman. But he never pays us on time. Usually I have to go up to the office on the second floor to get the money. We have to complain for days before we get paid."

Though Cecilia makes more than her coworkers, she still earns well below the minimum wage. "The other workers don't fight with me, because they know that in my heart I'm with them," she explains. "And they know I start work at seven thirty in the morning and work late, sometimes until midnight or one o'clock. They know I'm doing everything I can to get people their money, since it's my money, too."

At the moment, Herman Neiderman, who Cecilia calls a "nasty, nasty man," has more pressing concerns than this Bedford-Stuyvesant sweatshop. In October of 2003 Herman and an associate will be indicted by the federal government for conspiracy, mail fraud, and wire fraud in relation to a series of five suspicious fires set between 1987 and 1999 at a Williamsburg factory they owned. In an elaborate arson-for-profit endeavor, Neiderman and his associate pocketed $4.5 million from insurance companies using four different addresses for the same factory, according to government prosecutors. The case has been in court for more than a year, and if found guilty, Neiderman and his partner face a maximum prison sentence of five years and a fine of $250,000 for each count.

When I share this information with Cecilia, she isn't surprised. "I had heard people say he was in trouble with the government, but I didn't know what they were talking about," she says. Still, Cecilia is hoping to hold on to the job for as long as possible. "Yes, it's hard. But at least I don't have to pay rent for living down here. If I had to pay the high rents in this neighborhood, I don't know what I would do."

Each week, rolls of fabrics arrive on the factory floor and are taken upstairs to be cut and have designs ironed on. Upstairs the workers are male and, according to Cecilia, paid well. Within Neiderman's company a legitimate aboveground business exists, where people are paid according to the rules. But downstairs in the basement a shadow economy of payments in cash flourishes, and the two universes—male and female, legitimate and off the books—remain independent of each other. Juana told me that she didn't know any of the male workers, though they are both employed by the same company and depend on one another's labor, day after day.

Once the material comes down to the basement, it is stitched together by the women and slapped with a "Made in the U.S.A" label. After being folded and stuffed into boxes, the garments are picked up and shipped out to stores across the city. Cecilia is responsible for making sure that about five hundred dozen articles of clothing—six thousand pieces—are completed each week. When demand is high, it is not uncommon for Cecilia to put in ninety, even one-hundred-hour workweeks, while others like Juana clock in sixty to seventy hours. As would be expected in a shop where the workers make only a fraction of the minimum wage, overtime is out of the question. "We're happy just to get what he is supposed to pay," Juana says, looking less than happy.

As with many Brooklyn sweatshops, the garments produced here are sold locally at retail chains like Cookie's Department Store, which specializes in children's ware. Several days after my interview with Cecilia, I stop by a spacious Cookie's storefront on Fulton Street in downtown Brooklyn. Here, hanging on endless racks, are items that perhaps only days earlier were being stitched by Juana and folded and tagged by Cecilia. A purple and black shirt with a rose emblem sells for $8.99; a pair of pink stretch pants for $6.99.

And on another rack hang dozens of those gray and pink shirts that read "Dangerously Cute," each going for $4.99. A stout black-haired woman with a Mexican flag emblem on each of her socks is searching through the shirts as a skinny girl holding her hand points at the glitter that sparkles under the bright lights of the store. The price is right: the woman buys two shirts, size small.

A few weeks after my initial visit, I am back at the factory playing tag with Junior around the sewing machines. Cecilia comes over to greet me.

"Hola, Gabriel," she calls, extending her hand. "Look at how much energy that little guy has! You're no match for him," she says, laughing.

"No, but that's okay," I reply, gasping. "I could use the exercise anyway."

Cecilia smiles again, and then becomes serious. "You know, they have a day care upstairs, for the children of the bosses. It's set up real nice, where the kids can play and be taken care of. Maybe you should take him up there. We're the ones doing the hardest work, after all."

I nod in agreement and return to chasing after Junior, running around a factory while his mom stitches clothing for girls his age. If Juana is able to hold on to the job, she will make $4,680 in the coming year. Her wages can't support child care, nor can Cecilia's pay for the high rents of the neighborhood. In this factory, whose tags proudly read "Made in the U.S.A.," Juana has learned to turn the sweatshop into a child-care facility—and Cecilia, a permanent home.

CHAPTER 7

Escape from New York City

CANDELARIO, ENRIQUE'S BOSS at Speedy Car Service, is a compact, soft-spoken man with light brown skin and a boyish smile from a town named Las Calaveras ("the skulls"), less than a dozen miles from where Enrique grew up. Although Candelario's office is on a lot surrounded by broken-down cars and looks like a temporary workstation one might find at a construction site, he is always dirt-free and well groomed, as if he has just walked out of a barbershop.

While Juana is putting in eight-hour days at the sweatshop, Enrique has dramatically increased the number of hours he spends behind the wheel of his car. Not prone to moderation under normal conditions, Enrique is now working seven days a week and logging between twelve- and fourteen-hour shifts each day. Whenever I stop by his apartment I find it empty and eventually decide to try him at work.

Speedy Car Service consists of a small wooden trailer/shack combination situated on a large lot in the rapidly gentrifying neighborhood of Clinton Hill. The "base," as the headquarters of private car services are called, has a dispatcher sitting behind a Plexiglas window at all hours and an overhang that customers can stand beneath when it is raining. When I stop by one late summer afternoon, Enrique is out, dropping off a customer in Washington

Heights. I had heard of Candelario from Enrique and seen him several times around the base, but had never met him. Thinking he would be a compelling person to speak with, I ask the dispatcher if Candelario is in. He points toward the back without missing a beat from his rapid Spanish chatter, speaking with callers and confirming pickup locations.

As I step around to the back, I find Candelario behind a wooden desk in a cramped office, speaking on the phone. He glances at me briefly and motions for me to sit down, as if he has been expecting a visit. As he continues his conversation in Spanish, I look around. The room has just enough space for one desk, one computer, and two chairs. The walls and floor consist of unfinished, cracking plywood. On the walls hang various calendars and a few family portraits. A huge map of New York City is mounted behind the desk, and stickers with different prices show the fares for traveling to certain regions.

After several minutes Candelario concludes his conversation and swivels his chair in my direction. "What can I do for you?" he asks in clear English. I explain that I am a writer and a friend of Enrique's, and that I am hoping to arrange an interview with him sometime in the future.

"How about right now?" he asks. "Or is now not good for you?" I tell him that now works just fine, as if he is the one who has just popped up at my office without an appointment. He picks up the phone.

"Don't transfer calls to me, I'm busy," he says in Spanish to the dispatcher. "Okay, took care of that. Now, let's start." I proceed to ask him various questions about his life; without much prompting, he launches into lengthy answers, with the easy disposition of an immigrant who has made for himself a comfortable life in the United States.

After growing up in Las Calaveras, at sixteen Candelario moved to Mexico City, where he worked as a mechanic at a maquiladora that produced expensive couches. He eventually joined the Mexican army, and spent nine years as a bodyguard for then-president José Lopez Portillo. "That was an interesting job," he says, chuckling. "Lots of traveling, lots of fancy stuff, lots of important people." He gives me a mischievous look, as if to say: "If you only knew what I've seen."

In 1990 he came to the United States with a visa, planning a short trip to visit his older brother, Hector,* who had settled down in Brooklyn a decade earlier and had become a legal resident through the 1986 amnesty. "Originally, I was going to stay two, maybe three months," he explains. "But, you know, in life many times you don't know where you'll end up." Deciding to try his luck in the new country, he began working as a livery cab driver, and after four years decided to form his own company with Hector and five other drivers.

His timing was fortunate. In Manhattan roughly twelve thousand yellow cabs have served passengers since 1937, picking up people on the street. But in boroughs like Brooklyn, Queens, and the Bronx, yellow cabs are hard to find, so livery cabs have recently grown quickly to fill the need; in the last decade the number of cars has increased by about 50 percent. Livery cabs, unlike yellow cabs, are neighborhood-based, and passengers call ahead to schedule rides, with prearranged fares.

By 1996 Candelario's fleet had grown from six to fifty, and the next year jumped to nearly one hundred. On the best days—a busy Friday, for example—they were averaging between fourteen hundred and sixteen hundred calls from customers. With business

* Not his real name.

booming and the expansion of the fleet, Candelario was able to purchase the lot that has now become his base, and he tells me he is now preparing for a new endeavor.

"In six months we're going to begin building here. Instead of this little place we're going to have a seven-story building, with the business on the bottom floor. On the five floors above I'm going to make condos. My family will move into the top floor."

"Wow, so you're going to be living in a penthouse?" I ask.

"Well, more like a big apartment," he responds, not liking the sound of this description. "But I'll still be working here and driving cars, just like everybody else."

"You mean you still drive a car sometimes, even though you're the owner?"

"Of course. I drive every week. I like to drive. I drive on Christmas Day, on New Years Day—this is what I am . . . a driver."

Candelario can see that I find it strange that he is still driving passengers around in a car like a regular employee. To me, it was akin to the owner of a large garment factory still clocking in for regular shifts stitching fabrics. But to him, the divide between worker and boss is murky, and the work enjoyable.

I ask Candelario about his views of the recent crackdown on immigrant cab drivers. New York's Department of Motor Vehicles had begun a highly publicized effort to strip licenses from drivers who had provided false social security numbers, in the name of national security. Enrique had told me that a number of the drivers at Speedy Car Service could be affected, and that at least one driver had ventured to Wisconsin to renew his license. (At the time, Wisconsin was one of several states that still granted licenses to undocumented immigrants, a nice irony as Congressman James Sensenbrenner, one of the most consistently obnoxious anti-immigrant politicians on Capitol Hill, hails from that fine state.)

"Yes, that is the biggest problem we are facing right now," he says. "We come here to work, nothing more. It is so obvious to us that it seems silly to have to repeat it, but some people still don't understand. Immigrants come here for one reason: to improve their lives. What will happen if they take licenses away? People will not stop driving. Instead, we will have many drivers who continue to drive, but without licenses and without insurance. Who is that helping?"

I nod, and then ask what I think is an innocent question. "Was it through your brother that you ended up becoming a resident?" Candelario's easy posture tightens ever so slightly, and his round eyes squint at me. I immediately realize I've assumed too much, and try to mitigate the damage. "I'm just thinking that since you came after the nineteen eighty-six amnesty, it must have been hard for you. I know lots of people who are friends that haven't been able to make any progress on their immigration cases, especially after September eleventh. Like Enrique was lucky because he got here just in time, but anyone who came later has been pretty much screwed."

Candelario is still looking at me with a twinge of suspicion, but evidently decides I'm not out to cause any harm. "Yes, that is true . . . everyone here who came late is having a hard time. Like I said, we come to work, but for some reason people want to make life hard for us."

I nod again and put away my notebook. By now I have taken up an hour of his time, though he hasn't once looked at the clock. "I ought to be leaving so that you can get back to work."

He dismisses my concern. "Don't worry, the dispatcher is taking care of everything. But if you need to go, by all means, you should go." Again, I have the absurd sense that he feels he is somehow imposing on me—Candelario is an extremely polite man. I stand up and shake his hand, thanking him for his time.

"No problem. And if you really want to know about the life of Mexicans, you should go to Puebla and visit my hometown. I still have a brother who lives there. He never wanted to come north, happy to stay and farm in Las Calaveras. You let me know, and I'll call and tell him to expect you. One day in Las Calaveras, and you'll see why I decided to stay here. *No hay trabajo, no hay nada.*" There isn't any work, there isn't anything at all.

I call Enrique later that day. He laughs when I explain Candelario's reaction to my question. "He doesn't have any papers," Enrique tells me. "All the paperwork for the business is done in his brother's name. Why do you think he's so upset about how they're taking away the licenses? If they do, it means he can't drive, either."

Despite the fact that his work sucked up nearly every free moment, Enrique still found time to fish. Along with José and their friend Darío, a Mexican who worked at a pet shop in Manhattan, Enrique was an avid—albeit consistently unlucky—fisherman. Weather permitting—and this meant anything short of a blizzard—most Sundays would find the three men on some lonely bridge or aging boat, dreaming of twenty-pound trout. To make the $1,150 rent, Enrique was now working a full day on Sundays, so the three friends usually went out on what they called the evening shift, from 7:00 p.m. to early Monday morning, around 2:00 or 3:00 a.m.

I am not so intrepid: I wait to join them on a Sunday that Enrique has taken off from work. On the day of our expedition it is cold but clear, that moment in New York City's weather pattern between the humidity of summer and the ice of winter when the fall peeks through and offers a week or two of reasonable climate. I meet José at his Bedford-Stuyvesant apartment and we walk a few blocks to catch a bus to the subway station, where Darío is waiting for us. Enrique has already left with Juana and Junior earlier that morning, to purchase some clothing at a mall in Queens, and is now at our meeting place. We take the subway to the end of the line, and then hop on to another bus. After the hour-and-a-half jaunt we are in Rockaway Beach, right across the water from John F. Kennedy Airport.

Fishing in New York City is a bit like skiing in North Dakota: it's the same equipment, yes, but there's a whiff of desperation about it. During my youth I would spend a few weeks each summer visiting grandparents in Minnesota, fishing on lakes where even the occasional motorboats were seen as noise-producing nuisances. Fishing was an escape from the relative bustle of cities like Fargo and Minneapolis, a chance to be alone and clear one's head. Had it been a word in common usage by seventy-year-old Scandinavians, my grandfathers would probably have described it as "meditative."

In Queens, on the other hand, it feels like we are casting for fish in the middle of a polluted industrial plant. We set up shop on a narrow slab of sidewalk running along a bridge, divided only by a chain-link fence from cars zooming past at freeway speeds. Plastic bags and empty beer bottles litter the sidewalk, and the trash that isn't swirling around our feet is snagged in the fence, flapping in the wind. If that isn't enough to break the spell of the natural beauty that surrounds us, the roar of jets taking off and landing across the waterway surely does the trick.

José, Darío, and Enrique each have two fishing poles, and after sticking a concoction of animal guts on their hooks they cast their lines out. They then lean their poles against the rail and stand around, waiting for a bite. An hour passes, with little conversation. Enrique and Darío each have tugs on their lines and excitably reel in large catches of blue-green seaweed. It is getting cold. Juana has given up on witnessing anything of worth and is seated on an upside-down plastic bucket against the fence, with Junior on her lap. Her hood is pulled tight over her head, but still she shivers. The chill has even stopped Junior from his customary sprints and non-stop yelps.

"Boring, huh?" Darío says, looking out to sea. I don't want him to think I am as cold and miserable as I feel, so I try to put on a good face.

"Bored? No way, this is what I came to do," I reply with artificial cheer. "Have you guys been having luck around here?"

"Nah, not lately," Enrique replies, butting in. "Two weeks ago José caught a fish that was this big," and he holds his hands out three feet apart. "But I think we'll have good luck later on. Still too early."

Hearing his name, José wanders over. "I don't think they're biting here today. We should go to the ship."

"The ship?" I ask. "What ship?" I have taken the bait.

"Yeah, the ship!" Darío seizes on the opening. "The güero should see the ship. Let's stick around here until six, then do a round on the ship."

"You go out on the ship at night?" I ask. That sounds cold. Enrique explains enthusiastically that for only thirty-five dollars a seat could be reserved on a boat that leaves at dusk. If we go tonight, he tells me, we will get back by no later than 2:00 a.m. and be sure to reel in a few beauties.

Beauties or not, this doesn't sound enticing. "I don't know about you guys, but I've got to work tomorrow," I say, joking (they all have to work as well, and will be rising hours before me), but also serious. "I don't think I'll be joining you this time, but maybe in the future." They all smile and say sure, maybe some other time, but I have a feeling they are going to do their best to drag me along when the time comes.

We spend the next four hours huddled around the poles, waiting in vain for action. Baits are switched, then switched again. No luck. I have a hard time seeing what draws the three out here each week. Even though I don't have a pole myself, it can't be said that I am missing out on the experience. We are all "fishing": shuffling our feet, staring at the murky water, shivering. Juana and Junior have long ago given up on our failed experiment and returned to the warmth of the car. That sounds nice.

I begin to cough every few minutes. The coughs are dry, forced, but they fit into my plan of claiming a developing sickness if the men try to trap me into a trip on the boat. For some reason, the spirits of our group—notwithstanding my own, of course—remain high, despite the lack of action and freezing wind. I have retreated into a cold, silent bubble; Enrique, José, and Darío keep up a steady chatter that often ends in raucous laughter. José, normally quiet, has somehow located an endless string of jokes, which he tells at the rate of three a minute, his stoic face replaced with shrieks and giggles. Enrique, never quiet, has become even louder than normal, and his range and creative application of expletives is dizzying, bordering on the nonsensical. *Hijo de la chingada, eso puto fue más duro que su pinche madre, no? El cabrón anda de pendejo, la pinche chingadera* . . . . Darío is joining in the fun as well, recounting stories of the stupidly rich gringos who would pay several thousands dollars for dogs the size of rats. Every now and then Enrique walks over to me and— mid-expletive—slaps me soundly on the back, just to make sure I am still alive.

As I go through various strategies for getting out of the evening boat trip and continue to half listen to this strange band of brothers, I slowly begin to see what might be drawing them out here Sunday after Sunday. It surely isn't the fish, judging by how little they seem bothered by their lack of success. There is something more impor- tant than fish to be found during these hours, I start to realize. Here, there is some sort of power, peace of mind. No one is pestering them in English, no one is demanding to see identification. They are still immigrants in a bustling city, for sure, but they are also afforded some breathing room from their daily stresses. They can joke loudly, act ridiculously, and make the sorts of comments that men make when women aren't around. In what is at times a confusing and intimidating city (though perhaps not intimidating for Enrique—the word didn't seem to apply to him in any form), on this slab of pavement they are in charge. It is windy, ugly, cold, and uneventful, but at the moment this small corner of New York City real estate is absolutely theirs. No immigration officials, annoying bosses, or threatening landlords can ever reach them here.

My spirits are buoyed slightly by what I see as this little epiphany. It is now beginning to get dark, and the conversation again turns to the boat. Darío and Enrique are teasing José about his tendency to throw up whenever he's out at sea. The idea of spending another four hours watching José vomit while shivering with a crew of crusty fishermen holds little appeal. I again explain my desire to go home, which is now greeted with vociferous resistance.

"What?" Enrique yells, feigning outrage. "I thought you fucking said that you wanted to go fucking fishing with us"—as if I hadn't just spent six hours standing around and bullshitting in the freezing weather.

José chimes in. "Güero, you're going with us. Why do you need to go home anyway? It's early." He was apparently unconcerned about the inevitable retching that he'd soon be doing, and wanted me to share the experience.

I let out another round of dry coughs. "I think I might be getting sick," I say in the scratchiest voice I can conjure. No one seems moved. "Uhh, and I borrowed my girlfriend's bike to get to José's apartment, and she needs it back to go on a ride this evening." This, like the coughs, is a lie—who would bike at night in this weather?—but I am desperate to return to my warm apartment and watch some television.

"*La vieja?*" Darío asks incredulously, referring to my girlfriend. "You let her tell you what you can do?" We go back and forth like this for a while: me confirming that in fact my girlfriend called the shots, them laughing about my predicament and attempting to explain that I had mistakenly reversed the roles in the relationship. Thankfully, they eventually give in, and when we leave they drop me off at José's before heading out for the night session. Next time, I promise them, I will *really* go fishing and will block out at least a twelve-hour period of time so that we can get down to business.

When I call Enrique the following morning, he informs me that after five hours on the boat they had returned empty-handed. "But next week we're going to try a different spot. A man on the boat told me about a place on Long Island where the fish are always biting." I don't bother to ask what this man was doing on the boat if he had his own private paradise. I don't volunteer to join them again, either.

In the fall of 2003 Abram begins to work. At fourteen, he is too young to be legally employed, but at a car wash on Myrtle Avenue Abram finds a boss who will pay him off the books. At the car wash it seems everyone is paid in cash—Abram because he is too young, the other workers because they are undocumented. They all make the same amount, Abram explains: four dollars an hour—more than a dollar below the minimum wage. Still, as a fourteen-year-old, his wage is quadruple what his mother is earning.

Enrique was initially ambivalent about Abram working at the car wash. In some ways it was a slap in the face to his and Juana's journey north. Abram was a U.S. citizen, after all, who could speak English. He had no business cleaning cars like a mojado. That was the type of work Enrique had done when he first arrived, the type the second generation was supposed to skip over.

On the other hand, Enrique believes a job might build character in his stepson. "He has never worked before, and he thinks that this life is easy. Now he can learn that you have to struggle to get the things you want." Enrique was obsessive about the need for Abram to study hard and earn good grades so that he would graduate high school and land a professional job. But at the same time, the family needed the extra money. Enrique agreed that as long as Abram gave a small portion of his earnings to cover rent and continued to go to school, he was permitted to work.

School, however, was not going well. Abram is a big kid, perhaps five feet ten inches and two hundred pounds, but despite his size he is far from imposing. He has Juana's soft, permissive face, and some students at Boys & Girls High School, a large Bedford-Stuyvesant institution, evidently have identified him as an easy mark. There aren't many students of Mexican descent in the school, which is more than 90 percent African American and less than 1 percent white. Abram figured this was one of the reasons that certain kids were picking on him. Several times over the past month Abram had been hit, but he had simply walked away from the fights and started missing classes to avoid more problems. We are hanging around in the living room when Enrique lays out for Abram his philosophy on the bullies at school.

"If you keep letting them pick on you without fighting back, they're going to continue. You need to show them that you can fight, that you will stand up for yourself."

I don't agree, and I tell him as much. I know his own hard-wiring makes it virtually impossible for him to back down from a physical challenge. Abram, however, is closer to me in temperament: mellow, quiet, nonconfrontational. He certainly doesn't seem like someone who would feel comfortable in a brawl, and besides, parents are supposed to tell their kids *not* to fight, especially at school. But I don't press Enrique too hard on this point, because Abram clearly is not listening to his stepfather's advice. He is not going to fight—though he might not keep going to school, either.

A week later Enrique joins a group of my friends for dinner. He is relatively quiet during the conversation, though immensely impressed by the fact that several of my white friends speak Spanish. The next day he asks me if they had all gone to college. I tell him that they did.

"You see, you all know how important education is," he says. "That's what I'm trying to tell Abram. Learn computers, study hard, but he doesn't want to listen. He's different."

There are so many differences between Abram's school environment and that of my friends and me that it's hard to know where to begin. Boys & Girls High School is huge, with nearly four thousand students. More than half of the students, like Abram, qualify for the free lunch program. Of the students who began school in the year 2000, fewer than half had graduated four years later, with approximately one-quarter having dropped out entirely. Only one-third of the high school graduates in 2004 have taken the SAT, a good indicator of whether they plan to attend a four-year college. When I went to high school everyone was expected to go on to college, and even taking a year off (which I did) was viewed as risky, as evidence that one might be heading down a slippery slope. Parents spent thousands of dollars on SAT preparation classes, made sure their kids got into as many AP courses as possible. And I would venture to guess that not one student at my school qualified for free lunches; poverty was something to be studied, not to be endured.

"I don't know that Abram is so different than my friends," I begin. I point out that we all went to safe, quiet, and well-funded schools and that I actually didn't study all that much. I mention that most of my friends could afford special tutors when they ran into trouble and that Abram might be having problems because his school is overcrowded and overwhelming. I say that we all had large homes with desks in quiet rooms; no landlords were leaving us out in the cold, no rats were crawling at our feet.

Enrique, of course, doesn't agree. "Education is education, güero. You've just got to study." My nuanced reasoning is far from convincing. He had grown up in a village with only a primary school and a single teacher. Abram was living in a country that provided free high school, the same country where so many others—like me—went on to college. That was the only fact worth considering. But we dropped the conversation after a few more minutes of arguing: our friendship was made possible by, among other factors, our ability to agree to disagree. We were very different people, after all, with very different life experiences.

By the beginning of 2004 Enrique has begun mentioning that he is thinking about leaving the apartment, though he doesn't know where he and his family can go. "It's too much stress," he says one day while we are driving around. For several days he has been complaining about a recurring pain in his chest, and yesterday went to the doctor to have some blood work done. Though the results aren't back yet, Enrique has already diagnosed himself. "I think it's all the stress of the apartment, all the headaches. I'm hardly sleeping and we're all working, but the money is just too much."

Still, even if he is able to find a cheaper apartment, Enrique isn't eager to move. "You know how much we did to our place. You saw what it was like before, how everything was dirty. We built that place, with our labor. They should have a law that says if a tenant is abandoned and does his own work, then he becomes the owner of the building, no? That is what our campaign should be. Or else something to stop all of these Jews from forming corporations and just selling buildings back and forth to each other without fixing the violations." It is the first time I have heard Enrique speak negatively about "Jews" as opposed to landlords.

"Imagine doing everything we've done and then someone just kicking us out," he continues. "Me, I don't care if I'm alone. Fuck it, I can go sleep under a bridge or live in my car. I know I can survive like that. But now I've got Juana and Junior to worry about. So you tell me, where the fuck can we go if we get kicked out? How can we pay eleven hundred and fifty dollars a month? They want to make this city just for the rich people and move everyone who can't pay high rents into the shelters." We are driving on Atlantic Avenue, past an armory that is now a homeless shelter for single men, and he points it out to confirm his point.

I am silent. Normally an organizer would say something like: "Sure, it seems impossible, but you've just got to fight. Force the landlord to do more repairs, push for more affordable housing." And so on, and so on. But Enrique doesn't need agitating, or inspiration. He needs a solution, and I don't have one.

"Fuck it," he finally says when he sees I have nothing to offer. "We'll figure it out. I'm just tired of these games. *Chinga su madre,* I am tired."

In early February I call Enrique's home and am informed that the line has been disconnected. I call his cell phone. He picks up and tells me that they moved out last week, stuffed as many things into his car and drove to his brother Juan's place in Port Chester, north of New York City. He sounds exhausted, deflated.

"Maybe I can come up to see you."

"I'm still here in Brooklyn."

"Why?"

"In Port Chester my taxi license doesn't work, and I don't know any of the streets, so I'm still working here. I'm at Flaco's right now." I decide to come over and find Enrique nursing a large Styrofoam cup of coffee and bantering with Flaco.

"You look like shit," I tell him.

"Yeah, well you try going two days without sleeping, and we'll see how nice you look." He explains that the commute from Port Chester to Brooklyn is too expensive, what with the gas prices and tolls he has to pay. "Better to stay here during the week. That way at least I can work more." When he gets too tired, he says, he pulls his car into the lot of Speedy Car Service and sleeps for a few hours, leaving his radio on so if any calls come in he can take them.

"So what's the plan, though?" I ask. This does not seem like a sustainable way of life, and I've always counted on Enrique to have something up his sleeve.

"*Nada.* There is no plan. I'm going to try and get my taxi license transferred to Port Chester, might have to take another test. We're not coming back to Brooklyn soon, I can tell you that. I know when it is time to *correr,*" Enrique says, using the Spanish verb "to run," the same verb on his cell phone message. "So we ran, like we always have to."

And then he uses a familiar phrase, but this time it is missing the characteristic lightheartedness. "Fuck it, it's just real fucking stupid. I've got to get back to work. I'll see you later, güero."

CHAPTER 8

Only Twelve Violations!

MARIA (NO RELATION to Enrique), though standing well under five feet tall, has an air of fearlessness about her, like an undersized running back who has grown accustomed to charging into the front line and seeing much larger bodies scatter. She reminds me of Enrique—short, but not small.

I am standing in front of Maria's building on a cold February morning because Enrique stopped by my office two days after our brief encounter at Flaco's. He hadn't been back to Port Chester since, having spent four days essentially working around the clock. His hair was wild and he had the beginnings of a beard; he didn't smell all that great, either. He was finally on his way home, probably to sleep for a good fifteen hours. But he wanted to tell me what he had heard from his cousin Guadalupe about the family that lived next door to her.

"The same person owns the two buildings where my cousin and this other family live," he said. "The woman who lives next door, Maria, told my cousin that they had found lead in the apartment and that her daughter was poisoned. I think you should go check it out." Normally when Enrique told me about such events he would exhibit anger, but it looked like all his effort was being summoned just to keep his drooping eyes open.

When I knock on Maria's door a week later, a young woman peers out at me. I explain that I work on lead poisoning issues and that a neighbor had said someone's child had been poisoned.

"Maria, *un blanco* is here!" the woman yells through a doorway to the right of the entrance. A few moments later some rustling can be heard below, and then quick footsteps. Maria emerges, the top of her head even with my chest, a flashlight in hand. She looks at me, squinting and shading her eyes from the light. It looks like she's been belowground for quite some time. I explain that Enrique had referred me and that he had told me there was a problem with lead.

She nods. "Perfect timing," she says. "Though right now the biggest problem is the heat and hot water. Look, follow me." And she turns around and heads back through the doorway, needing no more introduction. We walk through what was presumably once a habitable apartment. Stacks of rotted plywood now clutter the area, most with rusty nails peeking through. In some areas they have been peeled away, leaving deep holes, and various electrical wires are taped against the cracked walls. "Careful going through here," she tells me. "Don't step on a nail . . . or a rat." I make a squeamish face and she laughs. "Don't worry, I'll go first."

I walk gingerly through the apartment and follow Maria down a flight of rickety stairs, which lead to a dark basement. In one corner is a man with a uniform fiddling with the boiler. "The city just got here to try and fix it," she says. "It hasn't been working for two weeks." She shines her flashlight on the contraption, doing her best to assist the inspector, who occasionally mutters obscenities as he taps here, adjusts there. The light bounces off the walls and ceiling, both of which are bulging and appear on the verge of collapse.

After about ten minutes the man stands up and shrugs. "This isn't going to work," he says in Spanish. "We're going to have to get a new one." He gathers his tools and we follow him upstairs, leaving him to write his report in the front yard as we continue on to the second floor.

It is in the low forties right now outside, and only marginally warmer in the living room of Maria's apartment, which she shares with her husband, Timoteo, and a friend from Mexico who arrived six months ago. We huddle around a space heater that sits next to the couch, and a young girl comes out from a bedroom pushing a baby stroller.

"This is my daughter, Reyna," Maria says. She leaves for the bedroom and returns with a stack of papers from the Department of Health. They show that the four-year-old tested with a blood lead level of 33 micrograms per deciliter earlier this year, and that her brother, Gary, also was poisoned, with a level of 14. Maria tells me that after receiving the notice from the health department explaining her two children were lead poisoned, the landlord came to the apartment and began scraping away the paint that was on the walls and windows, causing dangerous dust to be spread around the unit.

"At first he was angry, asking why we were causing these problems and saying that it would cost too much to fix," Maria says, angry herself. "So I told him that if he didn't fix, it we'd sue him. That's the only reason he ever came out."

After Maria threatened to sue, the landlord agreed that they would always be able to pay a rent of eight hundred dollars a month, and said he would pay the family an undisclosed amount of money for any special education classes that Maria's children might need to take. Since then, however, Maria hasn't heard a word from him; he hasn't even been by to collect the rent. Recently the pipes for the building burst, and for several days, Maria said, they hadn't had any water—not even cold water. She continued to leave messages for the landlord. When he did finally answer the phone, he told Maria that he had sold the building and that none of this was his problem anymore.

I told Maria I would try to get in touch with a lawyer for the lead case.

"And who are you, again, exactly?" she finally asks. In a city whose residents can be notoriously cold-shouldered, she has invited a stranger into her home and shared intimate information with very few questions herself. I explain my work, about Enrique and his cousin who lives next door, about the Mexican families that I've worked with—several of whom she knows.

"Yes, there are lots of people here from Mexico," she agrees. "Now I'm a permanent resident, but for the illegals it is much more difficult. Still, it's better than being back in Mexico. . . . I have a sister who is still in our hometown. Maybe you've heard of it? It's called Cacalutla."

"No, I don't think so. Is it in Puebla?"

"Guerrero. But near Puebla, like maybe an hour from the border. You said Enrique's from Chinantla; Cacalutla is not too far from Chinantla. But it's way out in the middle of nowhere, away from any cities. Almost no one really knows that it exists. There's nothing there. That's why everyone tries to leave to come here."

"How many people live there now?"

Maria lets out a little laugh. "I could list all the families that live there . . . the Menendez family, Jimenez, Gonzales, Sosa. That's how small it is. And it's not easy to get to. It used to be that everyone could walk there along this path from the nearest city." She pauses. "But not that many people walk the path anymore, because someone raped and killed my husband's sister, Reyna. She was walking during the day like everyone does. So now people have to wait for a ride. That's who she's named after." Maria points at her daughter, who has taken her doll out of the stroller and is wiping its face with a napkin. "My mom says she'll never leave Cacalutla, but for me Mexico can be very ugly. Dangerous."

"But your sister is still there?"

"Yes, she doesn't have a choice right now, because one of her sons is really sick. It takes all day to get to the city of Puebla, and my sister has to go every week to the capital with her son to visit the hospital. He's sick, with—how do you say it, some sort of cancer. Leukemia. Her husband now lives somewhere around here, with another woman, but I don't ever talk to him. Not after what he did to my sister."

"Maybe they can come here for medical treatment."

"No, I already tried that. See, because we live in a remote town that doesn't even have a hospital or phones, that's why I think she should come. But even though I'm a resident, they say I have to wait five years before I can bring anyone else. I've only been a resident two years. And how would she cross the desert with her three kids? Or get the money to pay a coyote to help her to cross?" Maria goes on to tell me that she came to the United States thirteen years ago with her husband, who works at a mattress factory in Sunset Park. Before moving here they lived for a decade on Kent Avenue, just two blocks away, "but then the landlord disappeared and no one came to do repairs, so we moved."

I am struck by the story of her sister, and not only because it reminds me of what happened between Angel and Angela. During the course of my organizing work I'd met many Mexicans who told me the most difficult aspect of immigrating illegally wasn't the occasional dangers at the border but the family dislocation. Temporary separations between spouses became permanent, young children were left with aunts and only vague memories of *mamá y papá*, elders died without ever seeing the grandchildren they heard so much about during long-distance phone calls. I mention how Enrique's father also left his mother in Mexico. "*Sí*, that is a big, big problem," Maria says. "There are a lot of people like my sister who have been left behind. And imagine, now she has to take care of her three kids alone and deal with trying to save Favian. That's the name of the one who has leukemia."

During our conversation I feel vaguely uneasy, and it takes thirty minutes to locate what's bothering me. Here is Maria—gregarious, yes. Maybe she has looked deep into my soul and concluded that I'm a trustworthy person. That would be nice. But it's still an odd experience to have someone share so much intimate information so quickly, and I don't think it has all that much to do with me. This has happened before: it is not that we're instant friends, it is that she is desperate for any sort of assistance. A white man might be able to help, after all. Earlier in my life I would have drawn a quick, self-serving conclusion—I'm a great organizer who people really relate to. Now I feel more like a strange interloper, peering into the private lives of immigrants while revealing little about myself. It can be quite lopsided, this game.

After saying good-bye, I descend the front steps, taking a moment to look at the small house next door, where Enrique's cousin Guadalupe lives. A tilting fence runs between the two, and as I pause a foot-long rat scurries under it, followed by another. I turn my back to the brazen creatures and retreat from the cold, infested, collapsing building.

Two weeks later, having spoken with an attorney who expressed interest in the case, I call Maria at home. The number has been disconnected. I call her cell phone, and she tells me they have moved in with friends because the heat still wasn't working and the temperature had dropped into the twenties. She tells me that she'll give the attorney a call and thanks me for all that I have done. Which was very little, actually.

In Port Chester, Juana is lonely. She misses the neighborhood. She misses the monthly meetings of our organization, where she enjoyed mingling with other Mexicans. "It is too quiet here," she tells me over the telephone during one of our conversations. "There is nothing to do." In Brooklyn she knew the people at the Mexican grocery stores, and she felt comfortable in the neighborhood. Living outside of New York City for the first time since having crossed the border, she is discovering stronger feelings for Brooklyn than she realized she harbored.

The only person who seems happy about the move is Abram. The school in Port Chester is quiet and orderly, and now that he is no longer working at the car wash he comes to class rested and ready to concentrate. "It's completely different than going to school in Brooklyn," he says. "The teachers are nice, and the other students don't bother me at all. There are even a lot of Mexicans all the way up here. I can speak Spanish with people during lunch." Without the threat of fights, Abram's attendance shoots up, and the D's he was receiving in Brooklyn are being replaced with B's and C's. It is the first time Abram has lived away from the inner city, and he is enjoying it. "You should see this place, Gabriel. It's like we're living in the country up here. You can do whatever you want, and no one is going to bother you."

But Enrique, like Juana, isn't as thrilled with their new neighborhood. For one thing, he is coming home only on the weekends, and spending five nights a week in his car is turning him into a wreck. He's found that the paperwork to transfer his taxi license is cumbersome, and he's not eager to relearn the streets of an entirely new area. So he stays in Brooklyn. A perpetually groggy, nearly sleepless cabbie: a nightmare scenario anywhere, much less the chaotic streets of New York City, which demand quick reflexes. And then, as seemed always to be the case, there was a problem with the housing. The apartment they shared with Juan was crowded, but Enrique had already anticipated this. The real issue was stability.

Juan had told Enrique that he had a lease for the apartment, which turned out to not be true. This made Enrique uneasy. They had moved north to Port Chester because of the cheaper rent, but they were also in search of a place that they wouldn't soon be chased out of. Enrique knew that without a lease they could be kicked out with only a month's notice. And then where would they go?

It wasn't only the lack of a lease that worried Enrique. For several days the apartment didn't have heat, and the landlord had been slow in fixing the boiler. To make matters worse, it wasn't as if they had found a bargain. Crowded, dilapidated housing, and they were paying nine hundred dollars a month. So while essentially living in his car, Enrique began to search for an apartment, scanning Bedford-Stuyvesant buildings for APARTMENT FOR RENT signs as he went about his work. He found some promising leads, but when he called the numbers listed all of the landlords wanted much more rent than he and Juana could afford. The neighborhood was now officially "up and coming" as bodegas began to be replaced by pet spas and Thai restaurants. For three months he struck out in the apartment search, and because he was either at work or sleeping in Port Chester, we rarely spoke.

In late May, after four months of living in Port Chester, Enrique calls. For the first time in a long while, he sounds like his usual chipper self. "What's up, you fucking alcoholic?" he asks, and I can clearly picture his grin on the other end of the line. I launch an appropriately vulgar greeting back his way, and then he tells me the good news. A relative of Enrique's lives on the first floor of a small building on Franklin Avenue, in Bedford-Stuyvesant. The family that was living on the second floor has moved out, and Enrique called the landlord earlier today, who said he and Juana could move in if they could manage paying nine hundred dollars a month. "So I want you to take a look at that magical computer of yours and tell me if the building has too many violations." Enrique, about as far from computer literate as one could be, was always asking me to look things up for him. Sometimes they were ridiculous requests—"Güero, I need you to look on your little computer and find me a house that I can buy for five thousand dollars!"—but this I could manage.

I pull up the city's violation database and find that the building has a dozen open violations. Broken or defective plastered surfaces. Missing banisters. Inadequate lighting. Defective fire escape. Exposed electrical wiring. Next to each violation is a STATUS column. The status is the same for all twelve violations. NOT COMPLIED.

"Only twelve?" is Enrique's reply. "Not bad, not fucking bad!" They move in two weeks later.

The first time I visit the new apartment is July 15, 2004—Enrique's thirty-fourth birthday and Juana's fortieth.* A dozen people are gathered in the small living room of the two-bedroom apartment (to cover the rent, they've already found a tenant for the second bedroom). Enrique's brother Angel, who recently moved from the Bronx to a public housing development in Harlem, is here. So are Juana's brother and his family and several friends from Speedy Car Service. Music is blasting loudly, and Junior is rampaging through the unit, dancing and jumping, screaming and laughing.

It's not exactly a beautiful apartment. Probably built around the turn of the century, it appears that the building has not

* Not only do Enrique and Juana share the same birthday, but they almost ended up having nearly identical names. Enrique told me that he received his name because in Mexico the *Día de Santo* for Saint Enrique (Henry) falls on July 15. Juana, with the same birthday, was almost named Enriqueta by her parents.

undergone any substantial renovations in the last fifty years. The kitchen ceiling is beginning to come down, and several cracks run alongside the living room wall, but Enrique isn't concerned. "Nothing I can't fix!" he shouts over the *ranchera* tunes. "Compared to the Dekalb apartment, this is nice!" With friends and family members crowded inside, despite its physical defects the apartment has a friendly feel. Enrique and Juana both seem to be elated to be back in Brooklyn.

He pulls me aside at one point and explains another new development. "Juana's got a little one on the way," he says with a grin

"Pregnant?"

"*Sí señor.*"

"Wow, congratulations! And where's Abram tonight?"

"Working! He's back at the car wash! Won't be home until the morning!" Then Enrique begins to tell the group about his stepson, who was born here and speaks perfect English but still insists on working like a mojado.

It takes less than two months after the move to Brooklyn before a new round of housing crises strike. The walls of the kitchen have begun to sprout cracks caused by leaks, and Enrique's calls to the landlord go unanswered, so he calls the city. On August 28 inspectors discover that the kitchen walls are covered in lead-based paint. Junior is now three, still at risk. Enrique calls me to tell me the news. "We can't get away from lead," he complains. "At least, though, we've got this new law. I just hope it actually works."

What followed was one of those rare occurrences in the life of a community organizer, where a law that an affected person helps push through comes back to actually help that person in a concrete fashion. Less than three weeks after the initial violation, the city reinspected the apartment and found that the landlord had not begun the process of abatement. So, with the quick deadlines of Local Law 1, the city hired their own certified contractor to do the lead work, and by the end of September the hazard had been removed from the home and the landlord billed for the work.

For Enrique, it was a sweet conclusion to the months he had spent arguing with housing officials, speaking in press conferences, and testifying at city hall, though he remained understated. "Yeah, it was nice, but I'm still sick of all this bullshit," he said, back to his old self: angry but not dispirited. "You see, it works when you fight. Sometimes."

CHAPTER 9

Murder and War

ON A SATURDAY night in early December 2004 I receive a cryptic message from Enrique on my cell phone. Most of it is rendered inaudible by static, but after replaying his words a few times I piece together a request: he is asking me to show up with him at Brooklyn's criminal court on Monday morning. I call him back, but he doesn't pick up. My imagination runs wild: has Enrique's temper landed him in jail? Has Juana been apprehended by immigration officials, sitting in a cell or already on a plane back to Mexico? Try as I might, no amount of convoluted reasoning can put a positive spin on his enigmatic request.

Thirty minutes later Enrique calls back. His twenty-two-year-old cousin, Adolfo, has been murdered, shot in the back and neck in front of his home. It appears that the shooting was related to a fight with another man over a girl, though this is all that Enrique knows at the moment.

"Right now we've got to take care of this quickly," Enrique tells me, his voice sounding uncharacteristically frantic. "The case is going to be in court on Monday, and we need to make sure we have a good prosecutor." In the background I can hear women sobbing.

"Where are you?" I ask.

"At the funeral home with Adolfo's sisters. They're going crazy. The people here say that they can't ship the body home to Mexico until January. They say they'll just store the body for a month."

"Store it where?"

"I don't know. Here, I guess. Maybe you can come by and talk to these fuckers, explain that he needs to be shipped to Mexico *now*."

"Well, to tell you the truth, I don't know anything about cases like this," I answer. "I have no idea what I can do."

"But you could at least talk to the sisters." I hear a woman again cry loudly in the background.

"What would I tell them?"

"Just say that you're a friend who works in the community and that you will be helping to get the body home. Right now they would appreciate it. If they know that a community representative is going to try and help them, they'll feel better." Though I know nothing about shipping dead bodies to Mexico or prosecuting people on murder charges, I agree to swing by the funeral home with Enrique the following night.

The Ortiz Funeral Home, where Adolfo's body is being shown, sits beneath the Brooklyn-Queens Expressway, quite possibly the ugliest highway in the United States. Congested with large diesel trucks and always undergoing construction, the BQE, as it is called, surely drops the property values of all buildings within sight. The funeral home is surrounded by check-cashing stores and tattered bodegas, and its broken windows are sealed with cinder blocks. On this cold and gray Sunday afternoon, it looks ready to lie down itself and die.

On the ride to the viewing, Enrique and his older brother Angel are discussing the details of the dilemma. Adolfo's parents in Cuicatlán—Angela's sister Teresa and her husband, Luis—distraught over the news of his death, want his body sent home immediately so that a quick burial can take place. But workers at the funeral home have told the relatives here that the body won't be shipped until late January, because all of the flights are booked with holiday travel. Apparently, regulations allow only two cadavers per flight, and with space at a premium the family can't come up with enough money to reserve a spot. Enrique and Angel can face the spiritual crisis brought by Adolfo's death; the material task of getting the body home soon seems much less manageable.

"We've got to do something," Angel says, turning around in the passenger seat and looking me straight in the eye. "What we need is a protest, some action." I gather that Enrique has explained to him my vocation as a community organizer, apparently leading Angel to believe that my foolproof solution to any problem is to get out in the streets. I'm not sure this tactic would work here, a view I share with Angel.

"Well, then what do we do?" asks Angel, as if I have failed to deliver on a solemn promise. "How can we get the body home?" I suggest they contact the Mexican consulate, and Angel seems to think that this is a worthwhile strategy. As we pull into the parking lot of the funeral home he's clearly mulling it over. "Of course," he tells me as we get out of the car, "if they don't do anything, we'll have no other choice but to protest." I nod and can't help but think that Angel is having a hard time facing the fact that a protest won't bring anyone back from the dead.

I've only attended two previous funerals in my life, one for a grandfather and the other for a great-aunt. Both were large gatherings in churches, and both clearly cost more than customers of the Ortiz Funeral Home can afford. I follow Enrique and Angel through the entrance door into a large lobby with checkerboard tiling, which is connected to various rooms—each with its own corpse and cadre of grieving friends and relatives. The largest room, where Adolfo's body has been placed, is doing its best impression of a 1970s motel room. Walls of imitation wood paneling are nailed haphazardly, and cheap lamps sit on awkward end tables in each corner. The room is dim, with the only overhead light coming from a large chandelier hanging in the middle, two of its mismatched bulbs no longer functioning. In many places the white foam ceiling is stained with water damage, brown and musty. Twenty-five folding chairs are arranged in rows, and a dusty beige couch sits on a stained beige carpet against the rear wall, where four children play handheld video games. Toward the front of the room, relatives have placed three large bouquets of flowers, and though the petals provide some relief from the drab surroundings, it doesn't feel like a dignified place to honor Adolfo's passing.

At the head of the room Adolfo lies in a casket, his body visible from the waist up. In death he appears younger than twenty-two; with his hair cut short and dressed in a suit, he looks more likely en route to a high school prom than the underground. Getting closer to his body, I see that the person in charge of makeup has laid it on thick, probably to cover up the exit wound in his neck from one of the bullets. A group of four people huddle in front of the body, staring. I retreat to the rear of the room and grab a seat next to the couch, feeling a bit like an intruder.

After twenty minutes of quiet conversation, Adolfo's uncle walks to the front and announces that it is time to pray. He kneels in front of the group and begins singing a hymn, with a voice that is not quite in tune but strong and haunting. At times the group joins in, quietly echoing his prayers. Once the singing is over, the reading of the rosary begins. From the back, through heads bobbing up and down in rhythm to the prayers, I can see Adolfo's face, oddly white but otherwise looking entirely alive. At the end of the reading of each rosary, during the pregnant silences of deep breathing, I imagine Adolfo raising up with a grin and hopping down, laughing at the success of his practical joke.

When the prayers are finished, we spill out into the lobby, and Enrique introduces me to Rosalina and Irma, Adolfo's two older sisters. Both have long black hair and bloodshot eyes. Enrique explains that I will be working to try to get Adolfo's body shipped out quickly, and then we head outside where a group of men, most appearing to be in their twenties, smoke cigarettes. The talk revolves around Adolfo's bad luck, and one man wearing baggy jeans assures those present that he has connections with people in jail who will see to it that his murderer is dealt with properly. Though I guess the young man is simply trying to make people feel better, Enrique tells me later that he is part of a neighborhood gang of Latinos, a group that has many members behind bars.

The details of Adolfo's death are sketchy, and people trade competing versions of what they think happened. According to Rosalina and Irma, Adolfo was preparing to leave for Manhattan with them to go shopping when he received a call on his cell phone from his girlfriend, Reina (who, making the matter even more confusing, is also a cousin of Enrique's—on his father's side). Though Reina had taken out an order of protection against Adolfo, forbidding him from talking to her, his sisters told me that this was routinely violated and that Adolfo and Reina still frequently hung out together. Though they don't know exactly what was said, Adolfo decided to stay back in Brooklyn. They left him just a few blocks from the apartment they shared.

When Rosalina and Irma returned home an hour later, they found an ambulance and police cars parked outside, with paramedics working on their brother. Adolfo was transported to Kings County Hospital, where he later died. The next day, a twenty-two-year-old man named Esteban, with whom Adolfo had had a previous altercation, was arrested for the murder. People think Reina has also been placed behind bars, though no one knows yet what the charges might be against her. Everyone seems convinced that she was in on the murder.

As we drive back from the funeral home, I wonder what Adolfo's life would have been like had he stayed in Mexico. I had listened to many Mexican parents blame the problems of their children on the fact that they had grown up without learning how to respect one another, a trait they deemed quintessentially American. Did leaving home and landing in a strange city as a teenager give Adolfo just enough of a nudge to head down a slippery, unsupervised slope? Or was he destined for trouble all along, a victim of his own temper and propensity toward violence? Such questions, of course, were probably impossible to answer; I'd never even met Adolfo, after all. And at the moment, my thoughts mostly rested with his parents, grieving in the tiny village of Cuicatlán. Their son's expedition north, whether motivated by the dream of higher wages or simply the excitement of living in a big city, had ended far too abruptly.

It's still dark out a month later when Enrique and Juana pick me up at my apartment. The case against Adolfo's alleged murderer has begun to wind its way through the courts, and by now the body of Enrique's cousin has been successfully flown home. All that was needed, it turned out, was a call to the Mexican consulate from the priest of his uncle's church. For recently arrived immigrants, the importance of such social ties—be they family, friends, or even related to a higher power—are impossible to exaggerate. Or, as expressed by Artemio Guerra, a Mexican friend of mine who worked with immigrants for several years while with a religious group in rural Georgia, "Without the church, you're screwed."

At six in the morning on this cold January day, the rain is falling in sheets of gray, already beginning to flood the sidewalks. Traffic is heavy in Manhattan, and twice while driving through New Jersey we hit huge pools of water and hydroplane. Whenever we pass one of the many big rigs on the road, they throw up gallons of water onto the windshield; during the moments before the wipers cut through the splashes it looks like we're driving through a dark and polluted lake. It doesn't seem to be a good time to take a long car ride.

In less than two weeks, Enrique's best friend, Manuel, is being shipped out to Iraq. He is stationed with his family at the Fort Bragg military base in North Carolina, and we're heading down to pay him a surprise visit. After a night on the compound, the plan is to continue on to South Carolina and stay with Enrique's father, Angel, who recently purchased a house in Columbia, the state capital. With crust in my eyes, peering through the blurred windshield, the bad weather seems to portend a difficult journey. Enrique, of course, is enjoying the challenge of safely maneuvering us through the obstacle course; for veteran cab drivers accustomed to the hustle and bustle of New York City, confidence on the road is never in short supply.

Once we cross into Virginia the sky opens up and the traffic thins. Junior is in the backseat, banging a Spider Man figure against the window. Despite this steady beating of plastic on glass, Juana lies fast asleep beside him under a yellow blanket. By now her stomach is the size of a ripe watermelon, but when I had earlier expressed concern about the prospect of a roadside delivery far from the nearest hospital, she had just shrugged. "That is how we've done it in Mexico for years," she said, oblivious to my anxiety. As we drive, Enrique and I discuss the history of his friendship with Manuel, which seems to have consisted mostly of drinking too much and narrowly avoiding serious trouble.

"Of all the people who used to hang out in Brooklyn, only a few of us made it," he explains. "Back then, let me tell you, it wasn't easy to go straight. A bunch of the guys in that neighborhood were fucking crazy. There was this one black guy, wasn't scared of anything."

"I don't think I've ever seen you scared, either," I say.

"No, this guy was different," Enrique insists. "One day we were hanging out in a park, not bothering anyone, when some cops came. This guy got angry about them just showing up and harassing us, and started talking shit to them. One of the cops took out his gun and smashed it across the guy's face. This crazy fucker just stood there. He wiped the blood from his face and told the cop, 'Now what? Is that all you can do?' The cops left after that, didn't want to mess with him anymore. *Loco.*"

"Where is he now?" I ask.

"Jail. Where else?"

As Enrique continued to list the near misses—of gunshots a few inches wide, of a last-minute cooling of tempers—he lifts his T-shirt, revealing a scar below his left ribs. "I was at a party in the Bronx, and I was talking to this girl but didn't know she had a boyfriend," he tells me. "He came up to me without saying any-thing and cut me right here." Enrique drew a line with his index finger across his stomach, with a hand that is also battle-scarred. He told me awhile ago about the origins of the lump between the two tendons, which occurred when Enrique punched a Puerto Rican who was trying to rob him on the subway in the 1980s.

It seems that nearly everybody from those years, except Manuel and Enrique, is either behind bars or dead. Living as a twenty-some-thing male in a rough-and-tumble neighborhood of Williamsburg, surrounded by gangsters and liquor stores, Enrique's long casualty list of former friends speaks to the difficulties of breaking free.

"I could have ended up like Adolfo," Enrique remarks. "But now things have settled down and I've got a family to take care of. That's why I want to make sure that the asshole who killed him goes to jail for a long, long time. I don't care if Adolfo wasn't perfect. He didn't deserve to die like that, with two bullets in his back."

I had actually wondered what was leading Enrique to take such a strong interest in the prosecution of Esteban. It was Enrique who met with the Mexican consulate, who arranged for the priest to make the call, who drove his cousins to court for each appointment and made sure they arrived early. At the most recent court date, the representative for the district attorney who was handling the case even had to explain to Enrique that she knew what she was doing, in order to put a stop to his endless suggestions about various legal strategies. Adolfo was a blood relative, of course, yet Enrique had also told me that he thought Adolfo was probably a "punk"—hardly the type of description one would give for an innocent bystander who had been wronged and demanded vengeance.

Yet Enrique, now thirty-four and with a new addition to his family on the way, was his own living proof that lives could be turned around, that early missteps don't necessarily determine later events, and it was precisely this opportunity at redemption that Esteban had stolen from Adolfo. Enrique looked at what he acknowledged was a young punk, and saw himself. So he followed the case closely, weeks after Adolfo's own friends and many of his relatives had lost interest, as if it were his very own.

We stop at a Denny's in Virginia to fill up on greasy omelets, served by a waitress from Veracruz who takes our orders in Spanish. Enrique explains to her—as he has begun to do at every opportunity, despite my pleas to desist—that I am writing a book about Mexican immigrants. She listens politely but doesn't look particularly impressed, and I hope this reception might encourage Enrique to stop parading around his gringo friend so garishly (a hope that, in the end, is in vain). "Did you see how she was looking at you?"

Enrique asks me as we pile back in the car. "She was definitely interested." I tell him he's delusional.

Back on the road, the rest of the trip through Virginia is uneventful. Mile after empty mile pass, with the only distractions being the gigantic billboards that tower over the rural countryside. One store claims to have rock-bottom prices for their three specialty products—gasoline, alcohol, and fireworks—which doesn't strike me as an especially bright combination. Motel rooms are advertised for $17.99 a night, a price I can't remember seeing since the 1980s; coming from New York City, they might as well be giving their rooms away. When I mention this to Enrique, he says it still seems too much to pay just to sleep in a room. "I've never stayed in a motel," he explains. "Why pay for something when you'll just be asleep? When you're tired, all you need is your car." He taps twice on his steering wheel to underscore his point.

I bunch up my sweatshirt into a pillow and lean against the door, preparing to sleep. Eyes closed, I think about his comment. I've spent many a night in fancy hotels—complete with room service, heated pools, and fitness centers; he has crisscrossed the country dozens of times in his car without once shelling out twenty bucks for a bed.

From the passenger seat at eighty-five miles per hour, there is nothing special about crossing the border of Virginia and entering North Carolina. A welcome sign, a quick pause at a rest stop with maps tacked up and various mileage charts, a chance to fuel up on sodas and snacks. Most of the people stretching their legs and relieving themselves in the bathrooms are white, and it seems an unlikely place for Latino history to be made.

Yet for the past ten years North Carolina has been experiencing the fastest growth of Spanish-speaking immigrants in the United

States. According to the census bureau, between 1990 and 2000 the Hispanic population of the state increased by an incredible 394 percent. The three fastest-growing Hispanic communities in the country are all located in North Carolina: Greensboro, with a spike of 694 percent; Charlotte, slightly less at 622 percent; and Raleigh, with 569 percent. Where once Latinos were present mostly in places like California and Texas, today states like North Carolina, Arkansas, and Georgia are seeing a massive influx of Latino immigrants.

An hour into North Carolina, heading south on Interstate 95, there is no hint of any such dramatic transformation. Here the land is still empty. No Latinos, no whites; not even any cows. Gazing out the window, where the expansive land blends seamlessly into the clear skies on the horizon, I think of Maria and her family crowded into their apartment in Brooklyn and contending with swarms of rats and spending winters without heat. For immigrants like Maria, forking over large sums of money to live in substandard housing, the draw south is proving hard to resist. Cheap rents, plenty of space, the promise of a quiet life—these are the benefits that New York City will never be able to provide.

We arrive in Fayetteville, the closest town to Fort Bragg, at dusk. Sleepy after the long drive, Enrique has rolled down his window and begun belting out lyrics, singing along with a tape of Chalino Sanchez that is rattling the stereo system: *"They call me one hundred deaths, because I deal in drug smuggling / I've murdered so many people, when I pass they know to turn away running."* It's too dark to make out much of the town, except for a few strip malls peppered with pawnshops and car dealerships. After several miles of generic suburbia we cross a river named Cape Fear and are greeted by a large "Welcome to Fort Bragg" sign.

Though difficult to appreciate at night, Fort Bragg—together with the nearby Pope Air Force Base—makes up one of the largest military installations in the world. The sprawling base is home to elite fighting forces like the Green Berets and Delta Force commandos, who are among the nearly thirty thousand people who live there. Including the military personnel, the median income for Cumberland County, where the base is located, is approximately twenty-nine thousand dollars a year. Take the military pay out of the equation, however, and the median income for the county drops to twenty-two thousand. Still, on the largest military base in the United States, in the most powerful nation the world has ever seen, poverty persists. Within its confines, 10 percent of the population lives on incomes below the poverty line—and more than one out of those ten are under eighteen years old. Indeed, when we visit a supermarket on the base, large signs are taped to the window, telling customers that food stamps are welcome here.

As we pull into the entrance of the base, a guard with an M-16 strapped to his back steps out to meet us.

"Are you military?" he asks. Enrique explains that we are here to surprise a friend who is leaving soon for Iraq. "Okay, then I'm going to need to see everyone's IDs and search the car," he states. When he comes to my side I mention that my driver's license, which was issued in Wyoming, has expired. He nods, takes a look at it, and hands it back to me. Enrique gives him his New York driver's license and Juana's Mexican passport. We all get out of the car.

"This is expired," the guard tells Enrique, holding up Juana's passport. "Pull your car over to the side here," he says, his words now sounding more like a command than a request. "I'm going to have to call my supervisor."

Enrique pulls his car next to the guard's outpost and we gather on the curb. Through the window of the station I can see the guard talking on the telephone while staring at Juana's passport. Although I don't know much about immigration enforcement, this doesn't feel like a good situation to be in. Juana and Enrique, however, don't seem concerned.

"Immigration is going to come here?" Juana asks, bemused. "What do they think, I'm a terrorist?" While Junior does laps around the car, even more hyper than usual after being confined for so many hours, Juana and Enrique seem more curious than frightened by the guard's actions. I pray that my quickened heartbeat is nothing more than paranoia.

Ten minutes later the guard steps out of the station. "I can't let you in here unless you want me to call the military police and have them run this information through their system," he tells us, his eyes focused on Juana. From his tone of voice, I can tell that he anticipates such a background check would likely land Juana in handcuffs. Turning to Enrique, he repeats the obvious. "This passport is expired." By now Enrique is angry. I have told him, perhaps unwisely, that I didn't have any trouble with my expired license.

"What is the damn problem?" Enrique asks me. "What's this guy going to do, call *la pinche migra?* Does he think Juana's a terrorist, or that we've got a bomb in the damn car?"

"Shut up," I snap. I'm relieved that the guard doesn't seem to understand Spanish, but *bomba* sounds all too much like its English equivalent. "Let's just forget it," I plead. "We can get out of here and call your friend. I bet he'll be able to get us in." Enrique pauses, staring at the guard who is awaiting our response with arms crossed. On Enrique's face is now a look I am all too familiar with—and which I normally appreciate: the look of rebellious and angry determination. *Not now,* I think to myself.

I do some extended cajoling, and Enrique finally decides to back off. We pile back into the car, turn around, and pull into a parking lot on the outskirts of the base, where Enrique calls Manuel. A few minutes later he pulls up in a car, followed in another by his friend

Raul. After introductions Raul gets behind the wheel of Enrique's car, and Juana and Junior join Manuel in his car. We drive to another entrance and both cars make it through without a problem.

On the quick ride, Raul, who is Puerto Rican and has family in the Bronx, explains that his regiment was sent off to Iraq yesterday. "I should be there with them," he says, not sounding totally convinced. "But I hurt my back—slipped a disk or something. The doctors don't know when it's going to get better."

Enrique, still fuming about the guard's behavior, asks Raul why they didn't have a problem with my license. "I don't know," he replies. "But after nine eleven the security has been really tight. Before, there weren't even any checkpoints to get into the base." This answer doesn't convince Enrique. Giddy with fatigue, and relieved to have avoided a confrontation with the guard, I take my own ridiculous stab at an explanation.

"The guy probably looked into my eyes and thought I was a soldier," I venture. "There's something about being a soldier—you have a look that lets everyone know you mean business. He could tell that I have that look. See?" I stick my jaw out and give a salute. Enrique and Raul burst out laughing and continue to chuckle until we arrive at Manuel's home. Had I ever aspirations for military service, their responses were far from encouraging.

Though the army has made Manuel a soldier—an occupation, I learn, he takes very seriously—with a goofy grin and a shaved head that accentuates his large ears, it is easy to imagine his previous life as a teenager getting into trouble with Enrique back in Brooklyn. His house is located in a development of identical houses; it feels more like a college campus or sprawling suburban apartment complex than a home for soldiers preparing for war in the Middle East.

When we enter his house, Manuel introduces us to his wife, Veronica, and their two daughters, and then pops open a round of Coronas. Junior and the girls run off into the living room to watch television. Raul shares with Manuel my notion that I could pass as a soldier. "Yeah, the güero does have the haircut, at least," Manuel agrees, to my surprise. The conversation quickly evolves into a pitch for me to enlist. Manuel grabs a sheet of paper with a graph outlining the pay scales for army soldiers.

"Look, if you enter to be an officer, you'll be making good money," he says. "Plus, you speak Spanish. That'll get you more money, too. If you do like I did, you can also get your degree. You want to get a degree?" I tell him I already graduated from college.

"No shit? Then you'll be making good money in no time," Manuel replies, closing the case. "You'll learn new skills. When I came here I didn't know how to cook, but now look at me—I'm a fucking chef." He points to a framed certificate hanging on the kitchen wall, which he has earned for his culinary skills. "And you won't believe this." He opens a sliding glass door and motions for us to follow him out.

"You see this?" Manuel asks, standing on a patio next to a barbecue grill. We gaze out at a large yard of neatly trimmed grass. "This is all my land—from here to the end of the lot. Try finding that kind of room to move in New York City."

We admire the space for a few more minutes and then head back inside, where Manuel cracks open another round of beers. A stack of photos is passed around, and while Enrique and Manuel catch up, Juana and I rifle through them. After a dozen shots of his family's recent trip to New York City, I pause at a photo. In my hands is a close-up snapshot of one of the World Trade Center towers with smoke billowing out of it. The second tower is nowhere to be seen.

"Where did this photo come from?" I ask. "Did you actually take this?"

"That's on nine eleven, right before the second tower went down," Manuel says. "I took that shot from outside of my office. I was working in Lower Manhattan that day. That was one fucking crazy day . . . fucking motherfucking crazy."

"After that day, nothing seemed to matter anymore," Manuel continues. "I knew that I had to do something for my country, so I joined. Walked right into a recruitment office. Never thought of joining before in my life."

When I ask Manuel what type of work he had been doing in Manhattan on September 11, he surprises me by launching into a five-minute rant about wetbacks. "I worked for a delivery company that moved things around the city. But once all the mojados like this guy started coming over," and he pauses to motion toward Enrique, "and working for almost nothing, they undercut us. They come here illegally and work for pennies, and we all get fucked."

It seems curious to me that Manuel—whose close friend had crossed the border illegally and even took pride in being a mojado—would have such antipathy toward Mexican immigrants. Enrique immediately jumps into the conversation, and as they debate loudly back and forth, I can tell this is not the first time they've had this conversation.

"And you, pendejo, how do you think you got here?" Enrique asks loudly with a slight smile on his face. "What do you think your parents did? If they hadn't crossed, you would be the same as me. You don't know what the fuck you're talking about. What are people supposed to do to survive? *Hay que comer.*" Enrique is using a phrase I have heard repeatedly when people from rural Mexican towns explain what led them to come north: a person has to eat.

"Fuck that," Manuel responds, nearly shouting. "That's just an excuse. There's work in Mexico. And my parents came from Mexico, but I'm one hundred percent American."

"Fuck you. You're a mojado who can't admit it." Their argument quickly degenerates into a series of competing "fucks" and "fuck you's," the volume growing ever louder.* Finally, after a few more minutes of trading vulgar insults they both give in, laughing. Juana and I, seated on kitchen stools, glance at each other, wondering who these madmen are. Manuel opens another round of beers.

"Let's see your tattoo," Enrique says to Manuel. "Just to show how confused you are." Manuel smiles a bit sheepishly and pulls up one of his sleeves, revealing three words etched in blue ink on his shoulder, *Viva la Raza,* a standard Mexican pride slogan. My head is beginning to spin with all the cognitive dissonance in the room.

"You got any Tigres del Norte?" Enrique asks, which I take for his attempt to officially declare a truce on the illegal immigration question. Manuel goes into the living room and returns with a CD of the classic Mexican band. While Enrique fiddles with the CD player, I ask Manuel where his parents are from, learning that his mother is from the Mexican state of Zacatecas, and his father is, like Enrique, from Puebla.

Suddenly, a song interrupts our conversation, blasting at full volume. It is one of the hits by Los Tigres del Norte, "América," and I realize this is just a creative rebuttal to Manuel's tirade. All conversation—even the children's shrieking from the living room—is halted by the deafening lyrics:

* I was surprised by such open profanity within earshot of Manuel and Veronica's daughters, until Enrique told me they had decided not to teach their children Spanish. When I asked Manuel about this decision, he shrugged and said his kids simply weren't interested in learning another language.

I was born the color of earth
And my inheritance was Spanish
Those from the north say I am Latino
They don't want to call me an American
I am *charrua* [Uruguayan], I am *jibaro* [Puerto Rican]
I am *chapin* [Guatemalan], Eskimo, a Mayan prince
I am a *guajiro* [Cuban], a Mexican *charro*
If he who is born in Europe is a European
And he who is born in Africa is African
And I was born in America, then I don't see why I can't be called
   an American
We might be different colors, but as children of God, we are
   brothers*

Enrique turns down the volume, nodding with the music. "If you're one hundred percent American, then so am I," he says to Manuel, jutting out his jaw in defiance. "Like Los Tigres say, America is a fucking continent, not a country." He cranks up the volume even louder for the final chorus of *"De América, yo soy"*—"From America, I am"—and then stops the disc.

"Listen good," he says to Manuel in the now quiet house. "Listen to Los Tigres and look at your arm every now and then, and you'll learn a thing or two about what I'm fucking talking about."

It is now a number of beers later. Manuel has spent the last hour explaining the endless benefits of enlisting, with Enrique and me mostly nodding along. By this point Veronica has left the kitchen

* For the translation of these lyrics, I consulted Héctor Tobar's wonderful book, *Translation Nation: Defining a New American Identity in the Spanish-Speaking United States* (Riverhead: 2005).

and Juana and Junior have gone to bed. It's unclear what Juana makes of Manuel; during the entire evening she utters only a few sentences.

As we're seated around the kitchen counter, Manuel takes an inventory of his army life. Rent: free. Electricity: free. Heat: free. Health care: free. While he talks he washes some dirt from his hands, and leaves the water running in the sink. Enrique reaches over and shuts it off.

"Fuck it," Manuel tells Enrique. "The army is paying for the water, too. They pay for everything."

"Yeah, but you have to pay now," Enrique retorts, tiring of the nonstop praise. "You've got to go to Iraq. That's not free."

"Of course I'm going to Iraq. The army has made me a soldier." Manuel looks at Enrique and me, as if we might challenge him on this point. "You think I'm afraid? Hell no. They have taught me everything I need to know to take care of myself out there. We're fucking prepared for *war.*" His emphasis on the word seems to be an attempt to communicate the idea that this is something we civilians will never quite comprehend. "You should see how much equipment I'm going to have out there in the desert. I'm more than ready for this shit."

It is odd to me that Manuel has not expressed any doubts whatsoever about the mission, or at the very least his personal safety, since so much of the recent news from Iraq has been negative. I don't want to get in a heated debate over the merits of the war—I'm an unannounced guest, after all—but I do want to engage him a little.

"I just met a journalist who got back from Iraq," I mention. "He was embedded with the army near Baghdad. He told me that one of the hardest things about being there is that so many of the Iraqis don't trust the U.S. soldiers, because Americans don't understand much about the culture over there. He also—"

"Your friend doesn't know shit." Manuel leans forward in his chair, his left foot bouncing up and down. "Or else the soldiers he was with were sleeping during their classes. They make sure we know about where we're going."

Manuel raises both of his arms and gives us a thumbs-up sign.

"For example, you know what this means to Iraqis?" Enrique and I shake our heads. "It means 'fuck you'!" He laughs, clearly impressed with his specialized knowledge. "And what about this?" He sits back in the chair and extends his legs up in the air, showing us his heels. I can't imagine the gesture meaning much of anything. "It is the same thing, basically, a sign of disrespect," he explains. "So if we're sitting around talking to them and I do this," and he lifts his legs and gives us a thumbs-up, "then I'm disrespecting them. People who don't pay attention in class don't remember this stuff. But me, I've been paying attention, so I know."

I wonder how often Manuel will end up sitting around a table chatting with Iraqis, as we are doing in his living room. Perhaps table etiquette has been covered, but is there a culturally respectable way of banging down people's doors in the middle of the night with guns drawn? I let the question go unasked.

"Plus, you should see all the gear we've got," he continues. Manuel steps out of the room for a moment and returns with a gas mask strapped to his face. In his arms is the rest of his gear: vest, helmet, and boots. "Anytime you hear the alarm, you snap this on," he tells us, his voice muffled and sounding robotic through the filter. He hands Enrique the vest and on my head places the helmet, which feels like a set of encyclopedias, then rattles off a list of ammunition this preventive equipment could guard against.

Veronica enters the kitchen while Manuel is listing the fourth projectile I no longer need to fear flying toward my head, and lets out a raucous laugh. I have to admit that we make a ridiculous sight:

three grown men playing army in the kitchen with beers in our hands (or two of us—Enrique's no-alcohol pledge is still in effect, and indeed continues more or less unbroken to the present). After she grabs something from the fridge and leaves, we hand over the helmet and vest so that we can see Manuel fully suited up. He puts on his desert boots, plops the helmet on his head, tightens a few sashes on his camouflage vest, stuffs the gas mask into its container attached to his belt, and stands at attention. Enrique and I both admit that he looks like he knows what he is doing.

"I told you, I am not going to die, because I am totally prepared," he agrees between gulps of beer. In the quiet kitchen of a quaint suburban home, after a few hours of alcohol and bullshitting about life in Brooklyn, the Iraqi desert seems a world away—not only for me and Enrique, but I sense for Manuel as well.

By midnight Manuel has drunk at least a six-pack and smoked some marijuana with Enrique. The equipment and uniform session has put him in a good mood, and as he grows sleepier I decide to ask him if he ever wished he hadn't joined, since he now has a family to worry about.

"Are you kidding me?" he answers, his droopy eyelids snapping open. "Joining the army was the best decision I ever made. It took me thirty-one years to realize it, but I was made for this. This is what I am supposed to do." He gazes past me for a moment, thinking, and then snaps his head up, looking like he's had some sort of epiphany. "It's like this: the more you do in the army, the more you want to do. And the more you do, the more people look up to you. I'm living a fantasy." I nod along.

"You just have to take our responsibility seriously. You've got to always remember the creed: 'I am an American soldier. I will always place the mission first. I will never accept defeat. I will never quit. I will never leave a fallen comrade. I am an American soldier.' I live by this creed." Manuel stands up, says good night, and goes to bed.

"I don't like to say it, but my friend is full of shit," Enrique tells me before heading off to bed himself. "That motherfucker Bush is sending all these people over to die for oil, and he's talking about some sort of bullshit creed."

A few hours of fitful sleep leaves me exhausted the next morning. "It's been proven that the human body only needs four hours of sleep each night," Manuel lectures as we settle into his car to get groceries for breakfast. "And you don't even need the four hours to be at one time. Sleep a little here, sleep a little there. As long as you've got four hours, you're good as new. It's been proven." Despite his insistence on the science behind the claim (he learned it during an army class, after all), the argument doesn't sound—much less feel—very convincing at the moment.

On the way to a gigantic supermarket we pass a building under construction. Though it's Sunday morning, a crew of laborers is already at work. "You see, the only people working right now are the immigrants," Enrique says. "Even here, in the middle of the base, you've got mojados."

"Those aren't fucking immigrants," answers Manuel, though they certainly look like they are to me. "And even if they are, you'll see it's different in the supermarket. All the people working there are white or black." With an emerging headache, I'm not looking forward to another round of immigration debate between the two. Thankfully Manuel becomes preoccupied with describing the layout of the base, pointing out a row of large houses that are set aside for officers, an area he hopes to move his family into when he returns from Iraq.

When we arrive at the grocery store we stop in at a coffee shop for a caffeine fix. No one is behind the counter, so Enrique gives a shout toward the back. A brown-skinned woman emerges, causing Enrique to let out a wild cackle, and the woman to look at him with concern. "Excuse me," he says in Spanish. "We would like three coffees. And could you tell me where you are from?"

"¡Tres cafés!" the woman yells. She turns back to Enrique and gives him a curious look. "I'm from Juarez. Why?"

"You see?" Enrique says, nudging Manuel. "Fucking Mexicans, we're everywhere."

With our stomachs full from a breakfast of bacon and eggs, Manuel and I sit down to watch television while Enrique and Juana pack up their belongings. After an especially ridiculous talk show I look over at Manuel, ready to make a comment, and see that he is fast asleep. So much for the four-hour rule. I'm laughing to myself when the doorbell rings, and Raul walks in with a tall white man, whose name I miss. They both join us on the couch.

Raul's companion is also a helicopter mechanic. "I'm originally from Upstate New York—just a country boy," he says, a friendly grin on his face. I imagine this is how he has been pegged since entering the army, and has learned he might as well be up front about his origins so as to avoid any future ribbing. I am immediately attracted to him for this act of self-deprecation—a trait that has been in short supply since we entered the base.

As we chat in the living room I learn that he spent five months in Afghanistan, but won't be going to Iraq because he hurt his knee and is being discharged next month. When I ask him about what he thought of his time in Afghanistan, it seems like the first time he has contemplated the question.

"Afghanistan? Fuck, what is there to say?" He looks at me and then back at the television, where a cartoon now plays. "It was okay, I guess. I got to meet Robin Williams and Joan Jett. That was pretty cool." He pauses for another moment, considering. "But it was hot as hell."

When I ask him about the local Afghanis, he appears equally unprepared for the question. "I didn't get to know anyone," he eventually decides. "We're not supposed to talk to them really. But from what I could tell they're okay. People said that all of the men are fairies, that they only have women around to make babies. Pretty weird, huh?"

In a half hour of conversation, this is the extent of the information I extract about his time abroad: he met two celebrities (if Joan Jett can still be considered a celebrity), it is hotter in Afghanistan than in New York, and all the men in Afghanistan are gay. Not exactly a poster child for the benefits of traveling abroad.

But when I tell him about Raul and Manuel's mission to get me to enlist, and ask what he thinks I should do, he pauses, and I can immediately tell that *this* is a question he has been contemplating.

"I wouldn't do it if I were you," he says. "It's not worth it. They tell you that you will get so many things out of it, but it doesn't really work that way. When I returned from Afghanistan you know how much money I had?" He waits for me to shake my head. "Eight thousand dollars for those five months. What can you do with money like that? And when you get back, there isn't shit to do on the base. Same thing, day after day after day. I can't wait till I get out of here and start doing normal work." He tells me he is planning on moving to South Carolina when he is discharged, and that he hopes to purchase a home with his wife.

By early afternoon it is time to leave for South Carolina. In the parking lot I pull out a camera and snap several quick shots of Manuel and Enrique. We say our good-byes, and as I hop into the backseat Enrique calls out to Manuel. "Be careful over there! Don't do anything stupid."

Manuel smiles at Enrique. "Don't worry about me. I know how to take care of myself." As we merge onto the highway toward South Carolina, Enrique looks at me and ruminates.

"I don't care how much training he says he's had—people with the same training are getting blown up every day. And so what if he is one hundred percent americano? No one gives a shit how you die—get shot in Brooklyn or get shot in Iraq. You're dead." He shakes his head slightly and sighs. "Fine, he survived Brooklyn, but you can't keep getting lucky forever."

CHAPTER 10

Under the Confederate Flag

THE BILLBOARDS WE pass on the way to Columbia serve as reminders that we are heading deep into so-called red state territory. "Get U.S. Out of the U.N.," reads one large sign sponsored by the John Birch Society. Another billboard, brought to us by a higher power, asks the ultimate question: "Is the road you're on going to get you here? —God." I normally don't think of life's decisions in such a starkly religious manner, but at the moment, we're on the road to visit a man named Angel—and there's even a Gabriel in the backseat—so I figure we're doing pretty well for ourselves.

Angel's house is on a quiet block surrounded by quiet blocks. In the driveway is parked a shiny blue truck with a series of scratches along the passenger side. The lights in the house are off, which again leads me to question the wisdom of Enrique's policy of conducting only surprise visits. "I never like to tell people that I'm coming," he had explained. "That way, if I can't make it, or if we're late, it won't matter." This was a policy he applied even to his trips to visit Angela in Mexico. The last time he had made the twenty-five-hundred-mile-long journey, he had pulled his car in front of her house and found a shocked Angela in the middle of a bucket bath.

Enrique disappears around the back of the house, leaving us to wait in the car. After several minutes the front door opens and

Enrique emerges, followed by a short man wearing a large cowboy hat. A stocky, light-skinned woman with a puffy face trails behind. Enrique introduces Angel and Leticia, and we gather our things from the truck, toss them in the living room, and settle down around the kitchen table, though Angel stays in the living room to watch a soccer game.

As soon as everyone is seated Leticia demands that we get back up. "Since you didn't call us to say you were coming, we don't have any food in the house for dinner." She looks at Enrique, who shrugs. "So come on, get up everyone! We've got to go shopping." I'm not quite ready to get back in the car, and Angel is not moving from his chair. Leticia is successful, however, in getting everyone else out of the house and on the way to Wal-Mart, which leaves Angel and me alone in front of the television.

He looks over at me in the empty house. "You're a friend of Enrique's?"

"Yes." I explain how I know Enrique, mentioning that I'm now writing a book about immigrants.

Angel raises his eyebrows. "*Interesante.*"

"Yes, I think so."

"So you came here with Enrique to take down my story? You know, I've been in this country a lot longer than him. Did he tell you that?"

"Yes. He said you came in nineteen seventy-one."

"That's right, nineteen seventy-one. Are you ready for my story?"

I nod, pulling out a notebook and pen.

Growing up, Angel never thought he would leave the hills of southern Mexico, much less end up in a metropolis like New York City. He was raised in a small adobe hut in the hot desert *cerros* that surround the village of Cuicatlán—itself less a village than a collection of two dozen other huts near a natural water source called La Pila. It was an hour's walk to Cuicatlán, and several more hours to Chinantla. Families survived in the hills by hunting, gathering, and planting. Nobody went to school; few left the hills for anything but a quick trip to La Pila for water or to Chinantla and neighboring Piaxtla to sell corn, beans, and squash. It wasn't uncommon for people to pass away without venturing much farther.

Sometime in the 1950s Angel met Angela while visiting Chinantla, and the two soon married, but he doesn't mention her name once as he describes his life in Mexico. Instead, he focuses on the chain reactions that led him to eventually apply and receive a visa and cross to *El Norte*. "People in town [Chinantla] had started to go to New York," he says. "I had two older brothers who heard about it, and then one of them left in nineteen sixty-eight. In nineteen seventy another one joined him." A year later, Angel followed.

The New York City that Angel found in 1971—where the overwhelming number of Spanish speakers were Puerto Rican or Dominican—initially made him feel out of place: it would be hard to find a locale more alien for a resident of Cuicatlán than the Big Apple, with its towering buildings and crowded sidewalks. Other Spanish speakers navigated the city with ease, speaking with strange accents and easily throwing English words into their rapid-fire sentences, which Angel often could not follow.

At times during those early years he must have felt as though he had taken the wrong turn and ended up in the northeast instead of out west, where more of his *paisanos* from other Mexican states had drifted. But though Mexicans were few and far between in Brooklyn, Angel arrived with that most important safety net in place beneath him: he had family. By the time Angel arrived, his two brothers were living in a five-bedroom apartment on Myrtle Avenue with three other Mexicans, and they quickly made room for the newest arrival. The building, 715 Myrtle Avenue, is just two blocks from Juana's sweatshop factory.

"When I arrived in New York there were only a few Mexicans," Angel says. "But that's how it always is. My nephew told me that when he first came to South Carolina there were no Mexicans, either. But now you can see *muchisimos mexicanos,* even here. There are people from Chiapas, Michoacán, Veracruz, Hidalgo, Guerrero . . . everywhere."

Within a week Angel was working at a nearby factory on Flushing Avenue that manufactured plastic pots for plants, where his two brothers were also employed. Asked about his earnings, he chuckles and tells me that his first paycheck for two weeks of work was eighty-two dollars. "We worked forty hours a week, Monday through Friday. That seems like nothing now, but back then I thought I was doing pretty good," he says, adding that the factory technically had a union but that none of the workers had actually met their representative. "Once I got settled down, I realized I could make more money elsewhere, so I switched."

Eighty-two dollars for eighty hours of work: to today's ears, it sounds like nothing. But not only was Angel's first factory job within a stone's throw of Juana's sweatshop, but his wages had been almost identical, at about one dollar an hour; counting for inflation, he was outearning Juana.

Midway through his second year at the plastics factory a machine exploded near Angel, injuring a Mexican worker from Chinantla. "He was bathed in burning plastic," Angel remembers, and though the man had many surgeries his face remained disfigured, and he eventually returned to Mexico.

The low pay and the industrial accident compelled Angel to begin searching for a new line of work. This plan was cut short, however, when immigration agents raided the factory and deported

Angel along with several dozen other Mexican immigrants. "So I went back to Mexico for a little while, and when I returned I went back to the same factory but started to look for new work," he explains. I try to ask him about what it was like to be back in Mexico, but he brushes aside the question and continues on with his narrative.

When he learned that the brother of the factory owner had a cleaning company, he changed jobs. For several years he worked for the Bushwick company, washing linens from hospitals and airports. Not only was the work less dangerous, but he was paid three hundred dollars every two weeks, nearly quadruple his old paycheck. He remained at the company for three years, until they relocated to New Jersey.

After that he drifted around, working in nearly all the industries that early immigrants gravitate toward: construction, food service, textiles. True stability finally came when he landed a job as a janitor at the Port Authority, where he was a member of 32BJ, the powerful Building Service Workers Union. For fifteen years he cleaned floors while living in an apartment in Williamsburg, and in 1999 he moved into the Tompkins housing projects in Bedford-Stuyvesant to live with Leticia. In 2001 he made a down payment on the sixty-five-thousand-dollar house in which we're sitting. He now collects a five-hundred-dollar pension while receiving another eight hundred dollars from social security.

With this steady income Angel was set for a life of leisure, but though he had come to South Carolina to retire, he didn't seem comfortable with the notion of sitting around. One of the first things he did after arriving in Columbia was to buy four new tortilla makers, medium-sized machines capable of producing thousands of tortillas a day. "There are so many Mexicans here, but no good place to buy real tortillas," he tells me. "There isn't a *tortilleria*.

If you want tortillas, you have to buy them at the grocery store. Some people even have to buy them at Wal-Mart!"

Though he had never made a single tortilla before, Angel was hoping to sell tortillas from his home. Word would spread quickly; Mexicans were desperate for decent tortillas. For now, though, the pristine machines sit on a small table in the kitchen, covered with a blanket. They didn't come with instructions, and I get the impression that Angel has no idea how to use them. Out of either stubbornness or embarrassment, he hasn't returned to the store to ask the sales representative how they work. "They're broken, I guess," he tells me, though the machines look like they've never been used before in their life.

Angel's thoughts about Mexico were bittersweet—mostly bitter. "I don't like my home country," he tells me several times during our two-day stay. "It doesn't have anything for me that I want or need." Enrique got nostalgic about Chinantla nearly every week; Angel's memories—never all that positive—seemed to increase in negativity with each year spent away. He explained that by now he was literally allergic to his previous country: "If I went to Mexico today, the water and food would make me sick."

Leticia, who had flown from Honduras to the United States with her uncle in 1971, held a much less negative feeling about her home country—"It is poor, yes, but also beautiful"—and expressed a desire to see Mexico. She had come legally to New York City with a visa and within the year was married to a Honduran man whom she described with one word, "drunk." At the time of their marriage Leticia was twenty, and they had two children together, a daughter and a son. "We fought all the time, if you know what I mean," Leticia explains, which I took to mean she was beaten. Still, the rocky relationship somehow held until 1990, when they were finally divorced. The next year, Leticia moved into the Tompkins projects.

In the early nineties, in addition to his job at the Port Authority, on weekends Angel was selling hot dogs out of a truck at the corner of Broadway and Marcus Garvey Avenues. One Saturday afternoon he made a sale to Leticia, who continued to come back each weekend to chat, and eventually to flirt. By 1999 Angel and Leticia were living together in Tompkins, and eventually married in 2004. Angel soon discovered that living with Leticia was much different than living with Angela. He could not boss Leticia around, and if anything she had more of an effect on him than he on her. Religion was a clear case in point. While watching television one day Leticia was moved by an advertisement for the Church of Latter-Day Saints. She called the telephone number on the screen and requested a copy of the Book of Mormon in Spanish. A few days later, three white missionaries speaking broken Spanish were knocking at her door in the projects. Not long after, she converted—and not long after that, so did Angel, though it took several minutes of prying before he finally confirmed to me that he was indeed now a Mormon. Late in life, Angel was finding the gender roles that seemed immutable in the campo were in fact quite elastic. Leticia, for her part, had come to her own conclusions regarding relationships: husbands were not to beat their wives, and wives did not have to unthinkingly agree to whatever their husbands said. Both, in their own ways, had been shaped by their time spent in the United States.

On our second day in Columbia we prepare to head out to a large flea market. Over a breakfast of Mexican pastries and weak coffee, Angel explains that he wants to get a decal for his new truck of the logo of the University of South Carolina Gamecocks. "Lots of people here watch them play *fútbol americano*," he explains.

"You're the first Mexican I've met that actually likes American football," I tell him. "Everyone else only cares about baseball and soccer. Are the Gamecocks any good?"

"Actually, I don't know," Angel says. "I don't watch the games. After all my years here, I still can't figure out what the rules are or how they keep score. All you see are a bunch of people standing around on a field. Real fat people. *Gordos.* Doesn't make much sense to me. But everyone here has that sticker on their car, and I like it."

A friend of Angel's has told him that he can get the decal at the Saturday flea market across town, so we pile into his truck and head out, with Enrique behind the wheel. (Angel's vision is failing, and when he is out of earshot Leticia tells me she doesn't feel safe when he drives. "He smashed the truck recently, and it was completely his fault," she murmurs, "but he's too proud to admit that he can't see.") Angel has traded his straw Mexican hat for a cap that bears the insignia of his union on the front and a militant statement on the back. "We Don't Play," it reads, which seems appropriate both for an aggressive union and for a man who rarely smiles.

On the way to the market we pass the state capitol building. Leticia, who is sitting beside me, taps my shoulder.

"Look, Gabriel," she says. "They still hang the racist flag here." Juana and I turn our heads upward just in time to see the Confederate flag blowing in the wind. In a state where the debate still rages on between whites and blacks over U.S. history, it hasn't taken long for Leticia to choose sides.

The flea market would prove a stimulating case study for sociologists. Half of the people here are white. Mixed among the Anglos are a decent number of blacks as well as a surprisingly large number of Latino immigrants. Judging from the clothing they wear—traditional *huarache* sandals, straw wide-brim hats, and Victoria beer T-shirts—many of the immigrants look to have recently arrived: one gets the feeling that the flea market's customers have been evolving quickly in recent years. Most of the people selling goods are individual entrepreneurs, hawking items out of their trucks. Here the Confederate flag is on display everywhere: on the T-shirt of the man selling boiled peanuts near the entrance, painted on the sides of oversized trucks parked in the lot, on pins sold for a dollar. The racist flag is apparently still a hot commodity, though I don't see any of the Latinos sporting it (nor, of course, the blacks).

A man near the concession stands is wearing a cap with the Confederate flag and has a large metal trunk sitting on his table with various Southern stickers. One sticker has a large Confederate flag with the slogan "Heritage, Not Hate." The next, however, seems to contradict this assertion, reading, "Happiness is a northbound Yankee." I wonder what recent Mexican immigrants make of all this as they weave in and out of the foot traffic, speaking in Spanish and wearing Mexican soccer jerseys. If I feel out of place, what must be going through their heads?

After thirty minutes of wandering around, Angel finds the decal he is looking for. He haggles with the seller for a bit, unsuccessfully, and eventually hands over twenty dollars for the red logo. With our mission completed, we leave.

That evening we decide to eat out at IHOP. Our party of six is seated at a large table in the middle of the restaurant, and the only other people in the place are an older white couple at a nearby booth, with menus in hand. As I translate the different options for Angel and Felicia, I sense that the two are staring at our group, and when I look up I lock eyes with both of them, then look away. As I continue to translate I can still feel their eyes on me. I look again, and this time I study their faces just as intently as they seem to be studying our little multicultural group. Both the man and the woman, for whatever reason, have looks of absolute disgust, which they are doing nothing to disguise.

Though his back is to them, Enrique, too, has noticed their stares. "Is it illegal to speak Spanish in this town?" he asks. Never one to back down, he pivots and returns their stare, and finally the couple looks away. Enrique holds his gaze for a moment longer and then, satisfied, turns back around. At the same time, the two slap their menus down on the table and get up, filing out of the restaurant without ordering. "Good," Enrique says as they leave. "We don't need any racists to watch us eat anyway."

I'm not normally one to notice unspoken hostility, but I agree with Enrique. The man and woman were clearly angry with us, though we weren't even conversing loudly. It was the Spanish that seems to have set them off. It makes me wonder, as more Latinos continue to move into Southern states where their labor is in high demand, what sorts of conflicts might arise in the coming decades. It could get ugly.

But for tonight, at least, our group quickly shrugs it off, and soon we're feasting on waffles and omelets. We talk about immigrants, about the United States, about Mexico. At one point I mention to Angel that I'm excited to see Mexico.

"You're going to Mexico?" he asks. I had assumed Enrique had already told Angel. As I explain our vague travel plans, he listens intently.

"I might want to go, too," Angel says. "To see my brothers for a last time."

"I would love to go!" exclaims Leticia. "I've always wanted to see where Angel is from. We should all go together!"

Enrique shrugs, waiting several beats before casting a hostile glance in my direction, when no one is looking. I shrug back; if our trip was a secret, you should have told me—that's what my shrug is supposed to communicate. Enrique looks down at his meal and grunts, either not comprehending or disagreeing.

The next morning we leave for Brooklyn, and it is a great relief to arrive home late that evening with a still-pregnant Juana. Although she is not due until mid-February, her stomach seems to me to be growing dangerously large, and her fingers are as swollen as the Polish hot dogs sold during baseball games. A few times on the long ride back I imagine being forced to deliver the baby parked along some remote highway, miles from the nearest hospital. I can't imagine two people less qualified for the job than Enrique and myself. "That's how you learn," Enrique tells me as he's dropping me off at my apartment. "Remember what you said? We invent things when we need to."

"You mean necessity is the mother of all inventions."

"Yeah, that's what I said. Now go get some sleep. We're leaving for Mexico soon. And thanks to you, we might have to bring along Angel."

CHAPTER 11

A Growing Family

ON FEBRUARY 4, 2005, Enrique and Juana gain a new family member, a seven pound, seven ounce boy named Feliciano, who at two days old already looks like he needs a haircut. Where Junior shares a mixture of both parents' features, little Feliciano has an almost spooky resemblance to Enrique, his boxy face and chubby cheeks making him look like a much smaller twin of his father. It is not an easy birth for Juana, who is now almost forty-one years old, and she spends several days in the hospital recovering. "It's the last one," she tells me, lying in her hospital recliner and sipping orange juice through a straw. Her face is still pale and she tells me that she feels weak, though better than yesterday. "*Ya basta,*" she says. Enough already.

A month after Feliciano's birth, I am at an evening tenant association meeting in Bedford-Stuyvesant, and when it concludes I call Enrique, who picks me up and drives me home. He is quiet; something is obviously bothering him, but as usual he doesn't start talking until we're in front of my apartment and the car engine has been turned off.

"Abram has stopped going to school."

"What? Since when?"

"How should I know, maybe a month. He just sleeps all day and stopped going. Says it was too far. I tell him, 'Why are you wasting your time at the fucking car wash?' He has his papers, he speaks the language, and he can get his education. But you can't talk with him, he won't listen to anything. Just wants to work like a mojado and buy his toys. What does he think he'll be doing in five years, still making four dollars an hour cleaning rich people's cars?"

"What are you going to do?"

"Fuck it. What can you tell him? I've already told him a thousand times: study now so you can have a real job. You've got everything you need. You don't have to pay rent, you don't have to buy your own food, as long as you finish school. If you stop going to school, you're just like me and Juana, just like a fucking mojado." Enrique stares through the windshield into the Brooklyn night. "He doesn't care. I'm real fucking tired of this. Real fucking tired. As far as I'm concerned, he should just go. If he wants to be an adult, stop going to school, that's fine with me. But he has to get his own place. Then he'll see how much he likes it."

"You can't just put him out."

"No? Why not? All he is doing is causing problems for me. Social workers keep calling the house. People from the school keep calling the house. I don't want to deal with this shit. Last week the school called and told Abram his papers were ready to be picked up so he could transfer back to a school in Brooklyn. Everything's ready. He got in the shower, put on clothes, and went out. Juana asked if he was going to pick up the papers. He told her, 'I don't know, maybe if I have time.' Next day, school calls again. He didn't go. What the fuck is he so busy doing that he can't pick up the papers? He thinks he's really fucking smart. 'So if you're so smart, then go live somewhere and pay your own bills. Don't disrespect your mother.'" As he speaks, Enrique's voice becomes louder and angrier.

"I asked him for two hundred dollars for rent today. He can't pay it, he says. Doesn't have any money. He could have said he didn't have two hundred dollars, but here's one hundred, here's fifty. He just bought a little music player for four hundred dollars, and he can't help pay rent?" Abram had recently purchased an iPod. "So fine, take your little toys and all your money and go. Go live like a fucking immigrant."

"Maybe I can talk to him."

"Fuck it. It's too late."

"Why?"

"It's just too late. He's not going to listen to you anyway."

"But why too late? I can stop by tomorrow."

"It's too late! I already put his things out. He plays all day on the computer, so I put it away. He plays those stupid videogames on the TV, so I put that away. All he does is sleep all day, so I put the fucking mattress out. It's too late. No more talking."

"He's sixteen," I protest. Abram might be making some bad decisions, but living on the streets isn't going to solve anyone's problems.

Enrique brings both of his hands down on the steering wheel with a thud and nods vigorously. "Exactly. *Exactamente.* That's exactly what I tell him, but he doesn't listen. He's not a kid anymore, he's not a fucking child. He has to start taking responsibility. That's why he has to go." We each, I realize, are dealing with different notions of life at sixteen: mine involved hanging around with friends and surfing in Santa Cruz while working a part-time job for spending money; Enrique's memories are of crossing the border with a group of strangers and landing in Brooklyn, working as a dishwasher, and struggling to learn English. What a middle-class suburbanite like me might see as uncommon hardships thrown in Abram's path—growing up poor in the inner city and attending substandard schools—Enrique saw as a soft and easy life.

"In my house you have to follow my rules," he says. "It's real simple. If not, that's it. He'll come home from work tonight and find out the way things work."

"And then what? Where is his mattress?"

"Don't worry about it, güero." Enrique turns the key and his car roars to life, his way of saying that the conversation is over. "It's not your problem. Now let me go try to make twenty bucks from someone who will actually pay."

I stop by the apartment the following week. Juana answers the door, and I feel a wave of relief pass over me when I see that Abram's mattress is where it has always been, with Abram asleep under a pile of blankets. "So he's back," I say.

Juana chuckles quietly. "Sí, sí, he never left. He came back and dragged the mattress into the house."

"And Enrique?" I haven't spoken to him since our evening conversation; I suppose I have been avoiding him because I simply didn't want to hear the details of what I feared had happened.

"He's at work. Look." Juana is standing over the crib. "Feliciano is sleeping on your pillow." I had purchased a red pillow with the letter "F" stitched onto it. "Look at how much hair he has already." It was true: Feliciano, not yet a month old, had a large mop that spilled across the pillow. If anything, he now looked even more like Enrique, as if someone had shrunk my friend down to size, slapped a diaper on him, and deposited him in the crib.

We sit down in the living room. As Juana talks about wanting to start working again soon—which seems like a crazy idea, considering what she's just been through—Abram begins the slow process of waking up. He waves at me, rolls out of bed, and goes to the bathroom. When he returns, Juana goes into the kitchen to prepare lunch while Abram and I watch a Spanish talk show. The guests, two women, keep lunging at each other, pulling at hair and trying to stomp each other with their high heels. They finally calm down long enough for viewers to discover that they are fighting over a man, who eventually emerges, setting off another round between the two women when they both try to slobber the potbellied man with kisses.

"Stupid, right?" Abram says. "They're trying to be like Jerry Springer."

"Right."

"And look at that guy. Who would want him?"

"Maybe it's an act." Abram considers this for a moment, nods his head. "Enrique says that you don't want to go back to school."

"Nah, not really. I heard about a job training program where I can get my GED. It's here on Dekalb Avenue. Maybe that would be better. What do you think—should I do it?"

"It sounds promising. Tell me a bit more about what's been going on."

Abram straightens up and mutes the television. "Okay," he finally says. "But it's all messed up."

After moving back to Brooklyn, Abram was determined to commute to the school in Port Chester, not wanting to abandon the relative tranquility of Westchester County after the chaos and fighting at Boys & Girls High School in Bedford-Stuyvesant. For five months he was able to endure the five-hour round-trip journey from Brooklyn and his forty-four-hour workweeks at the car wash. For those five months his schedule went something like this: wake at 5:00 a.m. for the trip north, return by 5:00 p.m., begin work at the car wash at 7:00 p.m., and get home around midnight. As grueling as the weekdays were, it was the weekends that were the hardest. On Saturday and Sunday he worked the graveyard shift, from 7:00 p.m. to 7:00 a.m., arriving home by 7:30 a.m. on Monday morning, taking a shower, and missing the first period of school. Most Mondays he couldn't keep his eyes awake. In February he began to miss a few days of school, and then—knowing that his absences would provoke his teacher's consternation—decided to stop going altogether.

"I liked the school, but I was always falling asleep in class," he tells me. "And when I wasn't tired, I had a hard time paying attention. I get distracted easily." He brings out his report card, which shows he was maintaining roughly a C average until he began to skip days. By the second quarter he was flunking all of his classes.

The day after Enrique put his mattress out, Juana and Abram had traveled to the Board of Education in downtown Brooklyn to see about having Abram enrolled in a New York City high school. At the Board of Education a man had told Abram that with his poor grades there were only three schools he could transfer to, but that they were all "bad, bad schools." Already knowing what this meant—overcrowding, gangs, the potential for more fights—Abram didn't want to return. He had been hoping to enroll in a nearby school, the Benjamin Banneker Academy, but was told that with his grades he didn't qualify. Instead, the man suggested that he enroll at the Brooklyn Job Corps Academy in Bedford-Stuyvesant, run by the Department of Labor for disadvantaged students. Through the academy, the man said, Abram could earn his GED and receive job training and career counseling. Abram, who liked computers (and especially computer video games), was excited about the possibility of working at Dell, one of the corporate partners.

"If I was working there I would make the minimum wage," Abram says. "At least I *hope* they would pay it." Abram had recently received a raise at the car wash, but he was still making just over four dollars an hour, nearly two dollars less than the recently increased New York State minimum wage of six dollars.

"So when would you start?" I ask.

"I don't know, probably in September. I don't want to start now, since it's almost summer." Hearing this, an idea pops into my head.

"Why don't you go with us to Mexico?" Enrique was always saying that Abram didn't understand how lucky he was; why not show him?

"To Mexico? With Enrique?" Abram makes a strange sound, which I take to mean he'd rather someone gouge out his eyeballs.

"Yeah, why not? You're not doing anything, and I know how well you and Enrique are getting along." He chuckles and dismisses my idea with a wave of his hand.

"Nah, I don't think so. Anyway, we're not really fighting anymore. At least not right now. But I don't want to see Mexico. I don't understand why you are going along in the first place."

"I think it will be fun," I argue. "We'll be able to see where Juana and Enrique grew up, see what the towns are like. I've been to Tijuana before, but I've never been to the parts of Mexico where everyone here is from. Also, we can go to the beach, maybe." This was unlikely—Puebla is a long way from the coast—but I thought the idea might interest Abram. "And I bet Enrique won't bother you so much if you came along. You can tell him that you'll go to Mexico with us, and then when you get back you can apply to that job program."

Abram stretches and yawns. "I don't think so. Juana says it's real hot in Mexico, and I don't like places that are real hot." He turns the volume of the television back on; the potbellied man is now crying loudly, begging for forgiveness from one or both of the women he is involved with. When the episode ends, I say good-bye to Abram and Juana and head home.

The next week, Juana calls. She says that Abram has decided to go with us to Mexico. As I suspected, the idea of traveling with Abram to Mexico intrigues Enrique. He sees it as a way of sharing with his stepson the struggles that immigrants like he and Juana had endured in Mexico. Though Enrique had lectured Abram many times about how lucky he was to grow up in the United States, instead of the campo in Mexico, he didn't think his words had had an effect. But what better way for Abram to appreciate his present advantages than to see the poor families who are still struggling to survive in Mexico? Plus, it will give Abram the chance to meet his grandmother—Juana's mother—before she passes away.

Several weeks later Enrique is driving me to John F. Kennedy Airport. Against his advice, I have decided to travel to the border to cover a group calling itself the Minutemen Project for an online magazine. The Minutemen promise to mobilize hundreds of volunteers to stand watch over the border during the month of April to report undocumented crossers. Or, to be more accurate, they are massing to stop an "illegal invasion" of "aliens" who are streaming across the U.S.-Mexico border in Arizona.

Enrique and I had discussed the Minutemen many times before he dropped me off at the airport for my flight to Arizona; mostly, he seemed amused by the actions of what he called "my paisanos"— my white brothers. In his eyes, they were fighting a misguided, hopeless battle. "We're already here, we're going to keep coming, and there's nothing that they or anyone else can do about it. Someone should tell the fuckers that they are the immigrants, not us. You know, when Columbus came here he enslaved all of the Indians in the supposed name of 'progress.' Fucking gringos and their fucking progress. It's a good thing I'm not going with you, because first I would have to give them a history lesson, and then I would have to kick their ass." I had recently given Enrique a Spanish copy of Howard Zinn's *A People's History of the United States,* and he was devouring it, rereading especially the first chapter on Columbus. He was amazed to find a writer who so clearly shared his views on immigration, and demanded that I find other titles by Zinn in Spanish so he could read those, too.

On the trip to the airport, Enrique shares with me a shocking piece of information that he has just learned. At thirty-four, he is going to be a grandfather. "Paula called me yesterday and told me Cristina is pregnant."

"What? How old is Cristina?"

"Fourteen."

"Wow. That's young." Enrique doesn't say anything in return, just nods. "Is the father that same boyfriend?"

"Yes. Who else would it be? You know I don't like him, we've had our problems. But there is nothing I can do about it now. Paula doesn't like it when I come over, because she gets upset. So all I can do is send my child support every month."

I ask a few more questions about Cristina, but Enrique is vague in his answers and clearly not interested in discussing the topic further. His frustration, however, is palpable; he has never had a good poker face. And I know his frustration stems from the fact that he had tried to prevent what he has just learned. He was not a person to wonder what success looked like. Education. Sobriety. Hard work. Sacrifice. And he also had his own recipe for disaster, for regression. There were two ingredients that guaranteed a lifetime of poverty: dropping out of school and becoming pregnant. This is what he had explained to Cristina, after all. This is why he had become so angry when he learned that Cristina had an older boyfriend and was cutting classes. Though his problems with Paula had made it difficult for him to remain connected to his daughters, they were still family. He wanted to see his daughters make it, with the same passion that he wanted his stepson and two sons to make it. Superando: the story of bettering oneself started with the immigrants and continued on to the second generation. But now Enrique's worst fears had materialized—his oldest child was backsliding, digging herself into a ditch, and he could only watch from a distance.

Enrique's detached response to the development—though not altogether healthy—showed a level of maturation. The younger, brasher Enrique would have gone over to the Broadway apartment after hearing the news and beaten Cristina's boyfriend silly. Now he was beginning to learn that there were some things out of his control. "She is going to do what she wants to do," he says to me as we approach the airport. Parents might gasp at this adjudication of responsibility—Cristina is only fourteen, after all—but the strained relations between Enrique and Paula had convinced him that further meddling would only make a bad situation worse. "I wish I could have been around more, to tell her about how life works, but it wasn't possible. Sometimes you just have to move forward."

When he drops me off, he gives me a final warning, changing the subject from Cristina to my personal safety. "Be careful, güero. No one plays around on the border. There's a lot of empty space, where you'll only find gangsters and drug smugglers." I tell him I will be sure to travel with a group.

He nods his approval of this plan. "And tell those Minutemen idiots that they've already lost, that it's too late. They can't get rid of Mexicans, *pobre racistas*. Just look at Cristina; we're like cockroaches. We're everywhere." He smiles sadly at this last observation, then gives me a hug, tells me to call his cell phone if I run into any trouble, and drives away.

PART II:
MEXICO

CHAPTER 12

On the Road

AFTER AN UNEVENTFUL week on the U.S.-Mexico border, where the biggest threat to the Minutemen wasn't invading hordes of aliens but the desert sun—pasty white faces quickly burned a lobster red—I am glad to return to Brooklyn. For the last two weeks of April, Enrique is working longer than normal hours in order to have enough money for our trip to Mexico, so I do not hear from him until a week before our departure date. He sounds tired but excited and tells me that Angel has confirmed he will be making the trek with us.

Having road-tripped with Enrique before, I know what type of message to expect on my answering machine the evening before our departure. It arrives as anticipated. "Gabriel, we're leaving tomorrow morning at five. Make sure to be ready to go by five—if you're not down by five-fifteen, we're leaving without you. We have to leave by five to get an early start and make it to South Carolina before dark. And then from South Carolina we'll cross Atlanta, and then we should be able to make it to Mobile by dawn. If we're at Mobile by dawn we'll . . ."

I erase the message before he has the chance to give me a play-by-play of our itinerary, but the tone in his voice confirms that this is not going to be a relaxed, see-the-sights-and-enjoy-the-conversation journey. Indeed, at 4:30 the next morning Enrique is in front of my building, leaning into long honks and hollering "Güero!" with his window rolled down, while Abram somehow sleeps in the backseat. I had set my alarm an hour early after hearing the first part of his rushed message, so I make it down the stairs before he manages to wake the entire block.

In truth, the alarm clock wasn't necessary; I was too excited about our trip to Mexico to get any real sleep, and also slightly anxious about one unresolved issue, the details of which are straightforward enough: We are heading to Chinantla, a small town of less than three thousand people. Angela still lives in Chinantla, having been abandoned by Angel twenty years ago. Angela and Angel haven't spoken or seen each other in years, and Angel has married another woman, Leticia. Leticia will be accompanying us on the trip. This seems problematic, to say the least, but each time I had asked Enrique about it he had only shrugged. I bring up these facts in the car to Enrique one last time as we cross a still-asleep Manhattan.

His reply is the familiar combination of belligerence and feigned ignorance. "So? What's the fucking big deal?" He shrugs and keeps looking forward, as if to say that this topic had been exhausted long ago. "Look, I told Angela that you want to come to Mexico to learn about our lives," he finally continues. "I said that Angel wanted to come along to visit his brothers, too, and asked her if that was okay. She said yes."

"But do you think Angel and Angela will see each other?" I ask.

"I am not bringing him to her house. No way. We'll drop them off at a hotel, and we'll stay with Angela. If he wants to go visit his brothers, I'll drive him around, and you can stay with Angela."

"But isn't Chinantla small? Won't they run into each other?"

"That's not my *pinche problema*. I told Angel I'm going to Mexico to visit my mother, and he knows that. I asked Angela if it was okay to bring Angel, and she said yes. Everything is cleared with everyone."

Well, not exactly everyone. Enrique's older brother Angel was against the plan. He told Enrique that bringing their father and his wife to Chinantla would make Angela sick, and even suggested that in her weak health the stress of the visit could kill her. But in Enrique's mind, the opinion that mattered most—the only opinion that mattered at all—was that of Angela. Since she had become sick the previous winter, Enrique had been waiting for a chance to see her; during his most recent weekly phone conversation with her he had broken down and cried in anticipation of the visit. Now that Feliciano was several months old and sleeping through the night, and Junior was in school most of the day, he saw this as his opportunity to go home. And if his mother said it was okay, who was he to argue?

If I was anxious about bringing Angel to Chinantla, it was partly because I would be to blame for any potential problems that his presence provoked. I was the one, after all, who had mentioned to Angel that I was planning on traveling to Mexico with Enrique in a few months. Angel then told Enrique that he wanted to come along, and that we could use his truck if we came to Columbia first to pick him up. Although he wasn't overjoyed at the prospect of traveling with Angel (they had recently had one of their frequent I'm-not-talking-to-you-ever-again arguments—which this time lasted two months), Enrique had grown concerned about his car's ability to endure another trip to Mexico. His Crown Victoria, now four years old, was approaching its last miles, soon to be discarded. Recently a light on the dashboard had appeared, advising the driver to check the engine, and though Enrique couldn't find anything wrong below the hood, this new development certainly increased the chances of our being stranded in the middle of the desert. So even though in Enrique's eyes Angel might not be the perfect companion, the offer to use his father's new truck was hard to resist.

But notwithstanding the pragmatic argument for bringing Angel so that we could use his truck, I harbored a suspicion that Enrique also hoped for an encounter between Angel and Angela. It was difficult to believe that Enrique hadn't contemplated what might happen if, say, we were wandering around the streets of tiny Chinantla one day with Angela and passed Angel and Leticia in the street. Maybe Enrique thought an all-out shouting match between the two might finally give his mother closure, allow her to forget about her previous husband once and for all. Yet if I was correct, and Enrique had given some thought to what might result from a chance encounter, he wasn't sharing his thoughts.

Nearing Columbia, Enrique and I get into an argument over whether we should stay the night at Angel's house. It will be dark in several hours, and I think it makes much more sense to get a good night's sleep before continuing on. Enrique, however, is already upset that it took thirteen hours to get to Columbia—it normally takes him twelve—and wants to continue on without stopping.

"But what's the big deal about one hour?" I ask, behind the wheel. "This is a long trip we're on, and it's not like we have to be in Mexico at a certain time. If we leave now, we're just going to be tired in a few hours. Better to relax somewhere with beds." By now I am wise enough to know that a motel is out of the question.

"The big deal?" Enrique snorts. "What do you mean, the big deal? In one hour we could go another eighty or ninety miles—at least! Do you want to get to Mexico or not? And don't worry about being tired, because I'm feeling wide-awake now. I can easily drive until two or three in the morning, and then you drive from three to six, and then I drive from six until nine." Not only does this sound like an awful plan, but five minutes later Enrique is rattling the windows with his congested snoring.

When we arrive in Columbia Angel and Leticia aren't home. Ten minutes later they pull into the driveway, Angel behind the wheel of his truck, which now has a half dozen more University of South Carolina decals—including a large "Go Cocks!" sticker along the driver side that to my out-of-state eyes looks to be less about a sports team and more about something less dignified.

While Enrique checks the truck's brakes and oil, Abram and I transfer our luggage from the car, and Angel instructs us to create a bed in the camper with a flattened cardboard box and a blanket. The thirteen-hour trip from Brooklyn behind us, we pull out of Angel's driveway less than an hour after we arrive, which still doesn't seem quick enough to satisfy Enrique, judging by the speed with which he navigates Columbia's streets en route to the freeway. I'm squeezed into the middle seat in the back with Abram and Leticia, where there is about as much legroom as a crowded church pew, and Enrique has Los Tigres del Norte blasting loud enough to make conversation impossible; this doesn't feel like it's going to be a sustainable journey. Abram, who has brought along his newly purchased handheld PlayStation, asks Enrique before we get on the freeway if we can stop briefly at a Best Buy so that he can purchase a game for the ride ahead—totally oblivious to Enrique's frenzied mind-set.

"Save your money for gas," Enrique replies, agitated. "We don't have time right now to stop if we're going to make it to Mobile by dawn." For good measure, he repeats our dilemma. "We're already late because it normally takes twelve hours to get to Columbia, but it took us thirteen." As we pass a Jiffy Lube before we enter the freeway (Tuesday is Ladies Day!), I wonder what has led Enrique to become so transfixed on the Mobile-at-dawn goal.

Picking up speed along the freeway, Leticia asks Angel if he has remembered his cell phone. After searching for a few moments he locates it in one of his pockets. "Your cell phone won't work in Mexico," Enrique tells him. "As soon as we cross the border you won't have a signal."

"Mine will work," replies Angel. "I took it in to the store yesterday, and they told me it will work all over Mexico."

"No, it won't," Enrique disagrees. "Trust me, I've been to Mexico many times with my phone, and it doesn't work. You can turn it on, and it looks like it will work, but the satellites in Mexico are different. The only way to get the phone to work is to find a cell phone store in Mexico. But after they install the microchip for it, when you return to South Carolina you'll have to go back to a store and have them take it out, or your phone won't work here."

Angel shook his head. "I spoke to a person at the AT&T store where I bought the phone, and he told me it would work in Mexico."

"Fine, we'll see if it works when we get there," Enrique says, giving up.

"There's nothing to see." Angel crosses his arms. "It will work. I checked with the store."

"I don't care what the store fucking told you. It won't work."

"It will work. If it doesn't work, I'll give you the phone." For whatever reason, the issue of the cell phone's functionality seems critical to Angel.

"You heard that, Gabriel?" Enrique calls to the backseat. "We're going to return to New York with a new phone!" Enrique laughs, Angel stares out the window, deadly serious, and I begin to worry about what other disagreements might be in store in the coming miles, and weeks.

By the time we arrive in Texas, Angel's phone is no longer working. I know we must have passed through Georgia, Alabama, and Louisiana during the night—and that I was behind the wheel for much of the time—but I am unable to remember anything about the journey, except that my eyes haven't been fully open for some time now. In the passenger seat while I drive, Angel continues to take his phone out of his pocket, stare at the screen—which confirms that he has no signal—and then place it back in his pocket. After a few seconds he then pulls it out of his pocket to see if anything has changed. Each time the visit to his pocket fails to jumpstart the phone, he curses the salesman in South Carolina. I'm already feeling sorry for the AT&T salesman; Angel has mentioned that his first order of business on returning will be to pay the "pendejo" a special visit.

In order to get his mind off the phone, I comment that I am eager to visit Puebla and see the state where so many people in Brooklyn come from. Angel doesn't reply. "You must be excited also, to see what life is like and how it has changed back in Mexico," I continue. "What do you think you will find? Do you think with so many people having left for the U.S. it will be very different?"

Either Angel hasn't understood my question or his dysfunctional phone has darkened his train of thought. "Many Hispanics are coming here to cause problems: to sell drugs, to fight, to abuse women, and to drive without licenses and cause accidents," he says, staring at his phone. "I'm not saying that Mexicans shouldn't come here, but they should do it the legal way." He nods and again places his phone into his pocket. It isn't clear to me if he if saying what he believes, what he thinks I as a white person want to hear, or if he has a growing suspicion that the AT&T salesman in Columbia is an undocumented immigrant.

"Maybe," I say, hoping to continue a line of conversation unrelated to the phone—with only a few hours of sleep under my belt, his incessant hand movements in my peripheral vision are beginning to drive me slightly batty. "But the Mexicans I know couldn't have gone through the legal channels, because they didn't have enough money to pay an attorney, and because the U.S. only lets in a small number of Mexicans each year."

"Sí, Gabriel, but look at me," he says. "I won't lie, when I came to the U.S. I came as a mojado. But one day I decided that I wanted to *legalizarme*. I woke up and determined it was time to fix my papers, so I went to talk to an attorney. I worked to get my papers together, I filled out the application, and I became legal. Other people should do the same thing, but now they just want to come as *ilegales* and do whatever they want. *Ilegales* in South Carolina are driving without licenses and causing accidents. These people are different. They are only coming to cause problems."

Angel's views were not unique; I had heard the same types of complaints from older Mexican immigrants back in Brooklyn. Many legal immigrants—and especially second-generation Mexican American citizens—are quick to distance themselves from the ongoing waves of illegal crossers, though their parents were once in the same situation. And it was ironic, if not also fertile ground for psychological exploration, that Angel saved his anger for the supreme injustice of undocumented immigrants causing accidents while driving without licenses. It was Angel, after all, who on our first visit to South Carolina had recently caused a serious accident by making a left-hand turn into oncoming traffic, and I noticed there was now a series of new scratches along the passenger side (which I later learned was from a run-in with a streetlight the previous week).

It was also interesting to hear Angel's citizenship saga as a result of personal agency, as if it was his determination to hunt down an attorney and fill out paperwork that enabled his transformation, a consequence of his dedicated effort to, as he put it, "legalize" himself. Not included in his tale, however, is the 1986 amnesty bill passed by Ronald Reagan that facilitated his determination—an amnesty that Angel qualified for but which subsequent waves of migrants have yet had the option of achieving, regardless of their work ethic or stomach for paperwork. In Angel's mind the legal/illegal problem was best understood as a moral issue: his new neighbors from Mexico, though following the same path he himself helped blaze thirty years ago, were coming to cause trouble and giving other legal immigrants a bad name. It was a variation on the same old adult yarn of "kids today being different" and "not showing the same respect," but with immigration status thrown into the mix.

Leticia, in the backseat and quiet up until now, doesn't agree with Angel's assessment. "*Este es un país de extranjeros,*" she says—this is a country of foreigners. "Without immigrants this country wouldn't exist. We do the hardest work, we earn the lowest wages, and we suffer the most discrimination. We come to work, yet they insist on calling us 'ilegales' even when they need us as much as we need them."

Perhaps feeling he was too harsh earlier on his paisanos, Angel partially agrees with Leticia's statement. "It is true that we do the hardest work," he says, turning toward me. "You are not going to go out into the fields and pick fruits and vegetables all day. That is a job you will never do, because you have better work available for you. But Mexicans, we come without knowing the language, without having an education. We come to work. *I* came to work."

As the late morning heat of Texas beat down, Angel continues to share his views of Mexican immigrants—which oscillate between those who come to work hard, support the U.S. economy, and become legal immigrants (like himself, the type of immigrants he supports), and those who come illegally and then go on to commit crimes like driving without a license (unlike him—except, of course, for the coming illegally part—the type of immigrants he believes are destroying the country and giving all Mexicans a bad name). After an hour of meandering conversation, it isn't clear to me which group—the hard workers or the lawbreakers—Angel thought was winning out. What is clear, however, is that the path Angel had taken to become a permanent resident, and that he regarded as the path more immigrants needed to follow, was no longer available.

As we pull into a gas station outside of Houston, Angel must intuit that I am having a hard time making sense of his comments. "If you really want to know about Mexican immigrants, I can help you out," he offers. "When we return I will write a report so that you can put the report in your book. That way you will know everything you need to know about Mexicans." I thank him and say I will appreciate whatever assistance he can give, then roust Enrique from the bed of the truck, climb in myself, and immediately pass out on the flattened cardboard box.

In contrast to the highly nuanced philosophy of Angel—with its many contradictions and inconsistencies—Leticia is a hardcore supporter of immigrants, legal or otherwise, and has a class-based ideology that always comes down on the side of those she perceives as underdogs.

While eating a quick lunch at a Wendy's near San Antonio, Enrique instructs us as to what we should say if Mexican police stop us on the way to Chinantla. "If we say we are heading to Puebla, they will know we are bringing lots of money with us and will demand a large *mordida*," he explains. In Spanish, mordida means "little bite," but in Mexico it also refers to the infamous practice of cops demanding bribes. "So we will tell them we are going to visit a friend in Monterrey, which is nearby. That way they'll just think we're making a day trip, and won't bother us as much."

This seems like a sensible plan to me, but the very notion that we have to prepare lies in the face of corrupt police sends Angel into a rage. "You can say what you want, but I will not make up a story for them!" he says loudly, prompting several white customers to glance in our direction. "I will say I am here to visit my country, which I have a perfect right to do. There is nothing wrong with coming home to see my land. What makes them think they can take our money? They are supposed to be protecting us, not stealing from us." As he speaks Angel's face and body language make it clear he is drawing a line in the sand that no reasoning can shift. It is the same look he had when insisting to Enrique that his phone was going to work in Mexico. *Terco* is the word Enrique has used a number of times to describe his father. Stubborn. I am beginning to agree.

But Leticia, who has never been to Mexico before, sees the potential mordida in class terms. "Don't be so stupid," she tells her husband. "I bet they are only doing what they have to do in order to survive. If they aren't being paid enough for their work, this is the only way they can put food on the table." In Leticia's eyes, if cops were demanding bribes it was less about an abuse of authority than making ends meet by transferring excess money from wealthier travelers into the dining rooms of hungry Mexicans.

"If they need more money, they should demand more money from the government!" Angel shouts. "If they ask me, I am going to tell them to go to hell!"

"Fine," Enrique says. "You can do what you want. We'll pick you up from jail on the way back."

As we are nearing the border town of Laredo, a Texas state trooper pulls me over for speeding on Interstate 35. I am convinced that after seeing Enrique lying down in the back of the truck he will write up one, if not two, tickets, but he instead lets me off with a warning. "What are you doing, anyway?" he asks, curious as to how I have gotten mixed up with a truck full of Mexicans. I tell him that I am a journalist and that we are heading to southern Mexico to visit the hometown of my friends.

"You know what's been going on around here, right?" I shake my head. "There have been thirty-eight abductions of U.S. citizens in Laredo so far this year, so it's best if you just drive right on through. This highway is a major avenue for drug trafficking, but since we have been intercepting so many drugs lately, people are now kidnapping Americans to make up for lost money." I thank him for the warning and assure him that we will not be spending any time on the border. I also make a mental note to not be in the back of the truck when we cross into Mexico, lest the authorities think Enrique and his gang have kidnapped me and are on their way to a safe house to await a ransom.

We pass through Laredo and creep in a line of cars toward Nuevo Laredo, the much larger sister city on the Mexican side of the border. Abram has finally put down his PlayStation and begun to peer out the window, eager to see Mexico. When we cross the line without incident and are still in a city, he is disappointed. "This is Mexico?" he asks me, a look of disbelief on his face. "People didn't say it would be like this. Everyone says that Mexico is just pure desert."

Winding through the streets of Nuevo Laredo in search of the tourist office to check-in, Abram is bewildered by the Mexican bustle, and after remaining silent for much of the trip he asks me a series of rapid-fire questions as if I am a tour guide. "How do they drive here without stoplights? Is that woman a hooker? That house, does someone actually live in that thing? What does that sign with the 'E' crossed out mean? Why is it so dirty here? Who is—hey! That car is playing Eminem! They listen to Eminem in Mexico?" Though he is of Mexican descent and a native Spanish speaker, Abram has the look of a virgin traveler, and I do my best to answer the questions I actually know the answer to (the signs with the "E" crossed out mean no parking).

After we check-in successfully we make our way through Nuevo Laredo toward the highway. Nuevo Laredo is—like many border cities—unevenly developed, with peasants begging in the streets in front of Hilton hotels, upscale nightclubs, and other pockets of pompous prosperity, which are mostly fueled by the city's out of control drug trade (several months later, the United States would temporarily close its embassy in Nuevo Laredo after a series of violent attacks by members of the drug cartels). Though I feel somewhat silly, I keep the tinted window rolled up, as the words of the Texas state trooper—"You know what's been going on here, right?"—keep playing in my head.

Exhausted after the sprint across the United States, I sleep on the cardboard bed in the back for the entire trip from Nuevo Laredo to Mexico City, waking up to find that the temperature has cooled off dramatically. Climbing through a mountain range, we suddenly find ourselves in the middle of a hailstorm. We safely make it through the city without being stopped by the police or sent off the road by the thin layer of ice that has developed on the highway, and head down a winding road into the state of Guerrero, where the temperature quickly rises again.

In Guerrero we pass men and women working in fields, cultivating corn and sugar cane. The people in the fields are darker than Enrique—some nearly black by a combination of sun and indigenous blood—but the occasional billboards selling Corona or

Modelo still have models with my skin hue. The land here is dry, dry and hot, and with cacti and scrub it reminds me more than anything of Joshua Tree National Park in Southern California. When I mention this to Enrique, he has his own comparison: "To me, it looks just like Africa."

We cross from Guerrero into the state of Puebla and stop to eat in the city of Izúcar de Matamoros, the hometown of Enrique's first wife, Paula. After eating I hop into the back of the truck for the last leg of the journey, which proves to be a mistake because the narrow road south from Matamoros winds up and then down steep hills. Only a few of the turns have guardrails, and from the vantage point of the camper, looking backward as we drive, Enrique seems to be driving much too fast, passing trucks on the two-lane road and then darting back into our lane before hitting oncoming traffic. Without a seat belt, I slide back and forth in the bed of the truck, banging up against the sides of the camper. My concerns for our safety are confirmed by the numerous *"Curva Peligrosa"* signs—dangerous curves—and the frequent white crosses along the road in remembrance of people who have lost their lives along this stretch. Enrique doesn't seem to be paying attention to the signs or the crosses, but as I bump along in the back they are impossible to miss.

We arrive at the turnoff to Chinantla at dusk, taking a right at an intersection called Las Palomas, where half a dozen minibuses are lined up waiting to take people to various locations. We stop for a moment, and I move into the backseat. After speeding along a flat road for five minutes, a few large houses begin to dot the landscape. On our right we pass a school, and then a series of speed bumps that feel more like curbs, and finally we see a sign that reads "Welcome to Chinantla: A Place of Friendship, Honesty, and Sincerity." Once he realizes that we are officially in Chinantla, Abram gives us his assessment. "This place looks so *boring,*" he says, raising his normally quiet voice to ensure that Enrique hears. "There's not going to be *anything* to do in this town. I bet they don't even have television."

Enrique, however, isn't listening to his stepson. "Let's go see if my cousin is around," he says, making a left from the main road into a dirt lot. We stop the truck and get out in front of a series of shops. Leading the way, Enrique walks up to the entrance of a small restaurant and yells, "*Primo!*"

A man sticks his head out, wearing khaki pants and a stained white tank top that hugs his protruding gut. "Primo!" he yells back. They exchange hugs and then Enrique introduces us all to his cousin Chimino, who is also the husband of Enrique's other cousin, Reina, the woman who was romantically involved in Brooklyn with Enrique's *other* cousin, Adolfo. As we are talking, a series of loud explosions go off. "You came at a good time," Chimino tells us. "There's a fiesta in section four this week." He then launches into the telling of last night's events, which include several hours of heavy drinking followed by a fight with a group of other men. While he recounts the episode, Enrique nods and laughs, occasionally slapping his cousin on the back. I can't tell how much of the fight story is true and how much is an embellishment for the sake of Enrique's enjoyment.

"The only thing was that this one fucker didn't just hit, he bit," Chimino says after recounting the reasons for the fight—none of which I really understand. Something about someone bumping into someone else. And then someone saying something. "I punched him and we went down, and then he took a bite out of my ear." Chimino points to his left ear, and for the first time I notice that his ear is swollen and bright red and has a chunk missing at the top, where pus is currently oozing down his cheek, mixing with dirt. "The pendejo thought he was Mike Tyson, but just like Mike, he got his ass kicked." Chimino laughs loudly at this joke and repeats it. Abram, Angel, Leticia, and I are silent, looking at the mess on Chimino's face, but Enrique is doubled over with laughter. Chimino tells the joke a third time. Enrique can barely breathe. Finally we say our good-byes and leave for the fourth section, to see what there is to see on the second night of the party.

When we arrive a crowd is already gathered around the bullring. We rent plastic seats for ten pesos a piece (about one dollar) and then, like the hundred or so other people, wait. A bull is already in the pen, and a *montador* is seated atop the rail, ready to ride, but the bull—instead of ferociously snorting and stamping its feet—is lying down on its stomach, looking disinterested in the whole affair. Five young men with cowboy hats begin to kick the bull to try to roust it from its slumber, without effect.

To keep the partygoers entertained during the lull, an eight-person brass band strikes up a ranchera song, and during the breaks an announcer on the public address system tells people to hold on for just a minute longer. The bull, meanwhile, appears to have fallen back asleep. Enrique gestures for me to follow him, and we walk over to the bullring to get a closer look at what the announcer has promised is an "angry, angry bull."

"So what do you think of Chinantla?" he asks.

"I like it so far. Your cousin is funny, but a little crazy."

"All my cousins are a little crazy," Enrique replies, grinning proudly.

"Do you think he'll come back here tonight, after what happened yesterday?"

Enrique laughs. "Of course he'll come back, *pinche güero*. This is where the party is. Fighting isn't such a big deal here, as long as people aren't using weapons."

"So you think they'll be another fight tonight?"

Enrique rolls his eyes at me. "Of course. There is precisely a one-hundred-percent chance that there will be a fight tonight. And if my cousin fights, I'll fight with him." Enrique surveys the crowd, pausing at a group of young men wearing baggy pants and gold necklaces. "Lots of gangsters here tonight. Definitely will be a fight. The *chamaco* gangsters [little kids] try to mess with the older people from the campo, but they always get their asses kicked." *Great,* I think. *Here we are, on our first night in Chinantla, and Enrique is already determined to back up his hard-drinking cousin with fists if need be.*

Just when it seems like the bull might actually stand on its own feet, a loud clap of thunder echoes through the air, and it begins to downpour. We rush back to the truck and drop Angel and Leticia off at one of the two hotels in Chinantla, then go look for Angela.

In Chinantla, Angela has three houses to look after, owned by her children—Juan, Angel, and Maria. We don't find her at Juan's or Angel's, so we head up a side road and down a long dirt driveway that leads to Maria's cinder block house. As Enrique turns off the truck's headlights, the front door swings open and a small dark woman flips on the porch light. Photos haven't prepared me for how short Angela is: she can't stand much taller than four feet; the top of her head is flush with the bottom windowsill to her right.

Her first smiling words are: "*Mi pinche hijo. Hijo de la chingada, por fin llegó.*" Rough translation: "My fucking son. Son of the fucked one, he finally arrived." Like mother, like son. Enrique hops out of the car and lets fly with his own round of cursing by way of greeting, and then swallows his mother up in an embrace. Next to Angela, Enrique looks like a giant. Like her bodyguard.

"*Y el güero vinó!*" she yells, surprised that I have actually come along with her son to Chinantla. After Enrique introduces Abram and me and we all sit down on folding chairs in the kitchen,

Enrique describes the details of our trip to Angela, and mentions the fiasco with Angel's cell phone.

"Pinche viejo," Angela exclaims as Enrique recounts Angel's anger. "*Pinche viejo viene aquí con su puta, chinga su madre.*" After this curse her face breaks out into a huge grin, and then she lets fly with another long string of nonstop expletives. Enrique joins in the cursing, and they laugh together—clearly elated to be reunited.

Several hours later, as we prepare to go to bed, Enrique tells me that he feels bad each time he thinks about Angela living alone in this house. I had expected something of a hut and am pleasantly surprised to find electricity, running water, and a working bathroom. "It seems like a pretty nice place to me," I reason. "It's definitely a lot safer than being an old person living alone in Brooklyn."

"Ah, but you haven't seen the scorpions yet, have you?"

I look at him and shrug, feigning disinterest. "Scorpions?"

"Angela, show the güero your collection!" Enrique shouts. Angela comes out from one of the rooms and grabs a glass jar from a ledge in the kitchen. She holds it out for me to take.

"Those are all the scorpions that she has caught here in the house," Enrique explains, pointing at the jar in my hands, which is filled to the brim with dead scorpions. "Mamá, when was the last time you saw one?"

"*Pues, ayer,*" she answers—yesterday. "And the last time that Maria came home to visit a scorpion stung her. We had to go to the clinic."

"Where was she sleeping when she got stung?" Enrique asks, now trying to control a building grin.

"*Allá, en la cama del güero,*"—over there, in the bed that I will be sleeping in. According to Angela, the venom of a scorpion will kill a person within thirty minutes if they don't get treatment (this turns out not to be true, a fact I don't learn until I'm back in Brooklyn). However, she tells me, I don't have to worry, because the glass jar is effective in warding off future scorpions.

"But you just said that you saw a scorpion yesterday," I argue.

"Of course, but the scorpion didn't sting me. They are still going to come, but they are afraid of stinging people as long as I keep the jar here."

After a three-day, twenty-five-hundred-mile journey, I am exhausted, and I want above all to believe Angela's words, to believe that she is correct in her assessment of the scorpions' fear. Still, that first night, sweating under a sheet and thinking about the bottle, I find sleep hard to come by.

CHAPTER 13

Capital of the World

OVER A BREAKFAST of coffee and *pan dulce*—sweetened bread that is dipped into the coffee and whose crumbs eventually give the drink a porridge-like texture—Enrique mentions that today we are going to visit Adolfo's parents, who still live in Cuicatlán, the small nearby village and birthplace of Enrique. Though I am eager to meet Luis and Teresa, I also want to have a moment alone to explore Chinantla on foot, so I head out for a quick walk while Enrique and Abram are taking bucket baths and Angela is hand-washing several of our grimy T-shirts.

After having read numerous journalistic accounts of Mexican villages emptied of all but the very young and very old—with those of working age gone to El Norte—I am surprised on my first meandering stroll to find so much life in the town. Compared to the towns of Nicaragua and Guatemala, which I have visited, Chinantla seems to have a thriving local economy: within ten minutes I pass numerous restaurants and a large construction business, two Internet cafés, and a well-maintained plaza, all while walking on what appear to be recently paved streets. Even the dogs wandering the streets with me on this early morning seem healthier and stockier than their Central American siblings. Instead of the scrawny, death-in-progress look of the mangy mutt that bit my leg one night in a small village in Guatemala—leading me to endure twelve painful antirabies shots around my belly button—many of the canines in Chinantla wag their tails at passersby, wearing colorful collars around their necks.

Down every street it is the rare one-story house that isn't in the process of having a second story built; most have cement blocks rising above the previous roof, with metal reinforcement rods sticking out crookedly, waiting for another round of cement and an eventual ceiling to support. From a distance, the houses look less like abodes and more like an assemblage of gigantic grey insects, their metallic antennae sprouting into the hot desert air.

Sprinkled throughout the ubiquitous development are a handful of houses that seem to have been transported directly from suburban American towns. Instead of cement cinder blocks, the walls of these homes are made of stucco and colored the gentle pastels favored by designers of the strip malls that now stretch from San Jose to Syracuse. These homes—of the Chinanteco families that have struck gold in the United States—come complete with oversized satellite-dish systems and are encircled by head-high metal fences that have less to do with security than status. The other thing these homes have in common is that, at least for the moment, they all appear to be empty, their owners back in Brooklyn or the Bronx.

Professor Robert C. Smith of Baruch College has spent more than fifteen years studying the town of Chinantla and its emigrants in New York City. In his book *Mexican New York* he estimates that between $3 and $5 million was sent from the United States to Chinantla each year in the early 1990s. In a survey he conducted in 1993, he found that one-third of the households received "99 percent or more of their income from remittances from the United States, and another 18.7 percent reported that 90 percent of their income came this way." Together, more than half of the households received at least 90 percent of their income from family members in the United States.[*]

I had learned the previous evening that Chinantla was divided into sections, like most Mexican towns. Angela lived in the first section; Natalia, Enrique's sister, lived in the second, where Enrique's brother Angel also had a home that he occasionally rented out; the third section was actually the first area that one passed when entering Chinantla from the highway; and the fourth was elevated and toward the neighboring town of Piaxtla. The last time Enrique's father had come to Chinantla, the third section had been mostly farmland, but with money sent from the United States, families had now constructed a number of large houses and it looked to soon be as developed as the other neighborhoods.

The *centro*, logically in the middle of town, is bustling with people. Several women are selling mangoes and oranges under the shade of a large cement gazebo, next to a line of empty taxicabs. A group of male drivers sits nearby, playing cards along one of the benches in the adjacent square. Rising above the centro to the west is Chinantla's church, reachable on foot by climbing an impressive series of steps, which two elderly ladies are slowly ascending, bunches of flowers in hand. On the far end of the centro are the town's government offices, where two men are presently painting the building a brilliant orange.

I am the only white person in sight, but people are either too busy to notice or simply disinterested, and pay me no mind. As I walk away from the plaza, I hear someone whistle, and turn around to see a thirty-something man sitting on a folding chair in front of Chimino's bike repair shop, wearing the baggy pants and oversized

---

[*] Robert Courtney Smith, *Mexican New York: Transnational Lives of New Immigrants* (University of California Press: 2005)

shirts that have become the ghetto standard. He motions for me to come over.

"What's up, son?" he greets me in urban English, almost accent-free. "You've come to visit Chinantla, son?" I explain that I am from Brooklyn and arrived yesterday with Enrique.

"Enrique, the son of Angel?" he asks. "Yo, that's my primo, son! Ask Enrique, I'm not bullshitting—ask him about Ray." I would soon learn that nearly everyone seemed to be a cousin of Enrique's. "How long are you staying here?" he asks, leaning forward in his chair, his breath reeking of alcohol.

"I'm not sure, at least a few weeks."

"Man, that nigga Enrique brought you to Chinantla at a good time, son. Next week is *la fiesta* in the first section—all week long. You need any pussy, son, just let me know, and I'll hook you up. You can't go back to Brooklyn without having some good Mexican pussy!" Ray cackles loudly, and I thank him for the offer but gently decline.

"Well, I'm sure I'll see you around," I say, realizing it's probably time to get back to the house.

"No doubt, son." We shake hands and I turn around and walk down a street that looks familiar. A block away I hear Ray call out after me in English.

"Welcome to Chinantla, son! Welcome to the fucking capital of the world!"

When I return to Angela's house we pile into the truck and head for Natalia's house. Angela has already left for her weekly trip to the nearby city of Acatlán to pick up her diabetes medicine. On the short drive over to Natalia's, I tell Enrique about Ray. "I don't remember the guy," he says. "But he might be a cousin. I can't always keep track of my relatives here."

Natalia is Enrique's only sibling who has chosen to remain in Chinantla, though she and her husband, Daniel—who, like Enrique, drives a cab—spent several years in the town of Port Chester during the 1990s, just north of New York City. During this period Natalia gave birth to two of her five sons; her seven-person family therefore has two members who can legally pass between the countries at will. While in Port Chester, Natalia worked at a Laundromat and Daniel at a bakery, the same bakery where Enrique's brother Juan is still employed. "They did what everyone says they are going to do," Enrique says on the drive over. "Go to the U.S. for a few years, save enough money to buy a home, and then return. But you already know that most Mexicans only say that, and then stay in the U.S."

As we park along the side of Natalia's house, I see that it is also in the process of having a second story built. Inside the small courtyard, which is shaded by a large tree, we find a compact, dark-skinned woman with a small boy on her lap. "Enrique!" she yells upon our arrival, getting up from a chair. "Welcome home!" Enrique introduces Abram and me, and we grab several chairs and join Natalia and her three-year-old son, Eduardo, who has some sort of disability that has caused his forehead to become enlarged and keeps him from talking.

"*Y el viejo?*" Natalia asks, wondering what we have done with Angel.

"We dropped him off at the hotel," Enrique replies. "We're staying with Angela. I'm not going to bring him over to Angela's house."

"So they didn't see each other?"

"No, of course not. But we're heading over to pick them up, and then going to see Luis and Teresa."

"*Y el güero?*" Natalia asks, referring to me (in Chinantla, as in Brooklyn, my name quickly becomes el güero). "What does he think of Chinantla?"

"So far, I really like it," I answer in my far-from-native Spanish. Natalia looks at Enrique in mock surprise.

"Look at that, your güero speaks Spanish."

"Yeah, the fucking güero speaks Spanish. About time that a few of them learned the language, since so many Mexicans like me speak perfect English. Right, güero?" Enrique says, now in English. "Me speaky perfect Eenglish." He chuckles loudly, but Natalia, a Spanish speaker, fails to get the humor.

"Gary!-Freddy!-Charlie!-Oscaaaarr!" Natalia belts out the names of her four other sons, in a booming voice that serves as proof that she shares the same gene pool as Enrique. The children come rushing from various rooms. Fourteen-year-old Gary is even larger than Abram, weighing more than two hundred pounds; Freddy, who is twelve, is skinny but nearly six feet tall; Charlie, seven, immediately begins to ask Abram questions about New York; and the precocious four-year-old Oscar introduces himself by plopping down on my lap.

"Güero, are you my uncle's brother?" he asks—causing everyone to laugh. I tell him that I am just a friend.

"Oscar, the güero came with your uncle and your grandfather," Natalia says. Oscar looks up at her in confusion. "He's never seen his *abuelo* before," she says, turning back to us. "Why don't you bring Oscar along to Cuicatlán, so that he can meet him?" Oscar quickly nods his approval of this plan.

"Anyone else want to go to Cuicatlán to meet your *abuelito?*" she asks the others. Freddy and Charlie decline, but Gary agrees to go along, so we hop into the truck, now with two grandsons whom Angel has never met, and head for the hotel.

In front of the hotel Leticia is standing alone while Angel wanders around the parking lot with a video camera in hand. As we pull up, Angel smiles and trains his camera on us. I notice as we park that Angela is sitting across the street on a folding chair, watching us behind the cover of a parked van. It appears that my concern about an inadvertent meeting between the two wasn't unfounded.

"Enrique, I can see Angela over there," I say before we get out. "What should we do?"

He glances over and waves at Angela, who ducks out of sight. "Do? What the fuck do you mean, do? There's nothing to do. She's just over there waiting for the bus to take her to Acatlán." Bus or not, it looks to me like she is staking out the hotel. Enrique takes another glance toward his mother. "Hey, that's her brother sitting next to her. Let's go say hello."

We get out, leaving the kids and Abram in the truck, and tell Angel and Leticia to wait for a moment. Leticia remains standing where she was, and Angel resumes his filming, this time capturing images of their hotel.

On the other side of the narrow street, Angela has an unobstructed view of her previous husband and his new wife, but neither Angel nor Leticia seem to have noticed her. It has been more than twenty years since she has last seen Angel. "He looks old, very old," she says to us, sounding satisfied. "And imagine him, just coming here to Chinantla with that bitch. Son of a bitch has no shame—but God is great and powerful. *Grande y poderoso.* He will be punished someday."

I don't know what to say, and Enrique has heard this all many times before, so he ignores her comment. We strike up a conversation with Angela's brother, chatting for a few minutes. Angela, however, has no use for our small talk and remains silent, her eyes fixed on Angel as he continues to film the hotel, oblivious.

Suddenly, a loud horn blows and a bus rumbles by us, belching blue smoke. "Shit!" Angela yells, jumping up from her chair with remarkable speed for a woman her age. She runs across the street after the bus, flailing her arms; I look over at Angel and Leticia, who are both staring with open mouths at Angela as she pursues the bus. The bus slows down, Angela gets on board, and we say good-bye to her brother and cross the street.

Back at the truck, Angel and Leticia don't mention anything about having seen Angela. We all pile in, and the silence feels heavy. I look at Angel to try to discern if he realizes he is in the presence of two of his grandkids, but his face betrays no emotion. Enrique, likewise, doesn't say a word. Oscar, however, lacks the stoic maturity of these much older men and can't remain quiet.

"Are you my grandfather?" he asks from the backseat. Angel slowly turns around.

"Yes, I probably am. And who are you?"

"My name is Oscar. This is Gary." Angel continues to look at Oscar. "My mom is Natalia."

"Yes, yes, then I am your grandfather. Nice to meet you." Angel looks at Oscar and Gary for a moment more and then turns back around. The silence returns, but it feels slightly less heavy.

To get to Cuicatlán we backtrack to Angela's house and then continue on a dirt path that winds between hills along a hot desert valley. Unattended goats scavenge for food, and we pass a gaunt donkey sitting in the shade, looking miserable.

"Look at all this land," Leticia comments, finally breaking the adult-imposed silence. "Why come to New York City when you could live out here with so much space?"

"Because this land isn't worth anything if there isn't any water," Enrique counters. "Tell her, Angel—if you can't grow crops, how are you going to survive?" Angel nods his agreement. We pass a dirt path that veers off to the right and is becoming overgrown by the desert brush.

"Who lives there now?" Angel asks, looking down the trail.

"I don't know," says Enrique. "We can ask Luis."

"One of my brothers had a house at the end of that road," Angel explains to Leticia. "It doesn't look like whoever is there now has been caring well for the area. If anyone even lives there anymore."

Deeper into the valley, we stop at the foot of a hill and get out. Angel and Leticia, who are heading farther to visit Angel's brother, continue along the road in his truck, and we begin to trudge up the steep path, following Enrique. As we hike we pass two barking dogs, several clucking roosters, a handful of donkeys, and then a church perched on the edge of the cliff to our right. Hearing the commotion that the animals are making, a slender man steps out from a small house in the distance—a room, really—with a large crack running along its side. He smiles and waves at our party.

"That's Luis, Adolfo's dad," Enrique says. Luis walks down to meet us halfway, and tears are in his eyes. He hugs Enrique and thanks him for helping get his son's body home, and then shakes my hand and thanks me as well for my assistance in the case—which was actually quite minimal. As we all turn around and trudge up the remainder of the path, Oscar runs ahead into a gathering of chickens, sending them off in frantic bunches of twos and threes.

In contrast to the modern cement homes that now dominate Chinantla, Luis and Teresa's house hasn't changed since they built it thirty years ago. Inside the single room are a bed, refrigerator, two chairs, and one counter that is filled with images of the Virgin of Guadalupe and a crucified Jesus. Yet despite the modesty, their house has one immediately apparent advantage over the much larger buildings in Chinantla: it is comfortable. Made from adobe—earth—the walls deflect much of the desert heat, and the cement floor remains cool and inviting. "Yes, I can't stand the houses in Chinantla," Luis mentions when I comment about the difference in temperature as we settle into the room. "Why would you want to spend all that money to live in an oven?"

Inside, Luis pours everyone a cup of Pepsi. Oscar gulps his down and then, blood coursing with the unneeded sugar, dashes outside to continue his battle with the chickens. Several moments later Teresa joins us. Teresa, Angela's older sister, is a stout, friendly woman who bursts into laughter at the slightest provocation—the perfect compliment to her husband, who is quiet in a way that seems to hint at ancient wisdom. While Teresa quickly dominates any conversation out of sheer exuberance, Luis spends most of his time listening, his brow furrowed and his head nodding along, encouraging the speaker to continue his or her story.

Between sips of ice-cold cola, Enrique asks Luis and Teresa about new developments in Cuicatlán and Chinantla. Though they do their best to engage in small talk, it is clear from the impatient looks on their faces that they are hungry for information about the case against Adolfo's alleged killer. Enrique, though, doesn't seem to notice and continues to chat about everything from the weather to next week's fiesta. Finally Teresa, no longer able to contain her curiosity, speaks up. "And what is happening in Brooklyn? How is the case going?"

Earlier, Enrique and I had discussed how to present the case against Esteban to Adolfo's parents, and agreed we should try to comfort them by emphasizing that the case was very strong—which it did seem to be. For half an hour Enrique explains everything he knows—about Esteban's confession, Reina's agreement to testify against Esteban in exchange for immunity, the district attorney's belief that they didn't have enough evidence to convict them both for the crime. While he speaks, even the garrulous Teresa doesn't utter a word, though she occasionally wrinkles her nose while rubbing her hands together. When Enrique finishes, Luis and Teresa both have the same question on their mind, which they ask simultaneously. "What about Reina?"

Enrique tells them again that Reina is the eyewitness and is testifying against Esteban in exchange for being granted immunity.

"But she *had* to have planned the killing with Esteban," Teresa insists. "Why else would she leave the house after seeing Adolfo get killed and go home without telling the police? If she cared about Adolfo, she would have gone to the police right away. After the shooting she went to her house and tried to hide. Why would an innocent person hide? She is as guilty as Esteban—it was them both!" Teresa's cheerfulness is gone, replaced with white-hot anger. As she speaks, the volume of her voice rises and her face becomes flushed, the round contours of her cheeks streamlining into a hardened triangle, ending at the point of her chin.

"Of course she knew," Enrique agrees. "Of course she is guilty. But the district attorney said there wasn't enough information to convict her, and that her testimony was the most important thing to make sure that Esteban is found guilty. If they tried to get both of them, they were afraid that instead they might lose both cases. They need to at least get the person who actually fired the bullets into Adolfo's back."

Neither Teresa nor Luis seems satisfied with this explanation, but they don't inquire further. The situation is out of their hands, and they trust Enrique; if he agrees with the district attorney, then the district attorney must be right.

"Adolfo was never scared of anything," Luis eventually remarks after several moments of silence, putting aside the topic of Reina's guilt. "Kids now think they will never get into trouble, but the world is dangerous if you think like that."

"Honestly, *tío*, I tried to talk with Adolfo about how things are different in the U.S. At a party a month before he was killed, I explained to him that he couldn't just go around hitting Reina whenever he was angry. I told him that it's not like here, where people won't catch you. Over there it is different. But he wouldn't listen. He said Reina was a bitch who didn't understand unless he hit her."

Luis shook his head. "I know, I know," he sighs, tears again welling up in his eyes. "I don't know why he never wanted to listen. I think maybe we did something to make him be like that, but I don't know what."

"No, tío, you gave him everything he needed. Look at your other kids—they aren't causing any problems. It's real simple. These *muchachos* today want to show everyone that they have balls, *huevos*. They go north and think they can do whatever they want. If someone does something stupid here, they can always run away. Where are you going to run in New York City?

"And it's not your fault or Teresa's fault. No one could tell Adolfo different. People leave and they get stupid. Look at his sisters, all working hard without causing trouble. Adolfo just wanted to do what he wanted to do. End of story."

After a lunch of handmade tortillas, beans, and unbelievably spicy salsa, it is time to head down the hill and meet up with Angel and Leticia for the trip back to Chinantla. Before we leave, Luis says he would like to give us a tour of their new church, which was built several years ago with money sent from relatives in the United States. We follow him through the large entrance door into the shaded sanctuary, which contains rows of wooden pews stained dark brown. Placards are screwed into the back of each pew, upon which is inscribed a family name. "Those are the families who have sent money from the U.S. to build our church," Luis says. "We would have liked to help, but our kids didn't have enough money to donate." Although they don't have a pew of their own, Luis has become the official caretaker of the church, opening it at five in the morning each Sunday for service.

After the tour of the church's interior we gather on the front steps, overlooking the valley. Amid the stark surroundings, the exterior of the church is simply glorious: made of red bricks and with a large ornate bell hanging from the entrance, it looks like it is out of a movie set in small-town, rural America. Gazing west from the top of the hill, the town of Cuicatlán seems to be little more than a few dozen small houses in a valley of scorched, yellow earth. While Chinantla has changed dramatically over the previous decades, it is hard to imagine how Cuicatlán could ever have been less prosperous. Luis confirms this lack of development. "The only change I can remember is this new church. Everything else is the same, people living like we do with animals and crops. And yet, this is how we like it. Simple. Quiet. *Tranquilo.*"

CHAPTER 14

Angela

"GABRIEL, YOU'VE GOT to get this down!" Efreín, a fifty-six-year-old elementary school teacher, is a very demanding conversationalist. Always dressed in a suit—school day or not—Efreín grew up in Chinantla but now lives and works in the capital city of Puebla. He is visiting his mother and already excitedly anticipating next week's party. I am passing by a small store when I hear him call out to me—*Güero!*—and duck inside with my tattered notebook in hand, stuffing it quickly in my pocket. An almost comically gregarious man, with short, slicked-back hair, Efreín sports an imposing mustache that partially covers his angular face. Though he is holding an open beer, and seems well into a six-pack judging by the empty bottles on his table, he notices this movement.

"What are you, a writer?" I nod sheepishly. "A writer!" he practically shouts. "Writers have power—you must choose your words carefully. *Con cuidado*—get it down! Write that down! Gabriel, write that down!" What I first thought was a suggestion is clearly an order, and I dutifully pull out my notebook. *Choose words carefully,* I scrawl.

Efreín, satisfied, launches into a story about his first trip to the United States. He came to Washington, D.C., with his wife on a tourist visa in 1970. He toured the Nixon White House and wandered around the capital city with his wife for several days, staying in a hotel next to a Greyhound bus depot; they had chosen the hotel because they were eventually going to head up to New York City. But on the day they entered the bus depot Efreín wasn't able to find anyone behind the counter who spoke Spanish, and no one understood that he wanted two tickets. After spending a frustrating and embarrassing hour without making any progress, they returned to the hotel, where they stayed two more days before getting up the courage to try again.

On their second trip to the ticket counter, confusion again was the order of the day, but this time a traveling sailor who spoke some Spanish eventually interceded and helped them purchase their tickets. "My wife was also pregnant at the time," Efreín says. "So she needed to use the bathroom often, but we couldn't figure out how to get in, because they were all locked. The sailor showed us that we had to pay a quarter to enter." He pauses uncharacteristically and takes a deep breath. He hasn't stopped talking since I wandered in, twenty minutes ago. "That is why I say I love America, because the people are friendly. The American people are willing to help."

I nod. I am finding it exhausting trying to keep up with Efreín's narrative; it is interesting, but he keeps looking at me in a way that makes me feel like a jerk if I don't nod vigorously and give a look that suggests the suspense of his tale is unbearable. So I keep scrunching up my face, trying to come up with a look that says: and then? And Then? AND THEN? But, concentrating on my facial distortions, I have forgotten about the notebook.

"Gabriel, you've got to get this down! The American people are willing to help! But your damn government, that damn Bush, he is the problem. Maybe you don't know this, but there are so many parents here who die without seeing their children, because they can't cross the border. In Mexico family is the most important thing, and it is a sad situation right now. So many families never see one another, so many parents are abandoned and can never come north." I nod and tell him that I know many people in Brooklyn who feel the same way.

"But you're an American," he interjects. "You're a writer and you're an American, why can't you go to speak to President Bush and tell him to allow the parents to come visit their children? You speak the language, you are a citizen, what can you do to fix the problem?" I tell him there are many things that I disagree with Bush about, but that I don't have any special power over him.

"Nonsense," he replies. "I think the first thing you do when you go home should be to go right up to the White House and go talk with him. They have to let you in, right? Go there and tell him there are Mexican families that are suffering now, and that he has to do something about it." As he speaks I listen and try to think of a way to explain in Spanish that I am not as powerful as my white skin might be leading him to believe. "Get that down," he says again; I have stopped writing while in thought.

"You should take down this story that needs to be told and bring it right to Bush. I don't want to hear about any excuses." He looks at his friend behind the counter, who is nodding off. "Imagine, an American who says he can't do anything! You can do *anything!*" I finish the beer he has purchased for me and leave, drained, but promise that if I do see Bush, I will definitely mention to him what we have discussed today.

After the visit to Luis and Teresa's, most of my first week in Chinantla is spent wandering around town bumping into characters like Efreín and hanging around the house with Angela. After being gone for twenty years, Angel had many brothers and cousins he wanted to visit, and since his eyesight was failing the task of chauffeur fell to

Enrique. Enrique, however, didn't complain. Angela was still upset after having seen Angel and Leticia at the hotel, and Enrique thought it would be good to try to keep his father out of town as much as possible, to minimize the chances of another awkward, stress-inducing encounter. Abram, who was constantly complaining about the heat and—like all good teenagers—that there was *"nothing* to do here," spent most of his days at Natalia's house, watching TV and showing off his handheld PlayStation to Charlie and Freddie. So while everyone else was occupied, I was left in the house with Angela.

I found myself feeling something verging on awe when in Angela's presence. Four and a half feet tall, always wearing a blue or white dress that highlighted her nearly black skin, she was a bundle of focused, relentless energy. Regardless of how late we stayed up chatting, she would rise each morning while it was still dark and begin cooking breakfast for Nico, who lived in the house behind Angela's. A large, bearded man who was always dressed in the same long-sleeved flannel shirt, Nico would pull up one of the plastic stools in the front yard and sit down next to the ledge at the entryway door, waiting quietly for Angela to hand over a heated bowl of beans and then begin tossing tortillas his way. Nico, Angela explained on the second day, was loco, and—though he usually seemed normal to me, if noncommunicative—she warned me that he had a habit of picking up large rocks and throwing them at whoever happened to wander into his sight.

Enrique confirmed this tendency: one evening during a previous trip, he was eating dinner on the front porch when between slurps of soup a softball-sized rock whizzed past him, missing his face by inches and shattering against the wall of the house. It was too dark to see much of anything, but Enrique took off running in the direction of Nico's house, only to see him disappear down a side street. Nico spent the evening elsewhere, but the next morning he was on his stool again, waiting for his breakfast. When Enrique confronted him about the rock throwing, Nico seemed confused and claimed he didn't remember the incident; Enrique felt he was "pretending to forget," and told him if it ever happened again he would first beat him and then kick him out of his house. While explaining this incident, Enrique couldn't help adding a juicy bit of questionable information. "Nico told me when we arrived that he doesn't like white people on his property, so keep your eyes open."

Once Nico had finished eating, not long after the sun had risen, Angela would begin shouting into my room. "Güero, get up! Hurry up! ¡Apúrate!" The first morning that this happened, I thought there might have been some kind of emergency and leapt out of bed in my boxer shorts to find Angela sitting at the kitchen table, eating a tortilla.

"Is something wrong?" She looked at me quizzically. No, nothing wrong. Breakfast wasn't even ready yet. I soon learned that she just liked to yell "Hurry up!" at me early each morning. Actually, "Hurry up!" was something of an anthem for her, used at all hours, without a clear purpose. If there is one time that hurrying up isn't necessary, it's when one is living in a rural town in southern Mexico and nothing much is going on. Still, by 6:30 each morning, I would be loudly encouraged to hurry up, and I'd stuff a pillow over my head and try to get back to sleep.

After Nico ate, Angela would heat up tortillas and beans for our breakfast, and then she and Nico would go down to the well and spend an hour or so drawing water and carrying it with buckets to dump in the rectangular pool of cement next to the outhouse. Part of the tacit agreement worked out years ago was that the price of Angela's cooking was this labor. This looked enjoyable to me, suffering as I was from a back-to-the-land fantasy, until I volunteered one morning to accompany Angela and found that the well's rope quickly turned my hands a bloody and blistered mess. Seeing that I was in trouble, Angela grabbed the rope from me and began pulling up the buckets at a lightning pace; from then on, she would draw the water and I would carry the buckets.

After fetching water, which always left my shirt drenched in sweat and my body in need of a nap, we would eat a lunch of rice and beans with tortillas, and then Angela would head off to the neighboring town of Piaxtla to buy more tortillas and run errands. I'd collapse for several hours, she'd return, and we'd eat dinner. After dinner the temperature had usually begun to cool off, so we would pull chairs onto the cement porch and she would tell me whatever was on her mind. I'd ask a question or two, and she'd be off, speaking in rapid-fire sentences for hours about her parents, about growing up in Chinantla, about her children—moving her hands back and forth almost violently to accentuate her points, looking like a shadow-boxing grandmother. As she spoke she would click her teeth repeatedly, a habit she picked up when she had a metal cap installed over a rotten tooth many years ago. As her excitement grew while she spoke, the pace of her clicking increased, and when the topic inevitably turned to Angel's betrayal of their marriage, it could sometimes be difficult to understand her, the words lost in the incessant click-click-clicking of her teeth and the punch-punch-punching of her whirling arms.

Angela was born several hundred feet from her current home, in an adobe house that had subsequently been torn down and rebuilt with concrete. When I asked her birth date she shrugged; she also wasn't certain of her age. Fishing into her bra she pulled out a plastic bag with several old photographs and ID's; according to one of the government-issued cards, she was born on September 29, 1937, which would make her sixty-seven years old.

When Angela was a child, her father didn't allow her to attend school, and she never learned how to read. "He didn't have the money for the supplies and for the uniforms," she said. "Instead, I worked with him in the fields." While a teenager she met Angel when he was visiting one day from his parent's home in Cuicatlán. Not long after that, they were celebrating their wedding in Chinantla's church.

After their wedding Angela moved from Chinantla to the hills outside of Cuicatlán to live with Angel in an adobe house near his parents. Life in Cuicatlán was a lot like life in Chinantla: they farmed the staple crops of beans, squash, and corn on land near the house. Not long after the move, Angela gave birth to the first of eight children, Sofia, in 1956. After Sofia came Juan, then Sabina, Angel, Maria, Sergio, Natalia, and Enrique. Today Sofia lives in Mexico City; Juan is in Port Chester, New York; Sabina in Brooklyn; Angel in Manhattan; Maria in Staten Island; Sergio in Alaska with his wife, who is in the military and stationed in Anchorage. Natalia is still in Chinantla; and Enrique in Brooklyn. In addition to eight children she also had two miscarriages.

Shortly after Enrique's birth in 1971, Angel decided he wanted to go to New York to work. Though Angela tried to convince him to stay, especially since Enrique was still an infant, he had made up his mind. One morning he caught a bus out of Chinantla for Mexico City and then made his way to Tijuana, where he crossed legally with a visa. After riding in a car to Los Angeles, he caught a flight to New York paid for by money borrowed from his brothers, and worked at the plastics factory but was eventually deported.

For the next two years Angel lived again with the family in Cuicatlán, but Angela could tell that he was itching to return to New York. In 1975 he crossed again in Tijuana, this time illegally with the help of a *coyote* since his visa had expired, and made his way back to Brooklyn. Sending money home occasionally, he didn't return to Mexico for another eleven years, after becoming a legal resident through Reagan's amnesty program in 1986.

When he returned to Cuicatlán that year he lived with Angela again. But after several weeks he told Angela that he had to return to New York in order to collect his retirement benefits from his job as a union janitor at the Port Authority. He would complete the needed paperwork, pack up his things, and return. "It was important to get the papers signed," Angela recalls him saying, "because then we would have checks sent to us each month that we could live on. Once he told me that, I agreed that he should return."

He also proposed to Angela that when he came back they should move to Mexico City and purchase their own home. Angela wasn't too excited about moving from the country into a big city, but she went along with the proposition. But, as she would remind me many times during our conversations, he never did come back—never even called to explain what had happened. She hadn't seen or talked to him since the day of his departure, a day when Angela was sad but also excited about the endless checks that her husband said would be coming soon. Imagine how wealthy the United States must be, she thought, that even ordinary workers in the country keep getting paid well even after they have stopped working! But that was the last she saw of Angel. Until, of course, we rolled into town last week.

Shortly after Angel's departure, Enrique, too, had left for Brooklyn. Still anticipating the quick return of Angel, Angela decided to move from Cuicatlán into Chinantla. With most of her children in the United States, and her youngest now out of the house, she was eager to return to her nearby hometown, where the houses had running water and one didn't have to embark on an hour-long trek just to socialize with friends. With financial assistance and donated labor from the town's government, she was able to obtain a small cement house that now sits abandoned, off to the left side of her front yard.

After Enrique left, though she was now living in town, Angela grew lonely. "You know how he is, he keeps things interesting, keeps good company," she says of her youngest son. "When he left everything seemed so quiet." But the fact that six of her eight children were living thousands of miles away was made bearable by the regular payments of money each of them sent every month to assist Angela. And since all six became legal residents through the amnesty, by 1988 they were able to visit Angela without worrying about how they would get back. Some, like Sergio in Alaska, rarely returned, but others like Enrique, Angel, and Sofia tried to visit at least once a year.

Two, three, four years went by without word from Angel. Had he petitioned for her residency so that she could join him in New York, she is not sure what she would have done. But the issue was never brought up. The phone calls stopped. Looking back, Angela couldn't remember a precise moment when she realized that he was in the United States for good. For Angela, time seemed to be much more about feelings than regimented demarcations; days, months, years were a blur, unimportant—strong memories, regardless of how long ago the corresponding events occurred, were talked about as if they had happened just yesterday.

But what Angela does remember is when she began to hear her children talk about Angel's desire for a divorce. Enrique was the first to tell her, during one of their Sunday evening conversations. She was never going to sign divorce papers, she said, with a stubbornness that made her son proud. They had committed to each other for life, and if she couldn't control Angel's philandering, she could certainly refuse to play along as if everything was okay. Eventually Angel had paid an attorney to make the divorce official, but in

Angela's mind the marriage had never ended, and as she explained this fact I sensed that she still clung to a stubborn hope that they might one day be reunited at last.

There is one topic that I don't quite know how to bring up with Angela. Enrique had mentioned many times his still-fresh anger at Angel for the beatings he used to administer on Angela and the children, but while listing her complaints against Angel she never said anything about physical abuse. On the fourth night, I ask her whether it was true that Angel had beaten her.

"Hijo de su pinche madre," she replies, astounded at my ignorance. "Of course he beat me. The son of a bitch beat me like a fucking donkey!" She held out her left arm. "See this scar?" she asked, pointing at a line that went along her left forearm and continued onto her hand. "Did he beat me? He gave me this!"

Relations between Angela and Angel hit their nadir soon after the birth of Natalia. One day, buckets of harvested corn were sitting in front of their house. Several of the buckets had tipped over, and a goat had begun to nibble at the food. Angela, who was inside the house, heard Angel whistle loudly. "Whenever he got angry he would whistle," she says. "It was his signal that something he didn't like was happening." Angela called for Sofia to gather the goats, but Sofia was caught up in her sewing and didn't move. Angela went outside to scare away the goats, just in time to see Angel coming at her with a machete. He raised it over his head and swung it at Angela. Had she not raised her hands in front of her, it probably would have struck her across the face. The blade, dulled from chopping brush, cut into her arm, but luckily it wasn't as deep a wound as it could have been.

"He always wanted everything to be exactly as he wanted it to be, and if something wasn't perfect, you never knew when he would lose his temper. He thought everyone had to obey him."

After being hit, Angela left immediately for a neighbor's house, where she stayed for three days, refusing to go outside. On the third day, Angel's mother visited, apologizing for her son's behavior and saying she would understand if Angela decided to leave him. Instead, Angela decided to go back to the house. "How could I leave? We had seven children in the house, and he didn't know how to take care of them."

When she returned, Angel was in the house, but they didn't talk. Instead, Angela simply went back to caring for the children; at this point Natalia was seven months old. "He never apologized for what he did, and he never asked for forgiveness. He was like the other men in the campo, thinking that women were just animals—animals they could hit whenever they wanted. They would hit us like we were nothing more than animals. Now, by the grace of God, we are in a different period, when women stand up for themselves. But back then what happened to me was normal."

I asked Angela if Angel ever hit her again after that, and she said he hadn't. Apparently, although he hadn't ever apologized for the attack, the episode had shaken Angel. But several days later Enrique and Natalia recounted an episode that contradicted their mother's claim, about an incident that occurred when Angel had returned to Cuicatlán after being deported. One day, when he discovered that the children had purchased slingshots, he became upset and hit Angela across the face with his sandals. Then, still enraged, he hit the other seven children with the sandals as well, including Enrique, who was then only three years old. Sofia, the oldest, was hit the hardest of all, multiple times across the back of her head, and began to bleed profusely.

Natalia, who was six years old, took off running for the house of Angel's mother. They then both rushed back to find Angel still hitting Enrique, and that was when Angel's mother stepped forward and put an end to everything with a single sentence. "If you want to beat someone, beat your own mother," she said. He immediately put down the sandals and was done for the day.

Sitting with her on the porch, I hadn't yet heard this other story, but what she had told me was awful enough. Even though Enrique had mentioned a number of times that Angel had administered frequent beatings, it was difficult to reconcile the mostly quiet and gentle Angel that I knew with the machete-wielding man who had attacked his wife and beaten his children. Yes, after talking with people from both Cuicatlán and Chinantla, I learned that it was considered almost normal for men to beat up their wives back in theose days. But attacking the mother of your children with a machete? I was beginning to see Angel's departure not as a tragic story of infidelity, but as a fortunate break for Angela.

I don't know what to say to Angela, except that she is better off without him. She curses and agrees, clicking her teeth. While we sit in silence Angel's truck roars into the dirt driveway, and Enrique jumps out of the driver's seat. "Come on, hurry up!" he yells at us. "The party has already started. They're getting ready to ride the bulls." Angela and I quickly get in the truck, and together we drive the several hundred feet to the bullring, where dozens of people are gathered around, awaiting the first rider. Looking for parking we pass Angel and Leticia, who are drinking sodas at one of the food booths. Angel waves at me, but luckily Angela doesn't see him. Normally, I would have waved back, but tonight I pretend I don't see him.

CHAPTER 15

La Fiesta

ALTHOUGH THE WEEKLONG party in Chinantla's *primera sección* will include live music, dancing, a beauty pageant, and bull-riding, for many men (and a few women), the ultimate draw is *peleas de gallo*—cockfighting. The signs advertising the matches, scheduled to run for three consecutive evenings, are posted on every conceivable landmark in town, and old men have been muttering about the event since we arrived. "If you want to know the real Mexico, you've got to see *las peleas de gallo*," an elderly storeowner had told me several days ago. "There, at *las peleas,* you will find true beauty." I had my doubts.

After we park the truck, Enrique, Abram, and I leave Angela with friends who are eating pizza at one of the newly erected food stands and head over to the action (Angela has long ago lost interest in the matches). Overnight, organizers have erected a large white tent that surrounds the neighborhood basketball court, and after paying fifty pesos each we walk through the entryway. In the middle of the court is the cockfighting ring, where large amounts of dirt have been dumped and spread out. The dirt is surrounded by a chest-high, oval-shaped ring, illuminated by a series of bulbs that hang from ropes wrapped around the arena's high ceiling beams. Encircling the ring are bleachers and folding chairs, and at one end are dozens of cages full of roosters. Loud music blasts from a stereo system, and a number of men in the stands already seem to be well on their way to inebriation.

Although we arrive an hour after the advertised start time, no fights have yet begun. The current action centers on one end of the ring, where a line of men patiently wait to weigh their birds on a metal scale, holding the creatures in front of their chests. The men are serious, silent. Their roosters, however, are frantic and squawk wildly at one another while ruffling their feathers; like boxers staring down an opponent before a match, they appear to be engaging in psychological warfare. Or suffering from sensory overload: it is loud in here.

A fierce-looking red-and-black rooster is refusing to stand still on the rusted scale and flaps its wings in anger, crowing loudly. Challenged, every bird raises its voice, and a few struggle mightily to free themselves from their owner's grip. The scene reeks of bloodlust, but the men here remain unruffled—all probably veterans of the cockfighting circuit—and with sure hands they calmly clamp down on their birds' legs. A few of them smile at the cacophony their creatures create: a loud bird, apparently, bodes well come fight time. Finally the owner of the red-and-black bird is able to calm it down by whispering soothingly in what I suppose are the bird's ears, and the animal perches uncomfortably on the platform just long enough for officials to take an accurate measurement.

The bizarre weigh-in scene is nothing if not photogenic. I take my camera out and am preparing to snap a photo when a mustached man in a cowboy hat taps me on the shoulder. "No photos here," he says sternly. "Something might happen tonight, so we don't allow people to take pictures of the ring." I shoot him a look of protest; cockfighting in Mexico isn't illegal, after all—but his face shows no sign of capitulation, so I turn off my camera and join

Enrique and Abram, who have settled down on folding chairs in the first row. Closer to the action than would be ideal, but I stay quiet.

As we wait for the rest of the birds to be weighed, Enrique explains the basic rules. One side of the ring is painted green and the other red, and each bird is assigned a color, which is used to identify them for betting purposes. When the fight begins, the trainers release their birds on opposite ends of the ring and then watch them battle it out. The bird that survives is the winner. If they both die, a tie is declared. Simple enough.

"Since it's your first time, it can seem ugly," Enrique warns. Neither Abram nor I have been to a cockfight before, but Enrique is directing the comment to me—probably because I am a vegetarian. "But you'll get used to it," he reassures me.

Thirty minutes pass, and by now the seats around the ring are nearly full. A chubby, ruddy-faced man wearing a dusty suit announces the first fight, pitting a white bird from Chinantla in the green corner—where we are seated—against the red-and-black bird, which is from the city of Tehuixtzingo, a region that Enrique explains is known for producing rugged fighters.

The Chinanteco trainer places something like a miniature suitcase on top of the ring's fence and opens it in front of us, revealing a vast collection of shiny blades. After several minutes of consideration, he makes his decision and attaches one of the glistening inch-long razors to the right leg of his bird with a piece of thin string. Although his input hasn't been solicited, Enrique lets the trainer know that he supports his choice of weaponry, to which the man nods and grants a half smile, half grimace. Excited but nervous, I presume.

Both of the birds are now armed with sharp blades that are hooked on one end, but they aren't quite in fighting form. For this they must be agitated, made hysterical. Several feet from us, the

Chinanteco trainer grabs his bird and lifts it upside down. He places his face where the rooster—it would seem, anyway—has its reproductive organ, and blows hard. Then he places the bird back on the ground and blows hard into its face. Not surprisingly, the bird doesn't care for such advances and begins to squawk and jump around, beating its wings. A similar dance is going on across the ring.

It would seem that the birds are now sufficiently riled up, but no: the soon-to-be combatants—still in their respective corners—are further frustrated when another bird is placed in front of them and allowed to fluff its feathers with impunity as the trainers restrain their fighters. The red-and-black rooster—which was already grumpy an hour ago—is now convulsing with rage at the sight of the brown bird that is hopping up and down just beyond the reach of its beak, and looks in danger of having an aneurysm before the match even gets under way.

While the birds are being agitated, two women dressed in skin-tight shirts and miniskirts wander around the ring, taking bets. With their heavy makeup and swinging gait, they are meant to be seductive, but circumstances have rendered this task virtually impossible: walking in stiletto heels along the uneven, rock-filled dirt floor, the smiling women trip repeatedly. At one point the taller of the two stumbles and falls to her knees, extending her arms just in time to avoid planting her face in the soil, a move that the men greet with a round of hoots. Consummate professional that she is, the woman simply brushes herself off and returns to her stumbling shuffle, all the while keeping a smile stapled across her face.

After ten more minutes of rooster agitation and bet collection (Enrique has placed one hundred pesos on the Tehuixtzingo bird, saying, "No one in Chinantla knows how to really train the best fighters") it is time to begin the first fight. By now both trainers are holding their birds close to their chests, stroking their wings rapidly and mumbling a string of unintelligible words into their ears. After several last-second pieces of advice, they place their birds on the ground, facing each other, and let them go. The arena falls silent. Even the drunks are concentrating on the ring, breathing heavily.

As soon as it is released, the red-and-black bird dashes at full speed for the enemy, while the white rooster seems momentarily confused and spends a precious second looking around the ring. With the red-and-black bird bearing down, it finally realizes that it needs to act, and at the last moment hurls its body into the air at the leaping opponent. They connect in a loud racket of flapping wings, swinging legs, and thrusting beaks. The birds bounce off each other, landing several feet apart, and leap again, colliding in another violent burst. Feathers go flying. This time, instead of separating they stay together, lunging repeatedly at each other with their beaks. Their movements are too quick for me to follow, but when they pull back briefly I see that the left wing of the white bird is drenched in blood. After several more leaping jousts they tumble to the ground and remain motionless. The white bird is now on top, resting its head on its opponent's body like a pillow. All the rage seems to have gone out of both birds as they cuddle, bodies heaving up and down, sucking for air.

"Is it over?" Abram gasps, his hands clenched in front of his chest.

Enrique shakes his head. "Can't you see that they're both still alive?" he asks, just as the trainers walk forward and grab their birds, bringing them back to their corners. Both birds look exhausted. The trainer of the white bird begins to administer something too close to CPR for my taste, his lips sucking and blowing, occasionally touching his creature's beak. Finally, after another round of genital molesting and face blowing, both birds are revived, angry. The truce is off.

They sprint into the middle and again collide in an orgy of flapping and clawing. After the birds tumble on the dirt for several seconds the crowd lets out a collective gasp. Though I am watching the match, I can't discern in the chaos what has caused the reaction. Then a spurt of blood shoots several feet up into the air—a thick red geyser—and I can see that the white bird has been cut badly along its body. Its entire white coat is quickly a sticky pink and red, and as the birds continue to wrestle it looks dazed. Sensing victory, the red-and-black rooster jumps up and slashes the bird's face with its razor blade. The white bird falls to the ground and is finished off with a series of hard pecks to the head. By the time the red-and-black bird is pulled off, it has what looks to be a section of brain in its mouth. The dirt surrounding the hemorrhaging white bird is mixing with blood, turning a few shades darker.

"Eeecthh," exclaims a woman sitting to my left, and I concur. Enrique and Abram, in contrast, are both enthralled, and begin to offer their own analysis of what happened, how the Chinantla bird's fighting "technique" went wrong.

"He wasn't using his blade in the air." "He started too slow." "The other bird was a better fighter on the ground." "He forgot to try and peck the eyes." And on and on. It strikes me as a kind of madness, this effort to decipher what we have just witnessed— an attempt to inject some sort of meaning into the match, to pretend that this, too, is a sweet science of sorts. Perhaps it is simply a lack of cultural awareness, but to my gringo eyes it looked more like two freaked-out roosters just spent a few minutes flailing unconsciously.

Skill or chance, the fight is now over. The trainer of the dead bird, who minutes earlier seemed unhealthily infatuated with his creature, picks up the corpse roughly by its legs and carries it out of the ring, tossing it into a far corner. Next round.

Each subsequent fight follows the same pattern: bird agitation; midair collision; birds fall on each other; separated and re-agitated; midair collision; one bird dies. All three of Chinantla's birds lose, while two fair-skinned men from Mexico City clean up, winning every one of their fights. By the time I leave it is nearly three o'clock in the morning, and at least two fights are still to come. Abram and Enrique don't get home until four-thirty, and when they do I am awakened by their noisy discussions of the fights, still debating exactly why the Chinantla birds didn't hold their own. My dreams that night, thankfully, are roosterless.

The next morning we rise early—Angela's *gritas* again—but slower than normal. Today is Mother's Day in Mexico, when all of the townspeople head to the cemetery to lay flowers at the graves of their mothers and grandmothers. By the time we eat breakfast and dress, Angela has already gone into town and returned with a bouquet of flowers, and is impatiently waiting our departure on the front porch. Apúrate.

The cemetery is on the southern end of town, built upon a sloping hill. To arrive there one passes the hotel where Leticia and Angel are staying, and then crosses a bridge over a dry riverbed, which is filled with tires and plastic bottles. Following the road as it curves to the right, a rusted archway comes into view, and on the other side of the archway lie generations of farmers and goatherds, hunters and teachers. Most of the headstones in the cemetery are simple, nothing more than a cement slab; in a town that has been transforming rapidly, the graveyard has remained largely unchanged, an anchor of stability in a whirling sea of development. Yet here, too, the careful observer can spot the results of payment in dollars: some of the wealthier families have constructed virtual houses for their dead, complete with locked front doors, aluminum roofs, and tile floors.

Her mother's grave is simple, only a small headstone. After Angela lays the flowers over the grave she begins a lengthy prayer in Spanish, and I notice Teresa and Luis in the middle of the cemetery and wander over. They are standing quietly over a six-foot-long section of freshly tilled earth. At one end of the pile is a headstone, clearly homemade, which in shaky handwriting reads "El Joven Adolfo Perez Soriano." At the other end is a wreath of flowers, now dry and yellowed, and a plastic soda bottle sliced in half with the remnants of a candle in its middle. It is by far the most modest grave I have seen in the cemetery.

Luis seems to be reading my mind. "We would have liked to have a nicer grave, but it cost too much. When we buried him, the flowers were beautiful. Sad but beautiful, with so many colors. We really should change the flowers soon. Don't you think, Teresa?" Luis's eyes are tearing up.

"Yes," Teresa says. "We can go into town after this, and I'll buy some new ones to place here." Teresa begins to cry softly. I make my way back to Angela's side, wanting to let them grieve in peace.

Angela has finished praying and is discussing her future plans with Enrique. "When I die, I want to be buried over there," she says, pointing toward the top of the hill. "You have to make sure I get a nice spot, up high so I can look out over the town."

Enrique waves his hand to shush her. "Mamá, you're too young to already be talking about this. We'll worry about it later."

"One never knows, *mi hijito,* when the time will come. Look at what happened to *pobre* Adolfo. One never knows what God has planned for us." She repeats one of her favorite phrases: *"Dios es grande y poderoso."*

After visiting the cemetery, Enrique, Abram, and I head north to see Juana's mother, Doña Luisa. She lives in Santa Ana Coatepec, a town near the large city of Atlixco—where José is from—which is famous for its flowers as well as a substantial maquiladora industry. Though less than forty miles north of Chinantla, the air is cooler and the yellow land has turned green, and as we make a right from the highway to enter Santa Ana we pass over a stream.

Juana had struggled over whether to permit Abram to see his grandmother (his grandfather had passed away many years ago). Juana herself hadn't seen her mother since she left for Brooklyn in 1984, but on each of Enrique's trips to visit Angela he had stopped off in Santa Ana, bringing presents and money. His reports back to Juana were discouraging: Doña Luisa was drinking, heavily. Several times she stayed up all night, first drinking beer and then moving on to hard alcohol, and even the much larger Enrique had a hard time keeping up. His assessment was pessimistic: "If she doesn't slow down, she'll be dead soon."

Juana wasn't a drinker, but she was afraid for Abram. His father had been a drunk, and with Doña Luisa's drinking problem, her son was at a high risk for alcoholism. Abram had told me that he had tried beer only two or three times, and that he hadn't liked the experience. But Juana was worried that Abram would either be ashamed of his grandmother or perhaps start to think that drinking was okay, so after hearing that Abram was actually interested in traveling with us to Mexico, she had been conflicted. Eventually, however, Juana agreed with Enrique, who believed it was important for Abram to see his grandmother before she passed away, drinking problem and all. "She is his family," Enrique told her. "That is the most important thing to remember."

One only need travel along the road leading from the highway into Santa Ana to know that the town isn't sharing in the same prosperity as Chinantla. Even in Angel's truck, Enrique is forced to proceed slowly around the large rocks and rough terrain of the dirt road, and where Chinantla teems with people on the streets and patronizing various local businesses, not a soul nor a store is in sight as we tour the town. It feels like what I had anticipated finding in Chinantla: a depressed, and depressing, ghost town.

I expected to find Doña Luisa living in a dirty shack of wood and aluminum, or an adobe hut like that of Luis and Teresa. Enrique had told Abram many tales about the hardscrabble life of poverty that his grandmother was forced to endure—usually when the two were arguing about his school attendance—so I am surprised when we park in front of a cement house and walk along a dirt path to its rear courtyard, which contains a large plot of land with many farm animals and various fruit and vegetable plants. Hunched over at a small folding table in the courtyard is an old, dark-skinned man with a straw hat on his head that reads "Texas Rodeo." At first he doesn't notice our presence, and continues to swing his flyswatter, mashing insects into the table. Each swing kills several bugs, which he flicks off the table with a long fingernail, but it is an endless task: there are flies everywhere. The result of his labor is a growing semi-circle of dead flies surrounding the table on the ground, but the table itself remains full of live flies walking about, unperturbed.

"Don Candido!" Enrique calls out. "*Buenas tardes.*" Don Candido looks up, momentarily confused, and then smiles once he recognizes Enrique.

"Luisa! ¡*Venga!*" the man yells. Doña Luisa steps out of a single room in the yard—it is obviously Doña Luisa, because she looks exactly like Juana, only more weathered and stooped—and shuffles over to greet us.

"Doña Luisa, this is your grandson Abram," Enrique says, pushing Abram forward.

Doña Luisa takes a look at Abram, crosses her heart, and places her hands on his shoulders, staring directly into his eyes. Abram fidgets and glances over at me, not sure what to do. "Hola," he eventually says. Doña Luisa steps back and gives Abram a thorough looking over, doing a complete circle.

"*Tan grande, y gordo,*" she says with a laugh. So big and fat. "I never thought I would see my grandson, but here he is, in my own home."

"He says he might want to stay here to live," Enrique says. "You know, learn how to farm. He could lose some weight and see how real Mexicans live." Abram smiles awkwardly, shaking his head.

Doña Luisa apparently thinks Enrique is being serious. "*Perfecto.* We have an extra room where he could sleep!"

"Naw," Abram says, looking slightly concerned. "I don't want to live in Mexico. We're only here to visit."

"You don't have to make a decision now," Doña Luisa says. "You just arrived. And I didn't even know you were coming today! Let me go prepare lunch for you." Doña Luisa ignores Enrique's insistence that we aren't hungry, and disappears back into the room from which she emerged.

We join Don Candido, the insect assassin, at the table. On closer inspection, he has the deepest facial wrinkles I have ever seen, which threaten to swallow his eyes when he smiles. He turns out to be ninety-one years old, and to have spent two years living in New Jersey with one of his sons in the 1980s. Sometime after that he returned to Santa Ana—he was born in a house two blocks away—and met Doña Luisa, and they have been living together for a decade. He tells us that at last count there were six hundred people living in the town, and probably twice that number from Santa Ana living in New York.

On Enrique's instructions, Abram and I head out to the town's store to buy sodas and beer. When we return, the soup that Doña Luisa has prepared is ready, and we slurp up the meal while Doña

Luisa, Don Candido, and I crack open beers. I am halfway through the beer when Doña Luisa opens her second, which she polishes off several minutes later and then opens up a third.

After Doña Luisa has finished a number of beers—somewhere between six and eight—the subject turns to Juana. "How is my daughter and the little baby?" she asks. "Why doesn't she ever want to come visit us so we can see her and the other children?"

"She wants to come, but you've got to remember that right now she can't, because her paperwork still isn't fixed," Enrique answers. "We're going to get married when I return, so she'll be able to come to Mexico, but right now it isn't possible."

"But she never even sends money," Doña Luisa replies, looking both hurt and angry. "She's like my other children, getting paid in dollars in the U.S. but forgetting to send money home to her mother. They all say they will send money, but money never arrives."

"Honestly, it's not as easy as you think," says Enrique. "Life isn't like they say it is in the U.S. Not everyone makes a lot of money. Things there are expensive, and I know that if Juana had any money she would send it, but she doesn't. Up there, Mexicans do the work that pays the least, and there usually isn't any money left over after we pay rent, pay for diapers, pay for food."

"They pay in dollars!" Doña Luisa shouts, unconvinced and on the verge of tears, her lips trembling. Her eyes are red, glassy. "How can there not be enough money? Look at us, we have nothing except what we can eat here and what our children send home. And now they want to take away our home. Where will we go if we are kicked out?" Doña Luisa begins to sob. Abram looks at me, and I feel both sorry for him and confused—who was kicking Doña Luisa out, and why? Enrique puts his arms around her, telling her softly that they will be able to stay in their home, and that Juana will come to visit as soon as her paperwork is fixed. Eventually Doña Luisa gathers herself together and shuffles into the kitchen to prepare dinner.

"What is she talking about?" I ask Enrique. "About having to leave?"

"This land belongs to the daughter of Don Candido. She lives in New York, but now supposedly she wants to come back to Mexico, and they think she wants to take over the property."

"And what, she would just kick out her ninety-one-year-old dad?"

"No, I think she would wait until he dies. Doña Luisa is afraid he will die soon, and then the daughter will tell her to leave. That's one of the reasons she wants Juana to come back to Mexico."

"Juana wouldn't want to come back here, would she?" I ask. I had never heard Juana express even a slight desire to return to Mexico to live.

"No, of course not. But we don't have to tell Doña Luisa that."

Doña Luisa's complaint was a common one. The thinking ran like this: child moves north for better economic opportunities and to support the family; arrives and finds work, sending money home; eventually forgets to send money, stops making phone calls; and abandons the very people the child left to assist.

It was a hard narrative to counter. How does one explain to Doña Luisa, who has never left her home state, much less Mexico, that her daughter is earning a mere one dollar an hour in one of the most expensive cities in the country? That the homes are full of cockroaches and rats, that the work is hard? How to explain that life in El Norte, much like life in Mexico, can be ugly and unfair?

One evening, gathered under the shade of the tree in Natalia and Daniel's yard, Angela had expressed similar misgivings about her children, upset that her sons and daughters didn't send money more frequently. "It's easy to forget the parents who stay behind," she said.

"Mamá, it's not like that," Enrique told her. "You don't understand what it is like as an immigrant there. You have no idea how immigrants live there, how hard the life can be." Angela didn't look impressed.

"Tell her, Gabriel," Enrique implored. "Tell her about the bottle in the taxi. Tell her about how I keep a fucking bottle in the car so that I can piss inside without having to miss a call, so that I can bring home a little more money for my family. Tell her about the housing we live in, about the rent we pay, about sleeping in a car overnight so I didn't have to pay gas when we were living with Juan."

Angela looked at me. I only nodded my assent; Enrique was never one whom I felt needed anyone to speak for him. The disbelieving look on Angela's face remained.

Daniel put it another way. "The people you hear talk about the U.S. as a great place are the people who make it, who are successful and come back with money. But you don't hear about all the people who *don't* make it, because what are they going to come back to say? And if they want, they can just make stuff up—who would know the difference?" His comments reminded me of a high school reunion, when everyone returns to put on their best face—and some even rent a fancy car for the day to give the impression of success. Who would want to return home from several years abroad with only stories of exploitation and suffering, bitterness and unrealized dreams?

Angela had apparently heard enough success stories, and had certainly witnessed the results of dollars sent home, to believe that life in the United States was easy, or at least a lot easier than in Mexico. In some ways, of course, she was correct: the homes that her daughter Maria and sons Angel and Juan had built were made possible with earning from abroad. And the fiestas, the paved roads, the renovated churches, all were a result of remittances sent home. For parents who had never left Chinantla, it might indeed appear that when their children failed to send money, it was because they were blowing it on unnecessary items, that they had become rich and greedy.

But no one could call Juana and Enrique rich or greedy. "I think Daniel's right," I told Angela. "Everyone I know in New York City is working very long hours for low pay. Let's say you're working in construction. In New York you might make eight or ten dollars an hour, or eighty dollars a day. How much do you make doing construction here in Chinantla?"

"One hundred pesos a day," Daniel answered. "That's what everyone pays here."

"Okay, so you'll be making almost ten times the money in construction in New York that you could make here." Angela nodded in agreement. "But how much does rent cost here? How much do you have to pay for your house?"

Angela looked at me. "I pay three hundred pesos to the town each year."

"And how much do you pay for rent each month?" I asked Enrique.

"Right now, eleven hundred dollars."

"So he's making more money, but he also has to pay eleven thousand pesos each *month* just to live in a small apartment."

"*Once mil?*" Angela asked. "You don't have to pay once mil . . ." but her voice trailed off; she was no longer so confident.

"I know people who pay way more than Enrique," I said. "Once mil is nothing. That's why it's so hard to save any money living there. I haven't been able to save anything, and I don't even have any kids to take care of."

"That's because he's an alcoholic," Enrique explained to his mother. "He spends it all on beer." Daniel, beer bottle in hand, gave a toast to alcoholics, and we moved on to other, less serious matters.

Two days later Angela asked me over breakfast if she had heard right. "Eleven thousand pesos? For each month?" I nodded. "Why in God's name would anyone want to live there?" I shrugged and continued eating my bowl of beans and salsa.

The next morning we leave the home of Doña Luisa and Don Candido, but Enrique promises to return in several days to take her to a dentist in Atlixco. Most of her teeth have become rotten, and one has begun to dig into her gums, causing an infection that is spreading throughout her mouth and making it difficult to eat. Still, even with assurances that he will be returning, our departure is a sad affair. After hugging Enrique and Abram, Doña Luisa follows us to our truck, unsteady on her feet, and begins wailing as we pull away.

"Everyone always leaves us!" she cries. "No one wants to stay!" She continues shouting, but as we pull away I can't make out any other words.

I am in the front seat, feeling awful and exhausted. Abram and I had slept in the truck overnight, and it was cold and cramped. Twice during the night Doña Luisa opened the passenger-side door and wailed drunkenly into the cabin about how she had been abandoned, before being led away by Enrique. Both times she scares the shit out of me—then leaves me feeling thoroughly depressed— though Abram doesn't seem to wake up.

"Did she even go to sleep last night?" I ask.

"No. Her son came over at midnight," Enrique says. "They were up all night drinking whiskey."

I glance back at Abram, to see how he is handling the tense scene of his wailing and drunk grandmother. He has his headphones on, his face buried in the PlayStation. He doesn't look up.

CHAPTER 16

Crisis

DANIEL, ENRIQUE'S BROTHER-in-law, spent several years living in the city of Port Chester, in Upstate New York. He worked at a bakery during this time, alongside Enrique's older brother Juan, while Natalia put in shifts at a Laundromat. During this period Daniel and Natalia spoke Spanish at home and at work, though Daniel did pick up a few odd English sayings. His favorite, which he repeats incessantly when I am around, is "Let's go, big boy." At the bakery his boss would use this phrase to encourage him to work faster. So each time he wanted me to go for a ride with him in his taxi, or do him a favor, or have a beer with him, he would ask in the same way: "Let's go, big boy."

By nature Daniel is soft-spoken, quietly intelligent. At work he becomes louder and is the unofficial leader of the cabbies, the person who organizes the card games at the centro and usually buys the beer for everyone. He banters with his passengers as consistently as Enrique, and through these work-time conversations he knows most of Chinantla's secrets. In a small town with its requisite rumor mill and family feuds, Daniel remains on good terms with everyone. The president of Chinantla is a good friend; so is the biggest *coyote* of the region, the person responsible for maneuvering people successfully across the border and into New York.

Daniel and Natalia are model immigrants of sorts. When recently arrived Mexicans in Brooklyn would tell me about their long-term plans, they envisioned something approximating Daniel and Natalia's life. They would spend several years—five at the most—in the United States, saving money. Then they were going to return to their hometowns and use the money to build a new house. That, in their heads, was the end of their traveling. They would settle down for good in Mexico, stretch their U.S. dollars, and focus on raising their children.

Such plans were almost always discarded. Many times, saving money didn't prove as easy as advertised. Life was expensive in New York City; this was what had happened to Enrique, to some extent. Or even if the migrants did earn enough to build a house in Mexico, they found themselves wanting to stay in the city they had grown to appreciate, especially once they had children who were U.S. citizens. They would return to Mexico during fiestas and spend a week or two in their new houses, but then they would get the itch to return.

Daniel never had that itch. "You can earn more money in America, but it is too crowded, way too busy," he tells me one afternoon as we're lounging on the unfinished second floor of his house. Daniel and Antonio, a construction worker, have just finished laying down another round of cinder blocks, and both have beads of sweat on their brow as they sip Victoria beers. Enrique, who is on vacation and not looking to do any home improvement in the near future, is asleep in the hammock that hangs between two trees in the front yard, and is snoring loudly.

Most people in town have told me that the going rate for construction workers in Chinantla is one hundred pesos a day (about ten dollars), but Daniel is paying Antonio twice that—with free beers thrown in as well. He can afford to be generous, because as a cab driver Daniel has one of the most lucrative jobs available, earning fifteen hundred pesos a week. During fiesta weeks, when Chinantla fills up with visiting families from the United States, he often pulls in two thousand pesos.

In all, thirty-five-year-old Daniel tells me, he has crossed the border illegally three times—in 1990, 1995, and 1998. The first time, he and Natalia made it through a border checkpoint in Tijuana with fake green cards. The second and third trips, when Natalia stayed back in Port Chester, he crossed with coyotes into Arizona. "The second time I crossed *la linea* [the line, or border] it was fine, but the third trip was ugly," he says. During that trip Daniel's group ventured on foot into Arizona near the border city of Nogales. The coyotes were drunk and during the evening trek raped one of the women in the group. That's about all Daniel wants to say of the experience. That, and he's never going to make the journey again.

Antonio has his head cocked to one side, listening with special interest to Daniel's tale, which makes sense when he tells me he is planning on making the trip in the near future, hoping to eventually return to Port Chester. The last time he crossed was in the 1980s, and for that journey he sprinted across the border near Tijuana with a group of other hopeful migrants. "That's what I'm going to do this time, too," Antonio explains, "so I don't have to face the dangers in Arizona. You don't have to walk for miles and miles—it's harder to get lost."

"No, you can't do that now," Daniel says. He explains that hardly anyone crosses in Tijuana anymore, because the border security has been increased, and that everyone instead goes to Arizona.[*] Antonio considers this statement. Like many Mexicans, he's heard a number of tragic stories about people disappearing in the desert.

[*] Daniel is correct. Operation Gatekeeper, launched under Clinton in 1994, dramatically beefed up the border patrol presence in the Tijuana-San Diego corridor. The architects of Operation Gatekeeper predicted that migrants seeking to cross would be forced into inhospitable areas—east heading into Arizona. They were right: today, more migrants are now apprehended in Arizona than California, New Mexico, and Texas combined. They were also right in characterizing the terrain that would become popular for crossers as inhospitable: the deserts and mountains of Arizona are claiming hundreds of lives each year. No one, however, pretends that the number of would-be crossers has been slowed.

"Maybe I'll go to Tijuana first and see if I have any luck," he eventually decides. "If not, God willing, I'll try Arizona."

I ask Antonio why he has waited so long to return to the United States, and he picks up a hammer and waves it. "There's always work here, if you know how to do construction. Everyone wants a bigger house, or a new house. All the people who are in New York are building these houses, so there's enough work—even if they don't pay as much. That's why so many people come here."

Daniel nods. "Zambo isn't originally from here," he says, referring to Gilberto, the cabdriver whom we had played cards with several days ago. "He's from Oaxaca."

"Yeah, lots of people come from Oaxaca to Chinantla," Antonio adds. "In Oaxaca, they say, people make forty pesos a day. Why work for forty pesos when you could make one hundred here?"

Later that day I stop by the centro to talk with Zambo, whose nickname is stenciled across the back of his cab. He is wearing his usual baggy jeans and slightly mischievous smile, sipping on a Coke while waiting for customers. I explain what Daniel and Antonio said about Oaxaqueños.

"Oh yeah, there are lots of people from Oaxaca here. Most only come temporarily, to work in construction for a short while. But there are a few others like me who came to work and then decided to stay." Zambo goes on to tell me that he left his hometown of Cuatemo with his parents' blessing when he was eleven, because "there wasn't enough food to eat." He found work outside of Oaxaca City, picking coffee beans and earning between five and ten pesos a day. "I stayed there for three years, and even though the work was hard and they paid little, I still enjoyed it . . . because at night it could be so beautiful." After each day's work Zambo and the other laborers would lie down under the trees and relax, staring into the stars before falling asleep, only to rise when it was still dark out and do it all over again.

Eventually he moved to the state of Mexico, where he harvested tomatoes, oranges, mangoes, and sugar cane. One day, a man who was related to the boss asked Zambo if he would want to come work for him in Chinantla, caring for his goats. "I told him, sure, since he was offering me more than I was making at the time. I've been here ever since. Now I've got a wife and two kids; my wife is from here, and both my kids were born here." For the last eight years he's driven a cab, making more money than he ever dreamed possible.

As such, he's been able to wire larger amounts of money home to his parents. Even when he was earning less than a dollar a day, he sent whatever little he could afford each month back to Oaxaca. Now, as an established member of Chinantla's middle class, he felt good about really being able to support his parents, who were no longer working. "Yesterday, for example, I sent them six hundred pesos. When I'm earning more, I send more . . . but I always, always send them at least something every month."

Migration is a ubiquitous, unstoppable force. Even here—in a town that began the exodus of Mexicans to New York in the 1940s; where the elders speak of being abandoned; where there are probably more Chinantecos living north of the Rio Grande than in the town itself; where nearly all of the infrastructure development is thanks to money sent back from the United States—people are arriving to work, and sending their own intra-country remittances. Listening to Zambo, who left his parents to officially join the workforce at only eleven years of age, it's hard to believe that fences and motion sensors—no matter how fortified or technologically advanced—stand a chance when up against the same age-old phenomena that compelled Moses to pick up his stakes and move on.

That evening, when I return to Angela's house, I immediately sense that something is wrong. Though she is always chattering and accusing me of being late for some nonexistent event, when I walk through the door Angela doesn't even say hello. Indeed, we have a problem. A big problem.

First of all, several hours ago, while Enrique was still enjoying a late afternoon nap in the hammock, Angela walked to the plaza of Piaxtla to purchase tortillas. En route she saw Angel and Leticia. They were smiling and talking to someone, and Angela became very angry. She turned around and stormed over to her daughter's house, entering the kitchen and yelling about "Angel and his bitch," then downing a beer quickly. "I don't want that bitch around here anymore!" she yelled. "They both need to get out!"

Second, after being woken up by his screaming mother, Enrique became upset as well—because of both the state of his mother and the idea that we would have to leave so soon. Although he hasn't had a drink in more than two years, he also gulps down a Victoria while trying to calm Angela and convince her that we should stay. She doesn't agree.

Third, Enrique has agreed that we will be leaving in two days. "So get everything done that you need to tomorrow," he says after filling me in on the recent developments. "Because we've got to get out of here."

I listen to everything Enrique says, nodding slightly—not agreeing exactly, only acknowledging that I comprehend his story. "We've got to get out of here," he repeats, louder. "I asked Angela if everything was okay. I asked if we could bring Angel and she said yes! . . . Why would she say yes if she really meant no? . . . If she had said no we would have come alone, there wouldn't have been any problems! . . . Why the fuck does Angel have to walk around town like an asshole? . . . This is all Angel's fault!" I again nod slightly at each verbal explosion, thinking this the safest bet (I was the person, after all, who advertised our Mexico trip to Angel in the first place, and I'd rather not find my name included in his agitated rundown).

By now Angela is squeezing pig fat from a Ziploc bag over a pot of rice on the stove, having listened to her son without comment. "Sit down," she tells us both. "Enough about this, it's time to eat. It would be okay for you to stay without Angel, but Angel has to leave—he has to leave. But enough. Sit down. Sit! The food's almost ready."

"Mamá, I'm not hungry right now," Enrique says. "All of this is making me sick. I have to go over to Natalia's and help them with their car, anyway." Enrique hops down the stairs and into Angel's truck, reversing hard out of the dirt driveway and disappearing behind a dust cloud of his own creation.

There's no way, of course, that I'm going to simply accept Enrique's proposal without a fight. While nodding, here is what I was thinking: *That's the most idiotic plan I've ever fucking heard.*

A quick consultation of an atlas was all the proof I needed. We had spent three practically sleepless days on the road, racing to get here. New York, New Jersey, Maryland, Virginia, North Carolina, South Carolina, Georgia, Alabama, Mississippi, Louisiana, Texas. After Texas came Mexico: Tamaulipas, Nuevo León, San Luis Potosí, Guanajuato, Querétaro, México, Morelos, Puebla. We'd been in Chinantla not yet ten days, and I had dozens of additional people I wanted to interview, another state to visit (Guerrero), as well as some background research for a magazine article that I was contracted to complete. The idea of turning around and spending another three days in the cramped truck was ridiculous, sadistic. And what would I do back in Brooklyn? I had set aside this time specifically to travel and write, not sit around in my apartment. If anything, as soon as we got back to Brooklyn I would probably have to pool all of my money together and purchase the cheapest plane ticket possible to Mexico City, then catch a bus to Puebla, than another to Chinantla. Idiotic.

As I ate dinner my mind whirled unhappily with such thoughts. On the margins of my mental meanderings, I wondered if I was being a self-centered brat. Should I be standing in solidarity with my friend, eager to help out in whatever way possible? Or encouraging our departure for the mental health of Angela, who at her age definitely didn't need additional stress?

After dinner I walk to the centro to call my girlfriend for consultation, saying I might end up back in Brooklyn sooner than anticipated. I stupidly think this will make her happy. Instead, she is adamantly opposed to the notion, telling me that it makes no sense to cut my trip short simply because of family issues. "You've been planning this trip to Mexico for ages," she says, which is true. "You quit your job for this," she adds—also true. "I'll be very, very upset if you come back now."

Okay, I figure, that settles it. Better to give them a bunch of money for gas and send them along their way. When I get back to the house Enrique is still out. I'm very nervous about suggesting to Enrique that I won't come along, so I figure a couple of trial runs will shore up my confidence.

"Angela, I think I might want to stay here in Mexico for a couple more weeks and then catch a flight home. Would it be okay if I stayed here and kept you company a little longer, after they leave?" Angela tells me that of course it would be fine. I head into one of the bedrooms, where Abram is playing his portable PlayStation.

"Abram, what do you think Enrique would say if I decided to stay here and not go back with you guys?" Abram looks up.

"Are you serious?"

"Yeah, I think so."

"Oh man. He'll be *pissed*," he warns. "When Enrique gets this way it's bad. You've never seen him really, really mad. He'll have to drive the whole way on his own. I wouldn't do it. He'll probably never talk to you again."

Enrique gets home around 10:00 p.m. Angela and I are seated in the kitchen, eating baked pumpkin seeds. Without saying hello, Enrique plops down on the floor, leaning his back against the wall. Though he looks exhausted, and in no mood for more drama, I feel like it's now or never.

"I was thinking," I start, pausing to take a deep breath. Enrique looks up. "I really need to be here for a while longer in order to do all of my research. This is the time I have set aside to travel and write, and if I leave with you guys now, I will just turn around when we get to Brooklyn and have to fly back here, which will leave me broke. I mean, I quit my job at PACC in order to come here." I was looking for a nod from Enrique, but he simply stares at me. "I think I'll stay back here and pay you for the gas to return. Then I can take a bus or a plane to get back to Brooklyn. What do you think about that?"

A switch flips in Enrique; he suddenly doesn't look the least bit tired. "Fine, that's fine," Enrique says, eyes ablaze. "What do I think? Who the fuck will drive? Angel can't see anything. I'll be the one driving all the way, fucking alone with that asshole. Everything would be tranquilo here if you hadn't mentioned to him that we were going to Mexico! We'd be able to stay here as long as we wanted; I could take you around to see all the people you need to see. But for some fucking reason you had to tell Angel that we were going. I don't know why the fuck you had to tell Angel! Now, after you caused the problem, you want to give it all to me and stay here? Fine. I'll drive the whole fucking way by myself! Good fucking plan!"

That didn't go so well. I leave the kitchen and walk into my bedroom, shutting the door behind me.

When I walk into the kitchen the following morning, Enrique is lying on his back on the floor with his eyes closed, holding his belly with his hands. I look at Angela, who is heating water. She tells me she is preparing a traditional tea to cure an upset stomach.

"I didn't sleep at all last night," Enrique says to no one in particular. "Too much stress with all this shit from Angela, and all your bullshit, güero."

I am relieved that Enrique is still speaking to me. As Angela continues to watch over the water on the stove, I speak to Enrique in English so that his mother doesn't understand.

"Look, I think we should be able to fix this. It's completely stupid for us to turn around already and go back. I think I should go and talk to Angel, explain what happened. If we can just make sure he isn't around for Angela to bump into, we shouldn't have anymore problems. Right?"

"The only reason she got upset is because she saw Angel. But you're not going to be able to talk to him. Forget that. He's more stubborn than Angela. You go over and try to talk to him, he'll just get real pissed off. You saw how he was with the cell phone. You can't talk to him about anything."

"So what do we do?"

"We need to think like organizers. Angela is the target. She is the only one who could change her mind. I have tried talking to her, but she isn't listening to me. The best thing is for you to speak with her. Tell her that you need to stay longer for your work. Then, whenever you go somewhere, you can take her along so she won't have to see Angel. That is the only problem. As long as she doesn't see Angel she is fine." Enrique sits up slowly and takes the tea that

Angela is offering. It's a good ten feet away from me, but the smell is strong, acrid. He takes a small sip.

"Uuhhaarg. This shit is bitter." Angela laughs at her son's grunt and pours a cup for herself, taking a healthy gulp without visible pain.

"Angela," I say in my most pleasant voice.

"*¿Qué?* You want some tea, too?"

"Ah, no. I was just thinking. So Enrique told me all about what happened yesterday with Angel."

"Pinche Angel, he brings his bitch here to my home, right in front of my face, chinga su madre—"

"Right, that was what Enrique was telling me. But I was thinking. You know that we came a long way by car to visit—"

"I told Enrique, if it was only him and you, güero, you could stay forever. I told him. But pinche Angel, chinga su madre, pinche—"

"Right, I know." I realize that I'm going to have to talk fast to avoid being interrupted again. "So what I was thinking is that maybe what would be best . . . well, here's my plan. I need to stay here for a while longer, because I'm working on this book. But if I don't go back with Enrique, then he would have to drive the whole way, because pinche Angel doesn't know how to drive. So maybe what we could do . . . the problem is, you shouldn't have to see Angel, right?"

"Sí, güero, it's no good. I don't want to see Angel and his *puta*—"

"So I was thinking that we could hang out, me and you. You know, so you don't have to worry about running into Angel. Plus, you don't really want Enrique to leave so soon, do you? He might not be able to come back for a while, you know. . . ."

I'm being a manipulative bastard; I'm desperate. Angela considers what I'm saying. "Güero, as long as I don't see Angel then I guess it's okay. But if I see him again, then—"

"No, we'll make sure he stays away from you," I promise.

"I'll take him in his truck out of town," Enrique offers. "He said he still wants to go to Puebla to shop for things, and to go to Guerrero to visit one of his brothers. We can make sure that he stays away."

"Sí, sí, like I said, I just don't want to see him anymore." Angela turns around and heads back to the stove. Enrique has a huge grin on his face, and offers his hand. We shake.

"Güero, you're a good friend," he says in English. "But honestly, after yesterday I was thinking I wasn't going to ever speak to you again. Let me tell you, I got so fucking mad."

"Yeah, I noticed. It's crazy how much pain Angel still causes for Angela. You'd think they broke up last week. And it not like their relationship was ever all that healthy."

"You don't understand how Mexicans like Angela think. We aren't always logical." He grins again. "Especially my family. We've got a lot of *coraje* [hot-bloodedness, anger], and we're stubborn."

"That's not good for you," I reply. Now I'm smiling broadly as well. "Got to learn to stay calm, like me."

"Fuck you." He laughs. Crisis averted.

CHAPTER 17

We Are Also Abandoned

FOR THE NEXT few days I accompany Angela on various trips. We go to the city of *Acatlán* to buy medicine and fruit. Daniel drives us to a northern town whose name I never catch, where, as tradition dictates, Angela asks a family for permission for one of her grandsons to marry their daughter, which is granted (both children live in Brooklyn). We travel with Enrique and Abram to Santa Ana Coatepec so that she can visit with Doña Luisa, who has four of her teeth extracted in the nearby city of Atlixco. Doña Luisa enjoys Angela's company and doesn't drink at all during our stay (the dentist has ordered her to stay away from alcohol while on the painkillers she has prescribed).

Now, with Angela ready to stay home, it's time to shift tactics, and it becomes Enrique's responsibility to make sure Angel is away and occupied. They make plans to visit brothers, go shopping in the expansive markets of Tlaxcala, and show Leticia various tourist sites. So now it's my chance to visit Cacalutla, where Maria's mother and sister live.

When I told Maria I would be traveling to Mexico, she had asked me to pay her family a visit to let them know everything was going well in Brooklyn. As she spoke, however, I sensed she didn't actually have much faith that I would make the journey. "Cacalutla isn't that far away from Chinantla, and if you look on a map it seems close." But looks were deceiving, she warned. "The town is very small, and even lots of people who live nearby don't know it exists, because it is so remote. If you do go, everyone will look at you like you're crazy, because they never see any whites all the way out there."

Indeed, no one in Chinantla that I speak to has heard of Cacalutla. I do learn, however, that buses for Jilotepec, which Maria had said was close to Cacalutla, leave every morning from the bus stop on the southern end of Chinantla, near the cemetery. So on the first day that Enrique, Angel, and Leticia have scheduled for sightseeing, I rise early and wait alone on a bench below an overhang, waiting for the bus.

After twenty minutes a small white van approaches, a vehicle that in these parts is called a *combi*. I hop in, pay the fare, and take a window seat. As we pass the cemetery I look out the window and then take out my lone article of navigational information, a torn piece of paper that Maria had given me. It contains two bits of scribbled information, which I reread: "*Mi mamá se llama Magdalena, y ella vive en Cacalutla.*" With no phones in the town, this is all I have to go on, and while the combi maneuvers expertly along the winding highway, I feel like a detective, or a participant in a transnational scavenger hunt. I am looking for someone who doesn't know me, doesn't know I am coming, doesn't even know I exist.

Cacalutla is in the state of Guerrero, which borders Puebla to the west. For an hour the bouncy combi rattles southwest along Highway 92, and we arrive in Tulcingo del Valle before 10:00 a.m. At Tulcingo I transfer to another combi going to Jilotepec, which is located just across the state line in Guerrero. From there, Maria had told me, it was possible to arrive at Cacalutla by foot, though she had also warned me that locals had stopped walking the path after

Timoteo's sister had been raped and killed. "Better to take a taxi," she argued. But when after a short drive I find myself in Jilotepec, the town is much smaller than its font size would suggest on my map. There are no taxis and no people, save for an old woman sitting on a folding chair beneath the shade of a large tree across Jilotepec's main street

"Could you please tell me how to get to Cacalutla?" I ask the woman.

She points back toward the highway. "Over there. Take the path where the sign is." I thank her, begin to walk away, then turn around.

"And it's possible to walk there, right?" I shout.

"*Claro*. It's only maybe ten, fifteen minutes," she calls to me.

I return to Highway 92 and this time notice a rusty and nearly illegible sign partially covered by foliage that reads CACALUTLA with an arrow pointing to the left. I cross the highway and begin walking. Though it is still early, I am quickly drenched in sweat. Several hundred feet from the highway, on the right side of the path, I pass a small cement monument. Getting closer, I can read the name on a cement slab in front of the shrine: Reyna Delgado Balbuena. Timoteo's sister. Underneath her name, in Spanish, it reads: "Died on the 29th of October, 2000. Made on November 7th." The words look like they have been scrawled with a twig in the wet cement, and lines are drawn with the same instrument below the words, in order to keep them relatively straight. Inside the shrine behind the slab are a statue of the Virgin of Guadalupe, a cross, and two empty jugs of wine. Several candles surround the cross, and one of them is currently burning.

From the monument the path slopes upward, and as I head farther into the countryside insects begin to hum loudly, sounding like the background noise of a poorly made audio recording. After another twenty minutes of walking I come across a dumpsite on the left side of the road, where several dogs are scavenging for sustenance amid empty plastic bottles and discarded food containers. When I pass, one black mutt looks up and barks several times, then begins to walk toward me, growling. I pick up a rock and he scurries back into the refuse.

An hour later, on the same path, I begin to wonder if I am heading in the right direction. I've been maintaining a fairly rapid clip, but still haven't passed anyone—either on foot or in a car—and by now I have finished the small bottle of water I had brought along. From the path the surrounding hills appear verdant; upon seeing a photograph of the terrain, a person would insist that the temperature couldn't be much higher than eighty degrees. Yet as I am beginning to learn, what looks green from a distance is often only desert camouflage, a mirage; get closer, and the green bristles reveal thirsty, dry ground.

Forty-five minutes of solitary walking later, I pass another monument to a fallen Mexican, this time for a man named Fausto Garcia. Though I had laughed off Maria's concern about the safety of the path, after two hours of walking in silence, and unsure about whether I am anywhere near my destination, my mind begins to conjure up less-than-pleasant scenarios. Two people murdered on one path; a white man walking alone with a digital camera and who-knows-how-much money; no one within screaming distance; rural Mexican bandits hiding in the hills, waiting months for what has finally arrived—it is stupid, probably, but I pick up the pace and start casting glances behind me.

Not too far after the second monument the hills widen into a valley, where several couples are farming. I call out to a stooped man, who tells me in a friendly voice that Cacalutla is just around the bend. I thank him and continue on, feeling the shame that comes with being a paranoid gringo, but also relieved.

The first house I come to reminds me that I am not in Chinantla anymore. Instead of cement it is made of wood and has a tin roof; with walls made of sticks it looks like nothing a strong gust of wind couldn't easily topple. In front of the house, two women are walking along a field, dropping seeds into the ground while shading themselves from the sun with umbrellas. Both look up when I pass, and we wave shyly at each other.

Farther up the path is the Vicente Guerrero grade school, a green and blue building with seven classrooms. Painted along one of its walls is a slogan: "*Cuesta mucho educar a un hombre, pero cuesta mas no educarlo.*" (It costs a lot to educate a man, but even more to not educate him.) In front of the classrooms is a basketball court, and though both backboards are missing rims, each has a carefully painted logo of Michael Jordan dunking a ball. Behind the classrooms is a soccer field of dirt, with two goalposts that are missing nets.

Past the school the town begins to take form, and I ask a woman seated in the doorway of her cement home if she knows where Magdalena lives. She looks through me for a moment, squinting, then without speaking points to the house next door. I thank her, walk up to the house, and knock. A dark-skinned man wearing a straw hat answers the door. He looks at me curiously, but doesn't say anything. I explain that I am a friend of Maria's from Brooklyn and am looking for Magdalena. He remains at the front door, still staring at me in silence.

"Is this the house of Magdalena?" I ask, realizing I might be at the wrong place entirely. He nods. "Do you think you could get her?" I ask. I repeat that I am a friend of Maria's from Brooklyn.

"Oh, you mean Cristina," he says, now smiling. His lips part, exposing mostly gums.

"Yes, Cristina." I don't know a Cristina from Cacalutla, but I've already caused this man enough confusion. He shuts the door gently, and when it opens a moment later there is a stout woman standing in front of me. I again begin to tell my story, which she interrupts.

"Come in, come in!" she exclaims. "Cristina didn't tell me that you would be coming, but come in. The place is a bit of a mess right now, because we're getting ready to plant our fields." I tell her that it can't be any worse than my apartment, and we settle down in the front room, surrounded by bags of fertilizer.

"How did you find your way here?" I pull out my trusty sheet of paper and tell her that Maria gave me the rough directions. "Is Maria the same person as Cristina?" I ask.

"Maria is Cristina's middle name," she says. "And how do you know her?"

"Well, I work with people in Brooklyn who have housing problems, so with all the things that Maria has been through, we started to work together." Magdalena looks at me blankly.

"*¿Qué problemas?*" It turns out that Magdalena hasn't heard anything about the poisoning of Reyna and Gary, so I spend ten minutes describing what has happened—the lead poisoning, the abandonment by her landlord, the recently filed lawsuit. As I recount the story, Magdalena nods with each new wrinkle of injustice. Once I have finished she fetches us each a soda and settles back into her chair.

"*Estamos abandonados también,*" she says. We are also abandoned. "Just like how her landlord left her alone, here the government leaves us to do everything by ourselves. They always say they have plans to make things better, but it's just talk. Talk, talk, talk. Last week, a man came to say they were going to be paving our roads, but I don't believe him. You saw how the road into town is all dirt and rocks, right? It's been like that forever. And another person said they were going to be installing a phone in the *centro*, so that we can make calls with phone cards. They've been saying that for a long time, too. The different political parties come and promise this, promise that. But they all only come into the *pueblo* when they are looking for votes. After that you never see them again. The only people who are actually making things better are those who go north. Everything you see here, it's all because people are sending money from *Nueva York.*"

Magdalena takes a swig of her Pepsi.

"Do you like it here? I'm sure you do. Even when it's dry it's beautiful. Here, you don't have to worry about breathing dirty air or eating bad food. How many cars have you heard pass by the house since we sat down? None. It's peaceful here, and quiet. I've seen pictures of New York on the television, and it looks crazy. Like everyone running around all day, everyone in a rush and wearing suits, right? Even if the government ignores us here, at least we know how to survive. We can farm and cook and go into Tulcingo to sell food. That's all we really need, you know. Here I was born, and it's here that I will die. I'm not saying I wouldn't want to visit New York someday, to see Maria and Timoteo and their kids. Where would I get the money for that, though?"

This is how Magdalena talks—long, pause-free paragraphs, raising questions that have no time to be answered. "Did Maria tell you about Diega and Favian? Diega is my other daughter, and Favian is one of my grandchildren. Pobre Favian has leukemia. That's where Diega and Favian are right now, in Puebla at the hospital. She has to go there every eight days for the therapy. Imagine having to take care of her son all alone! It's because her husband left her and is with another woman now. He left supposedly to improve the family and earn money, but that is what they all say. I guess you could say there has been a lot of abandonment around here." She smiles ruefully at this last comment, and as we both sip our ice-cold sodas, without much prompting she begins to explain her history.

Magdalena was born fifty-four years ago in a small gathering of homes in the hills surrounding Cacalutla—like Enrique, her family lived even beyond the most remote pueblo, areas where next to nothing has changed for generations. After a strenuous labor that lasted through the night, her mother gave birth at noon, but died several hours later from the loss of blood. Her father, not wanting to care for Magdalena alone, dropped her off at the house of an aunt in Cacalutla, who Magdalena grew to know as mamá. She never met her father.

Like most of the children in Cacalutla, she attended grade school only briefly. "Back then there was only one teacher for the town, and seventy or eighty students—not like now, when all the parents take their kids north. Imagine trying to learn with that many kids of all different ages . . . impossible!" After two years of enjoyable chaos, at the age of eight she began to work in the fields. "Once you were old enough to walk to the fields, you were ready to work" is how she explains the unwritten laws of the town.

Since then, Magdalena—like everyone else who has ever lived in Cacalutla—has planted crops to survive. "Here, there isn't any other work. Year after year we plant beans, corn, chile, peanuts, and squash. If you live here, you farm."

In 1972, when she was twenty-one years old, Magdalena gave birth to Maria, and then two years later to her second daughter, Diega. Shortly after Diega's birth, the father left Magdalena, and she declined to say anything more about him, preferring to let him fade away much like her own father. "If they aren't around and don't raise their own kids, they aren't really fathers," she explains. To this day, neither Maria nor Diega knows who their biological father is; Magdalena has refused to tell them even his first name. Though Cacalutla is a small town, making secrets hard to keep, Magdalena apparently ordered enough people to stay quiet. Diega and Maria will both tell me later that despite their efforts they do not know the identity of their biological father.

Shortly after Diega's birth, Magdalena married a man named Eduardo. It was a happy, if unusual, marriage. On the day of their wedding Magdalena was twenty-four; Eduardo sixty-five. Yet despite the difference in age, they remained together until Eduardo's death in 1995. In fact, for Magdalena, his age was the key to their success. "Older men are more stable. They are responsible. Younger men have too much coraje. They might drink too much or run away with another woman. But Eduardo wasn't like that at all." Magdalena was especially happy to have found a worthy man so that Maria and Diega could be raised with a father figure around, something she herself had been denied.

As children, Maria and Diega attended the same grade school as Magdalena, and once they had graduated from sixth grade they began working in the fields. As in Cuicatlán, education in Cacalutla stopped after primary school. "There was a high school in Tulcingo, but it was too expensive. Yes, you could go to school for free, but you had to pay for transportation every day, and then the books and supplies, which we didn't have money for," Magdalena says, echoing the earlier statements made by Angela.

I was especially curious about the details of Maria's departure. Had Magdalena encouraged her eldest daughter to head north in order to break free from a life of farming? Was it a move she supported in order to help provide for the family? And if so, why hadn't Diega followed her sister?

"Were you glad when Maria told you she wanted to leave Cacalutla?" I ask.

Magdalena looks at me and begins to chuckle. "Well, first of all, I don't know what Maria has told you about that. . . . Maria didn't *ask* me to leave. When she was sixteen she went to bed one night, in the same room as Diega. When we woke up, she was gone. Maria and Timoteo left together for New York in secret, without telling anyone in the family. I only heard about it because a day later Timoteo's mother came over and explained what had happened. Then a few months later I received a letter from them, saying they had arrived safely in Brooklyn and were looking for work. What could I do?" she asks, shrugging. "She was an adult, so she can make her own decisions."

After an hour of conversation Magdalena invites me to have lunch, and I follow her to the backyard, where she introduces me to Don Pedro, the man who answered the door and who is now living with Magdalena. As Magdalena prepares corn tortillas by hand, Don Pedro sorts through dried corn kernels that are in a storage hut made of mud and sticks. The hut, nearly ten feet tall, is called a *troja,* and Don Pedro tells me that each family in town has one, where corn is kept for future use. "Since the rainy season will begin soon, we are getting ready to plant the *milpa,* so I'm selecting the best seeds now," he tells me in his deep voice, looking pleased to share normally banal information with a curious stranger. He picks out a few large kernels and holds them up for inspection, then gives me a tour of the backyard, showing me where he has recently planted sesame and squash, as well as a large *platano* tree that he planted years ago.

During lunch Magdalena turns on the radio, and we listen to a news program called "The Voice of the Mountains," which broadcasts in Spanish and two other indigenous dialects. "All together there are seven languages spoken in the area," Magdalena says. "But we only know Spanish here. It's neat. You never know what language you are going to hear when you turn on the radio."

After lunch I mention that I ought to be leaving, since it is getting late and the last combi from Tulcingo to Chinantla will be leaving soon. Before leaving I ask if it would be possible for me to return on a day when they would be planting up in the field, which Magdalena has told me is an hour away by donkey. "Yes, of course," she replies. "We're going to be planting all next week. You can come any day you want. Just make sure to get here early, because we leave by 8:00 a.m." I promise to return and say good-bye, catching a ride with a group of men in a truck who are heading into Jilotepec to buy food for an upcoming wedding.

The following week, when I know that Enrique and Angel are away visiting relatives, I arrive in Tulcingo at dusk and check into a motel; in order to arrive at Cacalutla by 8:00 a.m. I figure I need to already be in Tulcingo the night before. Unfortunately, however, a family of mosquitoes has also checked into my room, and I sleep fitfully until the early morning hours, slapping my ears and scratching at rising welts on my forehead. Finally falling asleep around 4:00 a.m., I wake a sweaty and itchy mess at 10:00 a.m., many hours later than planned. I take a cold shower, catch a combi to Jilotepec, and arrive at Magdalena's house at noon. As promised, no one is home.

"Hola!" I call out toward her neighbor's home, to a shirtless man leaning against the doorway. "Do you know where Magdalena is?"

"Of course I know. She's planting."

"Do you know where her field is? I'm supposed to be planting with her, but I'm late."

The man looks me over, amused. I probably do look pretty funny, I realize, with my sunburned face and red bites covering my forehead and cheeks.

"*I* know where it is, but you won't be able to find it. It's a long way from here, up over the hills behind you. Better to wait until she gets back, or you'll get lost. It's too far to walk." I explain that my stomach is too big for my liking, and that a long walk will do me some good, but he again tells me that it would be too difficult a hike for me. "People go up there on *burro*. Better to wait here."

I again insist that I need the exercise, and he finally seems to realize there's no way I'm going to just sit around waiting, so he agrees to draw me a map. I hand him my notebook and a pen, and as he draws he talks me through the hike. "First you go left on this road here, and then you make a right at the first little hill, then a left at the green house, and then where the smaller church is—not the big church, the small church—you follow the ravine and go left at the first large tree that is behind . . ." I quickly lose track of what he is saying and instead focus my attention on the large pig that has waddled up and fallen asleep at my feet. After several more minutes of his direction chatter he hands me back my notebook.

"There, that should be all you need," he says. I look down at the map. Expecting a long list of landmarks after his thorough oral directions, I am surprised to see only one long and windy line, beginning in the lower left-hand corner of the sheet and ending in the upper right-hand corner. "As long as you stick to this path," he says, pointing out the line in case I am confused, "you'll get there fine." He traces the line with his finger for emphasis. "But be sure not to go off on any of the smaller paths," he reminds me, tapping the sole path. "*This* is the one you want."

It takes me thirty minutes just to get out of the town. For some reason, perhaps to honor the man's labor, I continue to pull out the notebook at each confusing intersection and consult with the line he has drawn, but it has little effect. Luckily, people relaxing in their doorways see me pondering my location and point me along the correct route, and eventually I am far above the town, convinced by the large amounts of donkey shit underfoot that I am finally on *the* path. For several hours I walk along, my only company being remarkably large iguanas scurrying along the path, until I run into a small boy with a herd of goats, who tells me that the field I am looking for is nearby. Soon I am at an intersection where the path I am on meets a dirt road, and following the boy's advice, I make a right. Ten minutes later I see a field to my left, where several people are working. After four hours, I have made it.

In the middle of the expansive field is a large *huamuchil* tree—taller than anything within sight—and beneath its shade sit two boys. As I turn off the path and head through the field the four farmers stop planting and turn to stare at me as if I were a desert apparition. As I get closer I recognize Magdalena and Don Pedro, who both wave. When I am within earshot, Magdalena calls out a hello and points at the third woman and a young boy. "This is my *hija* Diega!" she shouts. "Maria's sister! And that's her oldest son, Carmelo!"

I approach Diega, who is both taller and thicker than Maria, and she puts down the bucket of seeds she is holding to shake my hand. "How did you find us?" she asks.

"I asked for directions."

"Ha! They must have thought you were crazy! Who did you ask?"

"Your neighbor. Some other people. A small kid. Pretty much everyone."

"You're probably tired," Magdalena says. "You can go say hello to Davey and Favian if you want, rest for a bit under the tree. Those are my two other grandkids." I walk over to the tree and take a seat next to the boys.

"Hola," I say. Both boys laugh. "What are your names?"

The smaller of the two suddenly stands up and sprints around the tree. "I'm Davey!" he yells. "And I am a singer!" It's true. He begins belting out a tune as he runs circles around us. *"Todas las mujeres, me gustan todas! Todas las mujeres, me gustan todas!"* (All of the women, I like them all!)

"Davey, behave!" Diega yells, laughing. "Be polite to the güero!" He makes a final turn and then spills into Favian's lap, knocking him over.

"Davey!" Diega yells again. He brushes himself off and sits up quickly at attention, grinning.

Davey, who is six years old, asks me how to say a number of things in English. Cow (*vaca*); tree (*árbol*); field (campo); dog (*perro*); Davey (*Davey*). Favian, the eight-year-old with leukemia, listens without saying anything. After a few more minutes of fielding Davey's questions, the novelty of my presence wears off, and the two boys dash out onto the field to join the others, hopping along the berms that have been created by a plow, with the older boy, Favian, in the lead. There is nothing, to my mind, that suggests he is battling leukemia: he is at a healthy weight, has a full head of hair, and judging from the tumble he took when Davey landed on him, his brothers haven't been urged to treat him with any special care. I stand up and follow the boys into the field.

The rhythm of planting, especially when the scorching sun is hidden behind clouds, can be meditative. In my left hand is a bucket of seeds, given to me by Diega, which contains *calabasas* and *frijoles*—pumpkin seeds and beans. Carmelo, Diega, Magdalena, and Don Pedro each have their own bucket and their own row to sow, walking along the raised lines of tilled earth, straddling the miniature valley created by last week's plowing. Every several feet we drop exactly four seeds and then cover them with dirt with two swipes of our feet. "Five seeds doesn't give enough room for the plants to grow," Don Pedro tells me, "and three seeds won't give us enough food for the year."

For someone who has planted in these fields for their entire life, planting is probably just that—planting. But as I walk the lines and deposit my seeds, filling up the quiet by searching for an analogy, I settle upon a comparison: baseball. Like lazy afternoons of tossing the ball around, planting is an activity that seems to encourage long, meandering talks, and while Diega walks along her row to my left, she asks me about New York, gently correcting me when I toss the seeds too close to one another. "I have never been there, but I want to go one day, God willing," she says. "Favian would receive better treatment if we were there."

"He seems healthy to me," I say.

"Well, that is what they are saying now. Right now they say the sickness is almost all gone, after all the treatment. But we still have to go to the hospital every ten days for more tests." She mentions that they will be leaving first thing tomorrow morning, catching a bus from Tulcingo to Puebla. And she says sure, I can come along.

After an hour of planting, we gather together under the large tree and Magdalena pulls out a large container of corn soup, called *posoles,* along with tortillas and salsa. I open my pack and offer the kids some cookies, but none of them are interested. They are interested, however, in the bottles of Pepsi that Diega hands out. Davey and Favian are each handed their own, but begin to fight over a third bottle, playing tug-of-war. Diega snatches the bottle out of their hands and gives it to me. I dangle it above their heads, and they both leap, though neither comes close to grabbing it.

"You already have your bottle," I say. "Why do you need to drink so much?"

"They don't want to drink it," Diega tells me. "They want to win the game with the tops." Seeing that I am too tall, Davey and Favian begin to try to snatch each other's bottles.

"What kind of things can you win?" I ask them, stepping between the two to enforce a truce.

"Everything!" Davey yells.

"Yeah, everything!" Favian agrees enthusiastically.

"Like a new car?"

"No, like . . . ," Davey searches for the list of prizes he knows might be in store.

"Cookies!" Favian yells.

"Cookies!" Davey yells. The two race away, Favian in hot pursuit of Davey. Meanwhile, I sit down beneath the tree, take a long sip of the Pepsi, and have a cookie. Carmelo sits down next to me, and between gulps of soup I learn he will be starting fifth grade next year and goes to the school I passed entering the town. After sixth grade, he says, he won't continue on to Tulcingo.

"That's all the school they have here. When I'm done with the school, I can come out here all the time. I like it out here." I look at Diega, who is seated nearby.

"That's right," she says. "There is a high school in Tulcingo, but you have to buy the bus pass, and the books. How are we going to pay for that when all of my money is going for Favian?" This is a recurring, long-standing theme—bridging Angela's generation with Carmelo's. The first thing Mexico needs to do to get on track, it seems to me, is to start providing generous subsidies for children living in rural towns so that they can continue their education.

After lunch I help plant for another few hours, then make plans to meet Diega and Favian the next morning at the bus stop in Tulcingo del Valle. I say my good-byes and walk along the road that passes the field, hoping for a ride. None comes, so after the four-hour hike I find myself back in a Tulcingo motel, exhausted. Before I go to bed I wage a frustrated war with three mosquitoes, but am ultimately victorious.

I find Diega and Favian waiting for me at the stop, chatting with a man from the bus company whom they have grown to know well over the past two years. Eventually a yellow luxury bus pulls in and we board, finding seats near the rear. It's a five-hour trip into Puebla, so I have more than enough time to learn the details about Diega's life, and about the husband who failed to return.

Diega met Audon for the first time at a wedding in Cacalutla. Audon boldly approached Diega and asked her to dance. Flattered, she said yes. Not long after, they were married themselves; she was twenty and he eighteen. After their wedding in March 1994 they moved in with his parents, where they lived until December. "That was all I could take," Diega says. "His parents were always getting into our business, so I said we needed to get our own place."

They moved into another house, which they rented, and during the day they would work together in the field with Magdelena and Eduardo—the same field we had planted yesterday. During the dry season Eduardo worked construction in Cacalutla, building houses for people with money they had earned in the United States. During the first year of their marriage, Diega often spoke of following Maria and moving to Brooklyn, but Audon insisted on staying put. "He said he wanted to remain because his parents were here," she explains ruefully.

They had their first child, Carmelo, in 1995. Two years later they celebrated the birth of Favian, and then two years after that, Davey. One day, when Davey was two months old, Audon disappeared for a long stretch without alerting Diega. He arrived home in the evening and said he had spent the entire day at his parent's house. When Diega asked him what he had been doing, he matter-of-factly told her he was going to leave for New York in the morning. Diega learned that his parents had paid a coyote, who would be picking Audon up and transporting him along with several other people from Cacalutla.

"That was the first time I had heard about anything," she says, shaking her head. "I told him he couldn't leave me alone with the three kids, especially since Davey had just been born. But he had already made up his mind. He is the kind of person who does whatever his parents say he should do, so he wouldn't listen to me." By now other passengers in the bus are listening to Diega's story, and out of the corner of my eye I notice a woman sitting in the row behind us, nodding.

Audon had left at 5:00 a.m. the next morning, but before he did he promised Diega that he would return once he had made enough money to buy a plot of land, where they would build their new house. When he left, Diega moved with her three sons into the house of Eduardo's daughter, which they shared. Several times each month she would go to Tulcingo to speak to Audon over the phone. After three years of working in Brooklyn, Audon fulfilled his promise by purchasing a decent-sized piece of land in Cacalutla. During one of their phone conversations, Audon instructed Diega to begin collecting construction supplies that would be needed to build the home, which she did. At this point, it looked like the journey north hadn't been such a bad idea after all.

But then, shortly after she purchased most of the needed materials, Diega began to hear troubling rumors. Several people returned from Brooklyn and told her they had seen her husband with another woman. One even said she had heard he was living with this person. "I didn't want to believe what they were saying," recalls Diega. "The next day I called him and confronted him about the other woman. He told me that they were lying, that he would never cheat on me."

Still, the rumors persisted, until one day Audon admitted to Diega that he was indeed with another woman, and that he wouldn't be returning to Cacalutla. "I didn't know what to do. I had bought all of the material for the house, and it was just sitting there. The plan was for him to come home, we would build the house, and then live together here. But after that conversation I knew he wasn't coming back."

Audon did pay workers to have the house built, but his parents moved in. For Diega, this made the betrayal even harder to take.

Not long after the breakup, Diega noticed that Favian's energy level seemed to drop and found he had a fever. He spent several days in bed, but the fever remained. Normally rambunctious, he preferred to sleep throughout the day and only got up to use the bathroom. The nurse in the town's medical clinic didn't know what the problem was, so Diega took him into Puebla. It was there, on August 15, 2003, that she learned her son had leukemia.

"At first I didn't know what that meant," she says, shifting the sleeping Favian from one knee to the other. "But once I learned it was a type of cancer I knew it was serious." At the time of our conversation it has been nearly two years since he was diagnosed, and his most recent tests show that he is recovering well. Yet the costs of all the treatment are beginning to add up, forcing Diega to get creative. She has received two payments totaling four thousand pesos ($400 U.S.) from the president of Xochihuehuetlan, the Guerreran municipality in which Cacalutla is located. To receive the money, Diega had to get signatures from dozens of townspeople, attesting to the fact that she was flat broke. In addition, the bus line Oro, whose vehicle we are currently traveling on, has started to provide free tickets for her and Favian after receiving a letter from the hospital. Still, Diega currently owes approximately sixty-four thousand pesos to the hospital, or sixty-four hundred dollars, which she pays off in small amounts whenever she is able.

Last year, when Favian was interned at the hospital for eight days, Audon returned to Mexico. He visited his son and spoke briefly with Diega, promising to send money back each month to help with the costs. "He did send two hundred dollars a month for several months, but he hasn't recently. Maybe he has forgotten that we're still here and Favian is still sick." Despite it all, Diega lets out a laugh. "It's easy to forget something when you don't have to be reminded of it every day."

We are now on the outskirts of Puebla. Another five-hour journey is nearly completed—a journey that Diega and Favian have made more than one hundred times in the past two years. Diega taps Favian gently, and he wakes up smiling. Considering how hard the last two years of his short life have been, he seems almost impossibly upbeat and cheerful.

I have one last question.

"Do you think your children will go to New York when they get older?"

Favian looks up at his mom, awaiting the response. "I don't know. I guess it's up to them."

"But do you want them to go?"

She looks at me, then at Favian. "Of course not. I don't want to leave my children, and I don't want them to leave me. But like I said, it will be their decision, not mine." The bus begins to slow down. "This is our stop," she says. "Remember, if you want to eat what you have planted, you better come back in October. If not, we're not going to let it go to waste." She laughs. "When we have food, we eat." Before descending the bus she writes down a phone number where I can contact her. I give Favian a hug and shake Diega's hand, and then they are gone, off to the hospital. They'll spend the night there, and for eight hours tomorrow Favian will receive treatment and undergo further tests. Then it's back to the fields.

On the return trip to Chinantla, my thoughts are on Diega's mental toughness. Her husband is with another woman, her son is battling leukemia, and she now spends much of her time in transit or stuck in hospital rooms. Yet she somehow has found a way to remain cheerful, and if she hasn't forgiven Audon for what he has done, she also doesn't seem to obsess about it, either. Even though she has always lived in the countryside, and is preparing for a life much like her mother's—raising kids, farming, growing old among the familiar rhythms of life in Cacalutla—she is also a modern woman, able to fend for herself and able to realize when a man isn't worth destroying her life over. Remembering the toughness of Maria back in Brooklyn, when she told me not to be afraid of the rats in her basement, it seems this is the most important gift that Magdalena, who had been abandoned by her father and then left by her first husband, has passed on to her two daughters.

CHAPTER 18

Searching for Home

AFTER THREE WEEKS in Mexico, it is nearing time to leave. Our timeline of a monthlong journey shortens after I receive a phone call from my girlfriend, who is back in Brooklyn. She tells me that Juana had been complaining about stomach pains and had to be taken by ambulance to the hospital. The doctors diagnosed Juana's condition as gastritis, which occurs when the stomach lining becomes inflamed. It is as painful as it sounds. Within hours, having received medication, Juana was feeling better and is now back home, and she and Enrique spoke earlier today about his need to return to help care for Feliciano. After his conversation with Juana, I ask Enrique when we are leaving, and he is aggravatingly vague, as is his wont. "Just make sure to get everything you need in the next few days," he says, and refuses to elaborate.

Angel, for his part, has been ready to leave now for several days, his travels complete. "I wanted to do three things," he told me. "Now I have spoken with my brother, seen the town, and bought what I wanted, so I can die without ever coming back." After ten days of traveling around the area with Enrique, Angel and Leticia are now spending most of their time holed up at the hotel. When I bump into them in Chinantla, I can tell they are growing increasingly impatient, as they complain several times to me about the lack of hot water in the hotel. They are also beginning to see me as something of a traitor. "You're with her, aren't you?" Leticia asked me two days ago when we ran across each other in the centro. I knew she was referring to Angela. "She's filling your head with lies about Angel, and that's why you never want to stay with us." It wasn't true: the plan had always been for Enrique and me to stay with Angela—and anyway, Leticia and Angel were lodged in a single room with one bed. But I sensed that with their activities exhausted, Leticia and Angel were spending most of their days stewing, ready to return. But because Angel couldn't drive, because of his poor eyesight, they are stuck waiting for Enrique to determine the departure date.

There is one final trip I want to make, and I can't go without Enrique. During the entire time we have been in Mexico, Enrique has been promising me that we will go out on foot in search of his old house, deep in the hills of Cuicatlán. Each time I ask, however, he has found a reason to put off the trip, and at first I don't argue much: it is *hot*. I could see the narrow, shade-free trail winding up from behind Angela's house, where Enrique had said we would venture. When donkeys were walking along it they kicked up dust, and in the hazy afternoon heat it looked like steam rising up from a frying pan. Like it might just burn the rubber right off the soles of my shoes. I could wait.

Then, on what would prove to be our next to last day in Mexico, I wake in the midst of scorpion dreams to feel something on my foot and jump, only to find Enrique tapping me. "Today, we can go to where I grew up, if you still want to," he says, his face blurry through my squinting eyes. "It's a long hike, and you probably won't be able to make it all the way, but at least you'll be able to say you tried to do it."

I quickly throw on my shoes (but not so quickly that I don't remember to check for scorpions), drink a few glasses of water, and we are off. Enrique takes me through the yard behind Angela's house, past the home where she grew up, and we begin climbing the steep trail. "Whenever you hike along here you always carry a twenty-two," he tells me, holding his bottle of water as if it were a gun. "Always have to be ready for a rabbit that peeks its head out." He fires off a couple of water bullets, we share a quick drink, and he holsters the weapon.

It is still relatively cool, but it doesn't feel like it will remain that way for long. Within ten minutes, our backs are drenched with sweat, and from our elevated position one can see the sky in the distance beginning to turn a murky red from the burning of trash. After several more minutes of hiking Enrique bends down over a small cactus and plucks a small pink flower from its body. He hands it to me, and I hold it up to get a better view of the colors.

"It's nice," I say dumbly. Enrique continues to watch me watch the flower. I am not sure what more he is expecting. "It's pretty," I follow up.

"If you're not going to eat it, give it to me," Enrique says. He snatches the flower from my hand in mock anger and sticks it in his mouth. "This is what we used to keep our mouths wet on hot days, when they were blooming." He hands me another flower; it tastes sour in my mouth. "When the flowers weren't around, you could also use a stone. Anything just to keep the saliva going when you're walking." He points to a rock on the path, covered with a thin layer of dust and by now probably 130 degrees to the touch.

"That sounds good, maybe later," I say. "For now, how about passing me the water bottle?"

As we continue to climb, Enrique mentions that this is the first time he's ventured along this path since he left for New York. Still, twenty years later, he remembers each turn, each climb, each large rock or cactus. Every time he had to travel into Chinantla for food he would take this same path, walking alongside a donkey. "It looks like nothing here has changed at all," he says.

Ten minutes later we're still climbing, and the temperature feels like it is rising several degrees with each passing minute. Enrique takes his shirt off, droplets of sweat running down his back. Plodding along a few minutes later, my head down, I nearly bump into Enrique, who has stopped in the middle of the path and turns to face me with a silly smile on his face. He grabs his paunch with both hands and jiggles it up and down, sweat dropping from his forehead with each bounce. "If you lived out here you'd never need to go to a gym, huh? Just walk back and forth, back and forth. Stay skinny for life!"

I look at him and begin to say something, but my throat has gone dry. Instead, I grunt and gesture to the water bottle. He hands it over and I gulp greedily. "Whoah, güero, save some for later," he admonishes, grabbing it out of my hands. "That's got to last for a long time." He turns around and we resume hiking.

Where Enrique grew up, the three most important items were, in descending order: water, food, and shade. And as we continue to hike deeper into the hills, these also become the three things most prevalent on my mind, again in descending order—with water being far and away the most important necessity. "Angela told me we should bring two bottles of water, but I thought it might slow us down," Enrique says at one point as we hike. Now, with the bottle nearly empty early in the journey, he is having second thoughts about the wisdom of his decision.

"Are we close?" I ask.

"Yeah, just a little more."

Thirty minutes later, without a water break: "Are we close?"

"Yeah, just a little more."

Thirty minutes later, without a water break (I've been checking my watch repeatedly): "Are we close?"

"Yeah, just a little more." We must have lost a gallon of liquid between us in the last hour, and I'm starting to get hungry. My glasses are beginning to fog up from the heat, which is making it difficult to walk without stumbling.

"You bring any food?" I ask.

"No. But we've got plenty of food all around us." He stops and picks up a large rock on the side of the trail, then walks a few feet into the desert shrub, bends over for a minute, and returns with a bunch of small brown shells. "During the hardest times, we would eat these." He spreads the nuts across a flat rock and smashes them with the rock in his hand. "You eat whatever you can find in the desert."

The nuts taste surprisingly good (am I that hungry?), though it is hard to extract their meat from the shells, and I end up swallowing a few jagged casings. After our small meal we soldier on for another fifteen minutes and then sit under the shade of a thirty-foot cactus. "When you live out here you learn a lot about what things can be used for," Enrique says. "The branches of that tree over there are good for barbecuing, especially for barbecuing goats. If there are no goats, you can barbecue rabbits, if you can catch one. And if there are no rabbits, you barbecue lizards."

As if this is merely a movie set that Enrique has arranged in order to appear the wise desert guide, he lifts up a large rock to expose two foot-long lizards. They scurry away. "If you can't find lizards, then you're really in trouble, let me tell you. During some years I remember eating nuts and *ciruelas* (plums) day after day, because everything else was dead. When people from the campo say they come north *por necesidad,* this is what they mean. People in Chinantla think they have it hard, but the poorest people are the ones in the campo. To live here is to know suffering."

He raises his right arm, pointing. "See that tree over there? See those marks along it? People use machetes to collect sap from those trees, which they make into glue. Some people also like to burn the sap for different religious events. You can use almost everything out here for something," he repeats. "In New York we throw everything away, but here you learn to survive on anything you can. What was that saying that I liked?"

"You mean necessity is the mother of all inventions?"

Enrique nods and smiles, mulling over the phrase again. "Yeah, that's it. I like that. That's right. Okay, let's keep going."

Along a ridge we pass a woman on a donkey, who (of course) happens to be a distant cousin of Enrique's. Soon after our brief meeting the path opens into a clearing, with two gigantic cacti on the far end. "Look at that small house over there, next to the cactus. That was on the land of Angel's sister. When goatherds want to stop for the night, they sleep under its roof. Sometimes I would sleep under it, too, even though our house is close."

"Close?"

"Yeah, it's just a little farther. When I was a boy I would take the goats all around this area." He points to a far hill on the other side of the valley. "See that hill? I would go over to that hill, and then take the goats to the other side. We usually had about a hundred and fifty goats to watch after. You walk around with them all day, day after day. Think you could handle that?" I tell him I'd probably succumb to heat stroke. "Are you hot?" I roll my eyes at him, as we both have sweat pouring down our faces.

When we reach the large cacti we sit down again, at the top of a ridge. Nestled between the arms of the cacti are two bottles of water, which goatherds have stored to keep cool. It would be wrong, of course, but I'm tempted to drain them both when Enrique isn't looking. After we take two small swigs of our water, Enrique points out another lone house in the distance, which has a red roof. "That was the house of Angel's mother, Victoria. Over to the left of it you can see the house where I grew up." Although I try to follow his gestures, I'm not able to make it out.

Enrique lies down on his back with his fingers interlaced behind his head, appearing to be at peace despite the heat. "You hear those birds?" he asks. I hadn't, but now that I listen I realize there seem to be dozens of birds chirping and squawking around our heads. Amid the cacophony Enrique identifies several different types and gives his assessment on the flavor of their meat. It's amazing to witness this most unlikely of transformations: a streetwise cabbie of New York City morphing into a desert naturalist. He sits up quickly.

"Remember when I told you about the day when Angel was hitting everyone?" I nod. "That was when we were living in that house that I can't get you to see. Angel was going loco, and Natalia went running from the house to Victoria's house to get help. You can still see the path. See it?"

"No. I think I might need sunglasses." Maybe it's the heat or the lack of water; my eyesight has gone fuzzy.

We eventually stand up and plod along, to another ridge with a barbwire fence running along it. Enrique tells me that this spot is famous because many years ago a man killed his wife here—he's not sure how—when she said she was too tired to continue walking. Next to the fence is a medium-sized tree, which Enrique taps. "This is called the *mala mujer*"—the bad lady.

"Why is it called that?"

"Because it has thorns along its branches, and anytime you get involved with it you end up in pain." Considering where the tree was planted, I tell him it might better be named the abusive husband.

He laughs. "Yeah, well I think the men get to choose the names for things around here."

When we reach the house where Enrique was born, I can see why I wasn't able to find it from the hill—it is now just a pile of rubble, sandwiched between two trees not more than ten feet apart. "How big was the house?" I ask. "It doesn't look like there is very much room here."

"This is it. That space right there was the house. It was even smaller than Luis and Teresa's. But the next house where we lived is bigger. It had two rooms."

Enrique walks over to a nearby tree and reaches up to break off a thin branch. "These are the branches that Angel would hit us with." I catch what he says but don't pay much attention: I've spotted a ciruela tree nearby and scramble over to it and climb up, plopping the green fruit into my mouth. They are not quite ripe yet but still taste wonderful. This is the first real food I've eaten since last night's dinner.

"Oww! ¡*Hijo de la chingada!*" A sharp pain sears across my hamstrings, and I turn around to see Enrique holding a switch, grinning. Coupled with the burning sensation is a feeling of satisfaction: I've spontaneously cursed in Spanish for the first time in my life. Improvement.

"See, it hurts, doesn't it? That was just a love tap. Angel would swing it back like this and drop it down." He whipped the ground a few times, sending dust flying. "This fucking tree, always wanted to cut the damn thing down. If I had a saw right now I'd do it. He is nothing but a fucking *cobarde*, hitting his wife and kids." A coward. "A real man fights with other men."

"Or not at all," I say.

"Right, I was going to say that. Or not at all." He considers the switch, still in his hand. "Unless he has to."

We reach Enrique's second house after fifteen more minutes of walking. It is still standing, though its roof and one of its walls are collapsing. It walls are made of dried earth and rocks, which crumble to the touch, and inside are two rooms of equal size. I enter first and am greeted by a dozen startled bats flying past my face. Inside, the dirt floor of the house is littered with empty plastic bottles and some rusted metal tools. A two-foot-tall piece of rotted wood perched on four legs sits outside.

"This was the only toy we had," Enrique says. "I would sit on this all day, pretending that I was riding a bull." He sits down on the ground next to the animal. I join him.

"It is hard to imagine you living here."

"I know, that's how I feel sometimes. I'm surprised everything still looks like I remember it. I think maybe it was like a different life, that it wasn't me who lived here but someone else I knew. But that is how all immigrants feel, probably. You have to learn to change and live in new places, and you just do it. Your ancestors had to do the same thing, too."

"Do you ever think you'll come back to Mexico to live?"

And then a rare event transpires: Enrique thinks for several long beats before responding. Finally he answers.

"No."

It is the first time I have heard him admit what I have always suspected but never actually asked.

He explains. "What I wish we could do is have Angela move to New York City. But she doesn't want to do that, and I think she probably wouldn't like it there. Here, she has all her friends. She can do whatever she wants. She can talk with people. In New York she wouldn't be happy. She wouldn't know how to get around. Now that we have Feliciano and Junior, we wouldn't come back to Mexico until they are done with school. And by that time I'll be almost sixty, and Juana will be almost seventy. I want to buy my own house, maybe someplace that isn't New York City. But I don't think we'll come back to Mexico to stay. If Angela ever gets sick, I'll come down to take care of her. We're not used to living here, though. In New York there is so much happening, so many things to do. And that's where the rest of my family is, besides Angela. Fuck Angel, I don't need to talk to him ever again. But my brothers and sisters are all in New York. If we lived here it would feel like we were all alone.

"I will keep coming down. And I am going to bring Junior and Feliciano, and when Juana gets her papers she will come, too. I want them to be connected to Mexico, to not forget where they came from. And then when they are grown up, they will have good jobs, like your job, and can help support me and Juana. And we'll come back here together for la fiesta in January, all of us. You, too. So they will never forget that they are Mexican. They will never forget where they come from, how their parents and grandparents struggled. That's the most important thing. You see lots of kids like Abram, they are born in the U.S., and they don't even know anything about their history. You saw how Edgar's kids don't even know how to speak Spanish. My brother Sergio's kids, too. You try to speak to them in Spanish and they can't understand a fucking word. It's like everyone is fucking embarrassed about being an immigrant."

Having seen both of Enrique's previous houses, or what is left of them, we pick up the pace, heading downhill. It is mid-afternoon now, and we've been hiking for five hours with only plums and a few nuts for fuel. Angela surely is growing concerned about our extended absence and no doubt has a pile of warm tortillas and pots of rice and beans on the stove. As we walk down, though, I sense a hesitation in Enrique's stride. He begins to stoop at every desert flower and pause whenever he hears rustling, looking for lizards. Nearing the bottom of the hill, he sits down next to a small well where a gentle trickle of water flows and motions for me to join him.

"What do you think about this place, Gabe?" he asks, tossing a few rocks down the hill. He almost never calls me Gabe, and when he does it comes out more like "Gave." Whenever he addresses me in this way it's a sure sign that he is in a contemplative, serious mood. Seeing the houses—and the whipping tree especially—seems to have put Enrique in a pensive state.

He has asked me a variation of this question perhaps five times today. My answers have been banal. It is hot; it is dry; it is quiet; it is beautiful; it is very different than Brooklyn. Right now I'm mostly thinking that it's a place I'd like to leave so I can get some real food and purified water in my stomach.

"You know I like it out here," I say. "But I can tell that life out here must have been hard."

"Yes, that is exactly what I am thinking." He says nothing else for some time, throwing more rocks. "It was hard, that's for sure. But it was also fun. In New York Abram has all those games that he can play, and the computer . . . ," his voice trails off. "Here, all I had was a slingshot and that wooden bull. But I can tell that I was happier here than Abram is. And when you come from here, you know what it's like not to have anything. Not anything. And you learn to appreciate everything *mucho más*. The most important thing is family. Without family, you can't survive. And with a family, even living out here, you can keep going on. You can eat berries and nuts and rabbits, if you're lucky. And you know you don't need anything else."

Enrique had spent less than half of his thirty-five years out here, roaming the hills and sleeping in adobe houses. I have always pictured Enrique's natural environment to be Brooklyn, racing around the streets at a too-fast speed in his taxi, a larger-than-life personality. The quintessential New Yorker. Yet all it has taken is one day of tromping around in the desert to begin to see that Enrique's natural environment really is the campo, where most of the time is spent simply doing the things one needs to survive. Water, food, shade. And when that isn't enough, an illegal trip across the border to a foreign land. It's all about adapting, about scavenging. You can take this Mexican out of the campo, but you can't take the campo out of this Mexican.

"I didn't even ask Abram if he wanted to come with us, because I knew he would say no, and he couldn't make this walk anyway," he continues. "He's too fat and out of shape. But when Junior and Feliciano are older I will take them out here. I want them to see how people are living now, how their father and mother lived. Wouldn't you want your children to learn about your life?"

"Yes. I think that's a really good idea."

"Me, too. I'm pretty smart, right?"

"Sometimes."

"Ahh, pinche guero, you don't know what you're talking about! I'm a fucking genius. That's why you always have to hang out with me. You think if you ask me enough questions you'll become as smart as me."

I laugh. "Maybe."

Enrique lets out a long hissing sound. "Not maybe—yes! You güeros are all the same, can never admit when a Mexican is smarter than you." He stands up. "Okay, let's go back now. I can tell that you are too tired to stay out here in the campo. No way you'd be able to survive." As we head down the last steep decline of the hill, Enrique picks up the pace, bounding over rocks with an agility I would have never guessed he possessed. And as he bounds he begins to sing a song, but I fall too far behind to make out the words.

CHAPTER 19

Saying Good-bye

ON THE MORNING of our last day in Chinantla, Enrique and
I go to the centro to wait for Angel. Last night Enrique spoke with
Angel, who agreed to meet us with the truck at 8:00 a.m. It is now
7:45, and already hot.

Angel is always early, but by 8:15 he still hasn't arrived. This
makes Enrique angry, and while we are waiting he engages in some
brash brainstorming. "I don't think he's coming. Fuck it, we'll get
our stuff and take a bus to Mexico City. We can fly home from here.
I'll put it on my credit card. Fly to Columbia and pick up the car
and drive home. Let Angel try to get back on his own if he's going
to be playing games."

Thankfully, five minutes later Angel arrives with Leticia, driving
at a speed well under ten miles per hour, his body tense behind the
wheel. Enrique doesn't mention the fact that he is nearly half an
hour late. "We need to take your truck up to Angela's to get our
stuff," Enrique says brusquely. "You and Leticia can wait here and
we'll come back and pick you up."

"I'm not going to wait here," Angel says defiantly. "Where the
truck goes I go."

"Fine, but I'm driving."

"Fine."

Leticia gets out of the truck and says she'll wait. I'm guessing she's none too excited about the idea of seeing Angela. Abram and I climb into the back, and we head to Angela's. Instead of pulling into the driveway, Enrique parks on the street so that Angel is out of sight of the house. "Wait here," Enrique tells Angel.

Back at the house, Nico is fetching water from the well. Angela sits on the front steps, clucking her teeth and rubbing her sore foot. In my room I pack up my things. For once, the house is quiet. I finish packing and sit on the bed. From the other room I hear Enrique and Angela speaking softly. Then I can hear both of them crying. Enrique promises he will return soon. Angela tells him it isn't right for all of her children to live so far away. Enrique says nothing. When it comes time to leave, Abram and I wait halfway down the driveway with the luggage. Eventually Enrique emerges, walking slowly. We hop back into the truck and make our way to the centro in silence, where we find Leticia waiting angrily. We pile in, Enrique behind the wheel.

Abram has his face buried in his PlayStation. Leticia is looking out the window at nothing in particular. Angel, sitting next to Enrique in the passenger seat, has already fallen asleep.

Enrique is crying quietly; I can see his tears reflected in the windshield. He takes the Chinantla bumps with uncharacteristic slowness. We pass by Chimino's tire shop, then the Internet café, and finally the high school. Approaching the exit signpost, Enrique slows down and peers up at the familiar words: "Happy Travels— Chinantla Awaits Your Return." As we pass below the sign he crosses his chest twice, and then kisses his palm, as I have seen others do when leaving. With his left hand he wipes away his tears, and spots me watching him in the rearview mirror.

"Are you tired?" he asks. I shake my head.

"Good. No stopping this time. I can drive until lunch, then you drive until its gets dark. By that time we'll be in Texas. I'll get us through Texas, then you'll drive through Louisiana and Mississippi. I can take Alabama and Georgia. If we make good time we should be . . ." I close my eyes and smile as Enrique plans the trip back to Brooklyn, his words a blur of destinations.

Postscript

IMMIGRATION BECAME BIG news in 2006. Partly, the massive protests staged by immigrants were in reaction to HR 4437, a bill introduced by Wisconsin Republican James Sensenbrenner that passed the House of Representatives on December 12, 2005. This bill, officially titled the "Border Protection, Antiterrorism, and Illegal Immigration Control Act of 2005," called for seven hundred miles of additional border fencing along the U.S.-Mexico border and sought to make all undocumented immigrants instant felons—blocking any opportunity for eventual citizenship. Harsh, but not harsh enough: HR 4437 also would make a felon out of anyone who knowingly "assists" or "encourages" a person to reside in the United States "knowing or in reckless disregard of the fact that such person is an alien." One must imagine this broad definition to include a person who fights the evictions of undocumented immigrants in housing court. I would have been a proud criminal.

But anyone who walked along in solidarity with the immigrants at the marches knows that HR 4437 wasn't the whole story. People spoke of justice, honor, dignity—those catchall phrases that one will find scrawled on picket signs in the photo archives of the great progressive struggles of this country. And what made the immigrant explosion truly powerful was that Americans were forced to wake up to the reality that Mexican immigrants (for this is really what the bill was all about, after all) aren't just in California, Texas, Arizona, or New Mexico. Sixty thousand people turned up in Atlanta, Georgia; fifty thousand in Denver, Colorado; forty thousand in Salt Lake City, Utah. Thousands more took the streets in cities nation-wide: Nashville, Columbus, St. Paul, Des Moines, Indianapolis, Worcester . . . too long a list to compile here. Millions more turned up in massive demonstrations in Los Angeles, San Jose, New York City, Dallas: the scale of these quickly organized events was simply overwhelming. The writing is now on the wall. All of us—immi-grant-friendly or immigrant-fearing—will have brown-skinned neighbors in the coming years, no matter where we live.

After our trip to Mexico, Enrique's first big event came in October 2005 when he became a thirty-five-year-old grandfather. His daughter Cristina gave birth to a healthy baby girl; the father was Marcos—the boy Enrique had hit when Cristina was skipping school. Busy with the duties of motherhood, Cristina is no longer attending high school.

Esteban, the undocumented immigrant charged with the shooting death of Enrique's cousin Adolfo, was found guilty of second-degree murder in January 2006. On the day of his sen-tencing, the judge asked if any of the victim's family members wished to speak. Enrique stood up and testified for several minutes about Adolfo's dream of becoming a music star and showed the CD that Adolfo had made with a friend, along with a T-shirt of their band Sonido Azteca. "He had dreams and hopes, your honor," Enrique said, asking that Esteban receive the maximum sentence because he hadn't once shown remorse or apologized for his actions. After Enrique spoke, Esteban had the chance to address the court, saying he was sorry for the loss but that he had not even been at the scene of the crime—contradicting his earlier confession—and implored the judge to continue searching for the real killer. Unmoved, the judge sentenced Esteban to twenty-two years to life. Because he is an undocumented immigrant, when he finishes serving the sentence he will be deported to Mexico.

After serving a year in Iraq, Enrique's friend Manuel returned to the United States. He is now stationed in Washington, D.C., though Enrique doesn't know exactly what type of work he is doing in the capital.

Enrique and Juana were married on February 3, 2006, in Manhattan, just across the street from city hall, where Enrique had testified three years earlier regarding lead paint poisoning. Enrique's sister Sabina and I were the witnesses, along with Junior, who was sporting a new spiky hairdo, white dress shirt, and black tie for the occasion. Juana wore a light blue dress and high heels, and for the first time that I could remember she had on lipstick and earrings, though when I asked her if she was excited on her big day—it was the first time she had ever been married—she said no. Body language said otherwise: she smiled throughout the ceremony and throughout the post-wedding lunch at a buffet restaurant in Bushwick, where everyone ate way too much.

The plan was for Abram to return to the jobs center in Brooklyn upon our arrival from Mexico, so that he could enroll in job training while earning his GED. He made a phone call or two, but didn't hear back and failed to follow up. He has now quit his job at the car wash, and in the fall of 2005 began to work for his older sister Anayeli, who travels to Mexico to bring back goods that she then sells in the United States. Initially unexcited about ever seeing the home country of his mother and father, he now goes to Mexico multiple times each month and in June 2006 moved in with Anayeli and her husband, preferring the freedom to do what he wants without having to hear Enrique complain about the fact that he isn't in school.

Enrique tells me that the last time he spoke with Paula, she was planning on moving back to Mexico, because her daughter from a previous relationship had fallen ill, and was hoping to leave their three daughters and granddaughter with Enrique. He seems excited about this idea, though it will make for a very crowded apartment. If Paula does end up moving south, the tiny two-bedroom dwelling on Franklin Avenue will house two adults, a newborn, a one-year-old, three grade-school children, and the fourteen-year-old Cristina.

After spending a warm, if crowded, winter in their neighbor's apartment, Maria and Timoteo moved from the neighborhood of Bedford-Stuyvesant to Sunset Park. Maria says their new living arrangement is much better, especially since Timoteo is now within walking distance of the factory where he works. The lawyer I had put her in touch with did file a lawsuit against her pervious landlord for the lead poisoning of Reyna and Gary. Maria tells me that the suit is still pending.

Maria's sister, Diega, has had a hard year. Although Favian seemed to be in perfect health when I visited, and the tests were suggesting he was recovering well, he suffered a relapse in the fall. On December 8, 2005, the eight-year-old passed away. When I spoke to Diega in the spring she sounded sad, though she still managed to laugh when explaining that they had eaten all of the food I had planted and failed to return to harvest. Davey got on the phone briefly, too, and sang "Todas las mujeres, me gustan todas" several times before handing the phone back to his mom. I don't know if she thinks Favian would have received better treatment in the United States, and I didn't ask. I had taken several photographs of the family in the fields and sent one from Brooklyn that arrived in Tulcingo. In the photo Davey is grinning madly into the camera, with a straw-hatted Favian on his brother's back as they stand under the huamuchil tree.

In Mexico, Angela still waits for Enrique's phone call each Sunday and was overjoyed to hear about his marriage to Juana, hoping that it means one day she will finally be able to meet her new daughter-in-law when Juana becomes a permanent resident. Not to mention her two grandsons, Junior and Feliciano, whom she has heard so much about.

Enrique participated in the immigration marches that took the country by storm. Juana stayed at home, not wanting to bring the one-year-old Feliciano. "I would like to see my mom before she dies," Juana told me, "but I don't want to have to cross the desert." Having lived in the country since 1984, she would most likely be eligible for permanent residency if an immigration reform bill passes.

One final update. Not too long after I heard the sad news about Favian, I called José at work. It had been several months since we had last spoken, and Enrique had told me that on a recent fishing expedition José had landed a gigantic trout. This seemed to deserve a call of congratulations. After two rings, a woman picked up the phone.

"Hi, is José there?"

"We don't have a José here." Oh really?

"Yes, you do. Would you mind asking if he's around? He works in the back. He's the guy who paints all the jewelry."

She paused for a moment. "Oh, I know him!" She sounded pleased with herself. "Hold on a second." A minute passed. The woman returned to the phone. "I looked around, but I think he's out on lunch right now. Would you like to leave a message?"

"Yes, that'd be great. Can you tell him that Gabriel called?"

"Sure."

"Thanks."

Here's hoping next time she remembers.

Acknowledgments

First, a big thanks to all of the people in this book that allowed me to hang around with them. To you I owe a debt that cannot be repaid, though I do hope that someday soon this book will be translated into Spanish so I can hand out presents that will offer proof that all those little scribbles in my notebook weren't just doodles.

I am grateful to everyone at the Pratt Area Community Council that made my only "real" job thus far a wonderful experience: Hector Rivera, Enida Davis, Amy Laura Cahn, Deb Howard, Steve Aronson, Jedidah Baptiste, Jackie Mitchell, Julietta Padilla and Anne Lessy. It was at PACC that I first met Enrique and most of the other immigrants in this book; if Brooklyn remains a place where non-rich people are able to remain and thrive, it will in no small part be due to the grassroots work of groups like PACC.

A special thanks to Artemio Guerra, who not only hired me at PACC, but also has been a steady friend and troublemaking organizing companion. Always ready to feed me interesting stories to write, always ready to cut out from work early for a quick drink. I look forward to watching Sebastian, the smallest anarchist in Brooklyn, grow up and start raising a ruckus in the coming years.

Debbie Nathan, investigative journalist extraordinaire, took a young writer under her wing, offering sound advice, inspiration, and tangible proof that getting older doesn't mean becoming less curious, less passionate. Thanks also to my agent, Michael Bourret, of Dystel and Goderich Literary Management, and Carl Bromley of Nation Books, for providing solid critiques of the book.

My girlfriend, Daniella Ponet, was the one who first mentioned while I was still organizing that what I really wanted to be was a writer, which got my gears moving and helped give me the confidence to enter a crowded field of talented journalists. There's no other sabra I'd rather share my life with.

Finally, a big debt is owed to my family. I've been blessed to have a five-person cheerleading squad that supports whatever strange project that obsesses me. Marjorie Bjerkager and Ralph and Ivy Hietala are the best grandparents in the world (not an original statement, but true). My father, Jim Thompson, is the most intellectually curious person I know, and his empathy knows no bounds. He is my first editor and tireless cheerleader (and I mean *tireless*). And my mother . . . what to say about my mother? Some people are prone to wearing their hearts on their sleeves; Sandra Hietala is a walking, beating, bleeding heart. I often marvel at how exhausting it must be to so deeply feel other people's joys and sorrows-and yet continue to take action to create a few more joys and a few fewer sorrows. I've yet to find a better model for living a good life.

About the Author

Gabriel Thompson grew up in the Bay Area and graduated in 2001 from the Johnston Center for Integrative Studies at the University of Redlands, in southern California. After college he moved to New York City and spent four years as an organizer with the Pratt Area Community Council, a housing advocacy and organizing group active in Central Brooklyn. At PACC he worked with residents on a host of issues-displacement, landlord harassment, hazardous housing conditions-and met many of the Mexican immigrants described in *There's No José Here*. Thompson is now a freelance journalist based in Brooklyn, focusing especially on urban affairs and immigration. His writings have been published in *New York* magazine, the *Nation*, *In These Times*, *Color Lines*, *City Limits*, *Clamor* and the *Brooklyn Rail*. He has won two awards from the Independent Press Association-New York for his reporting for the *Brooklyn Rail* on labor and immigration. He can be reached through his Web site, www.wherethesilenceis.org.